THE LIGHT
POURS OUT
OF ME

THE LIGHT POURS OUT OF ME

The authorised biography of
JOHN McGEOCH

Rory Sullivan-Burke

OMNIBUS PRESS
London / New York / Paris / Sydney / Copenhagen / Berlin / Madrid / Tokyo

Copyright © 2022 Omnibus Press
(A division of the Wise Music Group
14–15 Berners Street, London, W1T 3LJ)

Cover and book design by Malcolm Garrett
Picture research by Rory Sullivan-Burke and Nigel Proktor

ISBN 978-1-913172-66-4
Signed edition ISBN 978-1-913172-76-3

Rory Sullivan-Burke hereby asserts his right to be identified as
the author of this work in accordance with Sections 77 to 78
of the Copyright, Designs and Patents Act 1988.

All rights reserved. No part of this book may be reproduced in any form or
by any electronic or mechanical means, including information storage
or retrieval systems, without permission in writing from the publisher,
except by a reviewer who may quote brief passages.

Every effort has been made to trace the copyright holders of the photographs
in this book but one or two were unreachable. We would be grateful
if the photographers concerned would contact us.

A catalogue record for this book is available from the British Library.

Typeset in Marr Sans by Palimpsest Book Production Ltd, Falkirk, Stirlingshire

Printed in the Czech Republic

www.omnibuspress.com

For Fianna and Jess

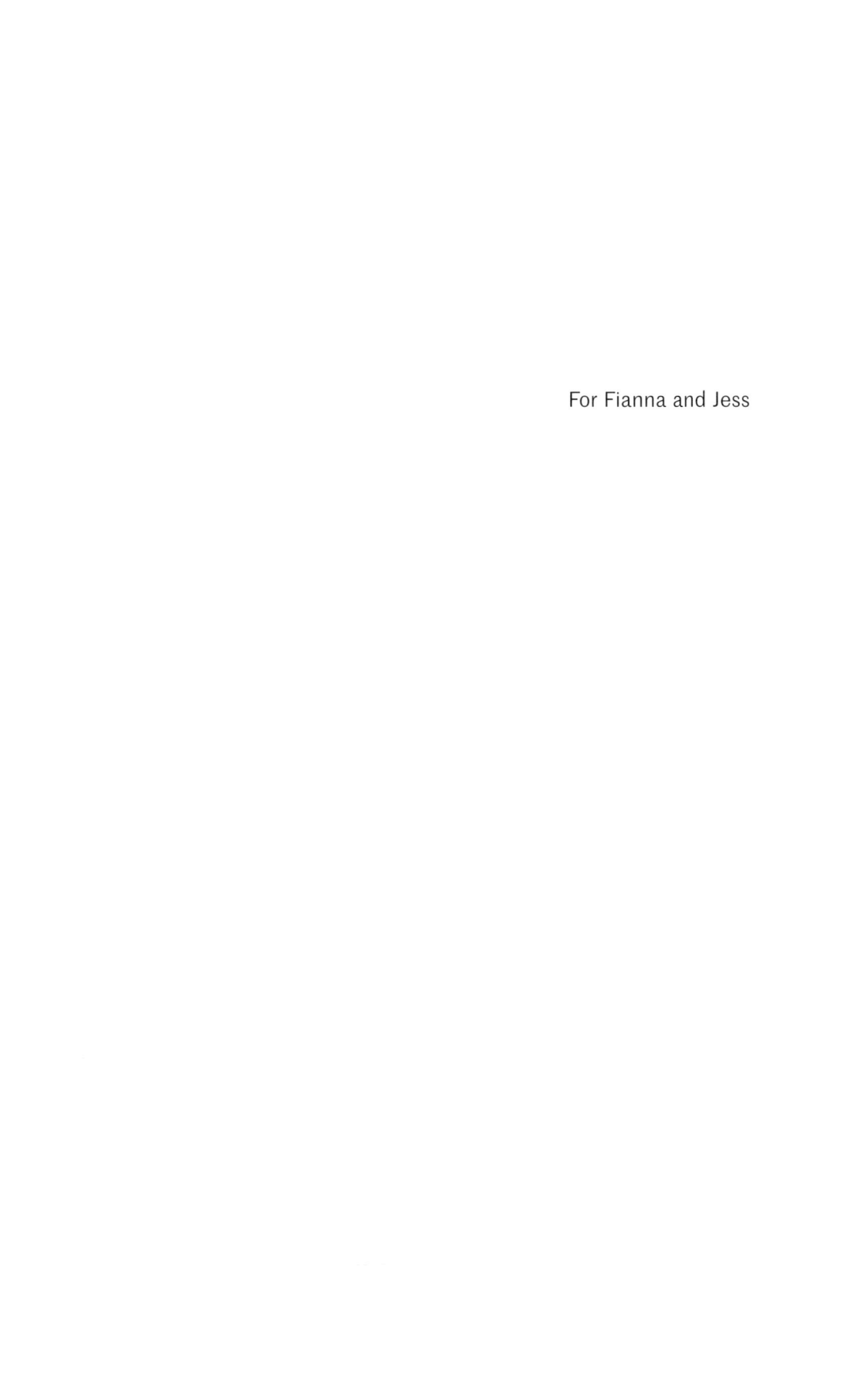

CONTENTS

FOREWORDS
EMILY McGEOCH   1
MALCOLM GARRETT   2
DAVE FORMULA   3
PAUL MORLEY   4
JOHNNY MARR   7

INTRODUCTION
JOHN McGEOCH   9
Taken from the fan information sheet, 'Secondhand Daylight'

ONE IAN   11
Childhood in Scotland and relocating to England

TWO FRIENDS OF MINE   21
Moving to Manchester to study fine art, and the first meeting
with Howard Devoto

THREE SECONDHAND INSIGHT   37
The formation, rise and fall of Magazine

FOUR STRANGE DAYS   79
A brief flirtation with the emerging New Romantic movement
courtesy of Visage

FIVE HAPPY HOUSE   83
John leaves Magazine and joins up with Siouxsie and
the Banshees

SIX WAITING FOR THE FLOODS   143
After his dismissal from the Banshees, John travels to
Sweden before forming the post-punk 'supergroup',
The Armoury Show

SEVEN BRAVE NEW WORLD 171
John joins John Lydon in Public Image Ltd

EIGHT DIAMOND 203
John as the family man, and starting up his own group, Pacific.

NINE HEAVENS INSIDE 217
John's later years and untimely death.

TEN THE ANTI-HERO 235
Tributes to John McGeoch from friends, family, contemporaries and admirers.

AFTERWORD 251

THANKS 257

FOREWORDS

Emily McGeoch

IT WAS A normal lockdown Wednesday, and ping, another message from another fan. This one, like many others before, was suggesting the prospect of writing a book about my father. I responded with my usual, pre-written response and expected to hear nothing more. Then, within a week, the emails started coming in from Dad's friends and colleagues. 'Who is this? Shall I speak to him? Have you heard?' and I started to take

John and his daughter Emily at home, 1991.
McGeoch family archive

notice – the industry chatter around the book in the first month was amazing. I spoke to my family and Dad's manager and we decided to look further into the project, and I'm so glad we did!

The first phone call with Rory was wonderful – we talked for over two hours. After hearing his passion and commitment to the project I knew it would be a success. Being able to contribute to this book has been a wonderful and emotional experience for me. It's brought a lot of people together and brought a lot of fantastic memories to the surface. Rory has provided John's family, friends, colleagues and fans with a chance to come together and honour the memory of a wonderful man, and for that I will be forever grateful.

Malcolm Garrett (the friend)

I REMEMBER DISTINCTLY the first time I met John. Well, not quite. I remember *where* it was, and *why* we met, and *who* he was with, but the actual detail of the meeting itself escapes me. He and his friend Liddy had come to look at, and subsequently move into, the flat in Rusholme where I had been living since starting the graphic design course at Manchester Polytechnic. Which makes it late 1975.

John, Liddy and I became friends immediately. John was cool. He was smart, witty, and really quite charming, speaking with a warmth that his just discernible Scottish accent gave his voice. He had on a well-worn black Lewis Leathers biker's jacket, which I (and others) coveted. At some point John explained to me how a good leather jacket moulds itself to your body, physically and visually. He showed me the best place to hide your drugs – underneath the zip at the cuffs – where the police wouldn't look if you were stopped and made to turn out your pockets. A year or so later I bought one the same style, but in red. To this day any jacket like this always reminds me of John.

The flat was on two floors above Cowlishaw's fish shop at 199 Wilmslow Road, with the entrance in the alleyway at the rear. It really was as dingy as it sounds. Yet it seemed OK at the time – it must have been, as I lived there for the full three years of my course.

The location of this flat was perfect. Rusholme sits at the edge of a swathe of student accommodation reaching all the way down Wilmslow Road to Didsbury, and back then had only a few Indian and Pakistani shops and restaurants. Across the way was Maine Road, Manchester City's football ground, and a few hundred metres heading towards the city centre was the Whitworth Art Gallery, Manchester University Students' Union, and (still within walking distance) the main poly campus at All Saints. And frequent buses to Piccadilly.

It was obvious why it appealed to John and myself. We could easily get to pretty much anywhere and always be able to walk home.

We ended up hanging out for the next couple of years. Going to gigs, clubs, parties, or just sitting at home watching television, arguing about who would change the channel when it was too cold to get up from the sofa. John made some home-brew beer, we took 'recreational' drugs, we enjoyed being students. We went to London to see Frank Zappa at Hammersmith Odeon, and he introduced me to his parents in Ilford.

Living in the flat at various times were David Atherton (who I knew from my home town of Northwich and had first invited me to move in), the enigmatic Trevor Green, and crazy Rob Dobson, who introduced me to the Ghulam (the best of the local Indian restaurants where we ate frequently). Everyone who lived in the flat was studying fine art, except me – and Judy Blame, who came up from Exeter to visit friends and never left. It is sobering to report that neither John, Trevor nor Judy are with us any longer.

All in all it was a remarkable collection of people who crossed the portal, not all of whom I have space to mention. John was to meet Howard Devoto, and me Pete Shelley, at a party we held in March 1977 – the outcomes of which precipitated what this book is about.

Now read on…

Dave Formula (the insider)

WITHOUT EXCEPTION, ALL the close friends I've had since the age of 16 have either been musicians or have been involved with music as part of their work and career. Thankfully, a couple are still around to share more thoughts, jokes, stories, recordings, experiences, often via a mutual musical shorthand that opens up the possibility of a friendship in the first place.

John McGeoch was one of those friends.

When I first joined Magazine it was close to a fresh start for me, not only musically but just as importantly, reacting personally and creatively with four young musicians I didn't know at all – apart from the couple of hours I'd spent a week earlier chatting and verbally auditioning for the job with Howard Devoto.

It was clear from the first rehearsal that John was a player who was hearing things in his head that translated into a uniquely uninhibited, highly exciting and challenging way of guitar playing. I was immediately hooked by what I heard.

I was quite a few years older than John and bass player Barry Adamson; musicians this young weren't supposed to be this good or as markedly original as John was. For me this was a chance to open up my own playing and ideas to contribute to, complement and expand within the existing songs, and then not so long afterwards, add my own melodies and changes for new Magazine songs.

If John's playing presented a welcome challenge to me musically, this, combined with his ability to socialise, his generosity and sense of the ridiculous, made it very easy to become friends. During the few years we were together in Magazine and for a couple of years afterwards, we shared an intense and creative musical sparring which played a big part in the sound of three albums, along with a great deal of conversation, laughs and adventures across the USA, Europe and the UK.

All too short, but long remembered and loved.

Paul Morley (the observer)

EVERY TIME JOHN McGeoch appeared – dramatically or delicately but always decisively – during the introduction to some of those great, tense and enigmatic pop songs that he specialised in playing on, particularly for Magazine and Siouxsie and the Banshees, he seemed to be introducing himself for the very first time. Not necessarily as a guitarist, or even as a musician or songwriter, but as someone – artist, thinker, dreamer, conversationalist, drifter, grand romantic, in an odd sort of way showman with incredible style – who was always working out his place in the world, and what he thought of the world, what a strange, wonderful and intimidating, messy, unstable and magnificent place it was. Here I am, here's what I am thinking, here's what I do, and here's the way I deal with life, all those twists, turns and tragedies, and try to make it a better, other, more blissful place, something it wasn't before I made these sounds and created this atmosphere.

He happened to use the guitar as his way of seeing, describing and feeling things, and he happened to find himself in at least two cathartic avant-garde pop groups experimenting with all sorts of ways of representing sensation, desperation and apprehension, groups that didn't need a 'rock' guitarist, or a 'punk' guitarist, or even a 'post-punk' guitarist, but someone whose playing continued a discreetly spectacular and isolated coastline first explored by such obsessive truth-seeking electric guitarists as Sterling Morrison, Michael Karoli, Lee Underwood, Tom Verlaine, Phil Manzanera, John Martyn, Allan Holdsworth, Robert Fripp, Richard Thompson, Fred Frith and Peter Hammill.

John was one of a number of Manchester guitarists with great record collections who appeared after punk, rearranging and rewiring the purpose and potential of the instrument, fleeing influence, imagining alternative futures, fighting a smudge-grey sky, escaping stress, finding something new under the sun, at a time when the idea of the guitarist, the aristocratic guitar hero, seemed to have sent rock music into a dull cul-de-sac.

Pete Shelley of Buzzcocks had generated a kind of critical return to zero, a reclaiming of power, with a brief, primitive, two-note guitar solo on 'Boredom', and from this radical begin-again event a new kind of liberated exploratory and immersive guitar playing developed that in Manchester led to Martin Bramah of The Fall and Blue Orchids, Bernard Sumner of Joy Division and New Order, Steve Diggle of Buzzcocks, Vini Reilly of Durutti Column, Johnny Marr of The Smiths and John McGeoch of the caustic, somewhere-else group Howard Devoto quickly formed after swiftly separating himself from Buzzcocks of 'Boredom' – Magazine.

The severe conceptualist correction of guitar expression in 'Boredom' flowered into suggestive new ways of handling and playing the guitar, and the fact that John was among the finest two or three of these original new Manchester players meant he was one of the finest of all the guitarists that arrived after punk, setting a new kind of poetic, emotional and investigative guitar playing in motion that, for what it's worth, would eventually make it through to U2, Nirvana and Radiohead.

For a few years John was in the right time and place, at the right age, finding the right personnel and the right local scenery, to have a serious role as a guitarist, technician, translator, conspirator and artist. You can hear him, alive and watchful, intuitive and shifting, technical and ghostly, daring and disciplined, sultry and tense, sad and savage, raging and reflective, meticulous and glittery, lonely and determined, noisy and urgent, down to earth and other-worldly, braiding darkness and light, imagining the shapes and dynamics that helped complete the singular, menacing visions and strange vocals of Howard Devoto and Siouxsie Sioux, which had the raw, ruthless power to turn you inside out and/or cut you open. Understanding their weird, bruised insides, their consummate use of the telling detail, their way of grappling with the hazards and potentials of their desires, their determination to contemplate the unseemly, to convey beauty and horror at the same time, in tune with their raging wit and whimsy, he played an irreplaceable psycho-spiritual guitar that elevated their songs into the extraordinary and sometimes the supernatural.

The anguish he must have felt later in life, exiled, burned out and adrift, when he couldn't find the right setting and collaborators – the right private space – to develop his playing and therefore his actual being was directly connected to the sensitivity, anxiety and self-consciousness he had as a human being that meant his guitar playing in the first place was so elegant, driven and provocative. For a while, for a few years that coincided with a time when discovering and falling for the right records was a matter of life and death, it all made sense, and he had a place, he was in the moment, on stage, connected, and he generously, almost anonymously, contributed to wonderful, mysterious, troubling records that may well echo into the future, long after the particular scenes and genres and musical fashions they belonged to have vanished into lost history.

He's still here, still there in two-hour Spotify playlists collecting his most notable freelance work, amid all of those millions of tracks, all those endless scenes, memories, classics, anthologies, introductions, all that information overload, introducing himself again and again, introducing densely shadowed dark fairy tales and various stories of unease, some of which once even made the pop charts, leaving traces of what was on his mind, of what he was remembering, craving, evading, and who he was loving, and in a way the pain he was feeling, the loss he could see coming. Ravishing little bursts of consciousness, miniature time capsules, dream fragments, precious moments, battle wounds, electric charges, weird stillness, neither dead nor alive, the distilling of huge amounts of time and space into a few transcendent guitar notes, bravely fighting the idea that one day his playing, his existence, the shimmering worlds he helped create, would all be forgotten.

I can never forget his guitar playing; it's always in my head, somewhere, part of me, as he introduces himself, defeating boredom, filled with life, allowing Devoto to be angry, ill and as ugly as sin, and Siouxsie to follow the footsteps of a rag doll dance, giving the listener something to reach for, the introduction to a fantastic new world.

Johnny Marr (the admirer)

I DIDN'T EVER think this book would exist. Not because the subject is unworthy, far from it, but because John McGeoch is one of those people whose approach to his work is so tasteful and intelligent that to draw too much attention to himself as a personality would've almost gone against his artistic sensibilities. So, I was pleasantly surprised, and more than a little intrigued, to be contacted by Rory Sullivan-Burke, who said he was writing a book about someone I regard as an unsung hero.

For years I've been part of a group of musicians, mostly guitar players, who when we met would inevitably share our appreciation of John McGeoch's work: in the studio with John Frusciante from the Chili Peppers, backstage with Radiohead's Ed O'Brien, in an airport with Roddy Frame from Aztec Camera. It's like a secret society of players who are still in awe of the riffs, sounds and arrangements on those records by Magazine, Siouxsie and the Banshees and PiL. The conversation would inevitably move on to John's playing in The Armoury Show, then the Yamaha SG, and then always on to 'Spellbound'.

I was 14 when 'Shot by Both Sides' came out, and although I was already keenly aware of all the bands of 1978, that first Magazine single made everyone who heard it take notice, particularly of the guitar. It was complex, modern and, crucially, it sounded like it had an agenda.

That first introduction to the playing of John McGeoch was the start of his fascinating career as a pioneer of postmodern guitar. He would continue to move on, experiment and sometimes confound, while remaining as interesting as ever, bringing his unmistakable approach to every band he joined.

As the years have gone on and I've made my own records, I'm sometimes reminded of John McGeoch's influence on my playing. It's not that much of a surprise given that I was such a fan of the Banshees, and that *The Correct Use of Soap* has remained one of my all-time favourite albums. If anything, the passing of time has served to prove just what an impressive musician John McGeoch really was, and it's a privilege to make a contribution to his story.

The voices that Rory has skilfully and attentively documented in this book are the voices of John's friends, colleagues, family and musical comrades. They share their memories of a man they admired, loved and respected, and in doing so they pay tribute to a singular and brilliant talent whose legacy deserves to be remembered and celebrated.

———————————————

INTRODUCTION BY JOHN MCGEOCH*

BORN IN RANKIN Hospital, Greenock, an industrial town about 25 miles from Glasgow. Went to Lady Alice School, then Larkfield Primary School. I have one brother who has dabbled at the guitar for as long as me – except that he was only seven when he started. I started playing guitar after receiving one as a twelfth birthday present. Gave up piano lessons (which I had been attending since the age of seven). First time on stage – playing Edelweiss on acoustic guitar at school Christmas party. Attended Redbridge, then Thurrock Technical Colleges. During this period I played a lot of experimental material with Ciaran Harte, a multi-instrumentalist guitarist, and Joe Barry, a bassist and trumpet player. Moved on to Greenock High School. Formed my first group – the 2d Sparklers. Saved up and bought my first electric guitar at fourteen – a Commodore for £25.00 (I used it on the first few Magazine gigs and still play it at home). The 2d Sparklers became 'Slugband' comprising of myself and Dougie Campbell (guitar), Alistair Cameron (bass), George McClarkin (drums) and Ray Wallace (vocals). I was the youngest member, playing my first gig while still fourteen.

    At sixteen moved with my family to Goodmayes, near Romford, Essex. Then moved to Manchester to become a painting student at the Poly. Started playing the sax as a result of rooming with a saxophonist – Steph Birkin. Around this time I was going to see local bands at the Electric Circus including Buzzcocks, Slaughter and the Dogs, Drones.

    Moved around a lot in early 1977. Malcolm Garrett (designs record sleeves for Buzzcocks, Members, Magazine, Betty Bright) and I threw a punk party where I met P. Shelley and Howard. Shortly afterwards

---

* This piece appears exactly as it did in the original publication, and John's errors have not been corrected.

Howard left Buzzcocks and soon he contacted me to try out a few ideas. He had already written 'Shot By Both Sides', but together we wrote 'The Light Pours Out Of Me', 'Touch and Go' and a few other ideas materialised, which were then developed on 'Real Life'. Howard then advertised for musicians while I worked in London for a few weeks to make some money. When I got back he and Barry (bass), Martin Jackson (drums), Bob Dickinson (keyboards) and John Scott (guitar), and I was back working with Howard.

On stage I use a Yamaha SG 1000 and a Les Paul through a MXR Compressor and Flanger pedals into a Marshall 50W Valve Combo. My sax is an old Conn Alto. In the studio I use the same set-up along with a Stratocaster and a twelve string Ibanez electric. On *Secondhand Daylight* I also experimented with a guitar synthesizer and with playing a guitar through a Leslie Cabinet which gives a great sound. On the instrumental 'The Thin Air', which I wrote, I played a few keyboards including three notes on a grand piano.

'Secondhand Daylight' fan publication, 1979

John, 1979.
Dave Formula

ONE

IAN
Childhood in Scotland and relocating to England

All summer and all autumn: this grey town
That pipes the morning up before the lark
With shrieking steam, and from a hundred stalks
Lacquers the sooty sky; where hammers clang
On iron hulls, and cranes in harbours creak
Rattle and swing, whole cargoes on their necks;
Where men sweat gold that others hoard or spend,
And lurk like vermin in their narrow streets [...]
[...] And wastes his passion like a prodigal
Right royally; and here her golden gains
Free-handed as a harlot autumn spends;
And here are men to know, women to love.

Taken from 'Greenock' by John Davidson

JOHN ALEXANDER MCGEOCH'S story begins in the western Scottish town of Greenock on the banks of the Clyde, on the morning of 25 August 1955. John's mother remembers his first moments of life with a smile: 'He was born at twenty past five in the morning. Now, in those days the fathers weren't at the hospital when the babies were born. So, Ian's [John's] dad phoned up at half five to see if anything had happened – he told me later that he'd not had a minute's sleep from when I went into the hospital at around two in the morning. The person who took the call popped her head out of the office door and said, "There's a Mr McGeoch on the phone wanting to know if there's any word on his wife Annie." The nurse smiled and went in and picked Ian up, who was screaming blue murder! She held him up to the phone, so within ten minutes of being born he was on the phone. Ian's dad used to say, "From ten minutes old he was on the phone and he's never been off it since!" Ian was always using the telephone!'

Greenock is a tough and proudly working-class town famous for its docks and the ships that unloaded their goods and trawled from there. A place where the inequities of class politics and the divides they create are evident. To this day it remains one of the most disadvantaged towns in Scotland. Unemployment and addiction are high and with the demise of its shipbuilding, it – in common with the mining towns and industrial cities of the north of England – has suffered terribly. Yet it was here that the young boy who became the man who would inspire a generation of music lovers and came to find his place in the world was raised. John was a man of many talents, but he was nobody's fool, imbued as he was with the tough spirit of the town. In many ways Greenock was the antithesis of what he would go on to experience in his later life, but his upbringing there shaped him for his forty-eight years and is integral to his story. Without it, this book may never have been written. For all the plaudits that would eventually come his way, John never forgot who he was and where he had come from. Whether walking the streets of Santa Monica or performing in New York City, he was always the boy from Greenock.

Affectionately known by his family and friends as Ian (derived from the Scottish Gaelic version of John), he would make his debut on television long before the arrival of John the musician. As his mother Annie remembers, 'When he was a toddler he was on television. STV started, which was the Scottish equivalent of ITV, and we went from Greenock on a coach to the studios in Glasgow. We went over there – Ian, his granny and myself – and we got a seat at the front. The show was called *The One O'Clock Gang* and it was hosted by a man called Larry Marshall, who was a bit of a comedian, and Sheila Matthews, who was the singer. They used to do little sketches and the children loved it. Sheila was pregnant at the time, and we'd brought a couple of bibs and a rattle which we'd parcelled up to hand to her. Larry used to collect lollipops for the local orphanage and so we'd brought a load of those too to give to him. The cameras went on Ian when Larry was collecting the lollipops and he was talking to Ian and then Ian handed Sheila her gift. When we came home and were walking back to the house, people that I knew would stop me and say, "We've just seen you on television!" So, he was on television at about the age of 2.'

He attended Lady Alice and Larkfield, both primary schools, as Annie explains: 'They changed the districts, and I was most annoyed. Ian was 11 and his brother William was 7 at the time. I said to the headmaster, "The 11-year-olds should not be moved." It ended up with a whole class of children being moved. There was a lot of redevelopment going on at the time, a new estate was built. I was worried about the effect the disruption would have on Ian because he had been top of the class every year without fail.' John's intelligence and aptitude for learning were natural to him. Annie takes up the story of what happened after John had sat his 11-plus: 'His marks for the 11-plus were so high, they wouldn't accept it, and Ian got taken into the headmaster's study and was made to re-sit. This was all because the education authorities said, "How does a child of 11 complete that?", as Ian had answered everything correctly. He was made to do a similar exam under supervision of the headmaster, and he came out with top marks again. I always remember that, you know, Ian's dad was quite annoyed because they hadn't informed us. We came to know about it when Ian came home and told us that he'd been taken into the headmaster's study and given an exam. So, we went down to the school to find out what it was about, and we were told that Edinburgh, where the exam papers went, couldn't see a child doing so well.'

Was it an example of institutionalised class bias? Was it, 'How can a child from Greenock be so academically gifted?' John would go on to study at Greenock High, a stern-looking building set against the hilly backdrop of the Clyde Basin.

John was a keen artist from his earliest days. He was happiest with a scrap of paper and pencil in hand, and would sit for many an hour on the floor, sketching away. His artistic talents didn't go unnoticed: as a Cub Scout at the age of 7, he won the silver cup for a drawing he had entered as part of a competition that covered the

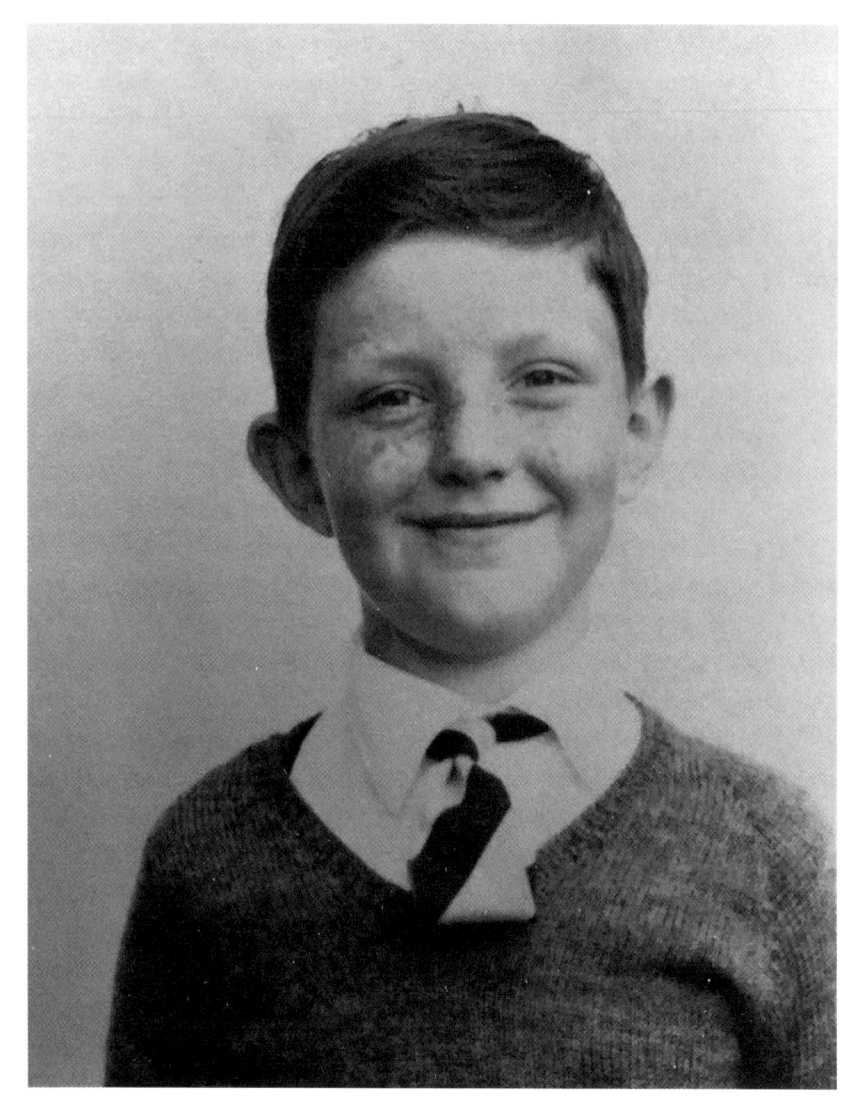

Ian McGeoch at school, early 1960s.
McGeoch family archive

whole of Renfrewshire. Amid the harsh realities of life in an industrial port town, he found support and encouragement from his family – good, hard-working people, moulded in the Protestant ethic of graft and tenacity. It is fair to say that John's parents were of a different background from their neighbours in that, especially on his mother's side, they were middle class. Both parents had aspirations for their boys – John and his brother William – that would ultimately see them move south of the border in search of greater opportunities. This wasn't a move made out of snobbery, but they recognised only too well that Greenock was a town in decline and the opportunities were decreasing year on year. John's creativity was only ever encouraged: and as well as indulging his love of visual arts, he was taken to piano lessons, which would eventually lead him to the instrument he is synonymous with. As Annie remembers, 'At 7 he started piano lessons, which he kept up with until he was 16. It was at 12 years old that he began classical guitar lessons, which he did for four years, and that came about because his brother, William, wanted to learn the guitar and had been going to the same place for music lessons. William told the neighbours that he was going to learn the guitar because he really didn't want to learn the piano. So, William started to learn the guitar and Ian would pick it up, and after about a year we decided to put him in for that as well.'

As well as lessons in music, his mother wanted to make sure that her boys had the gift of eloquence. The unusual move to equip them with this skill may go a long way to explain John's effective use of language in later life. As Annie explains: 'Both Ian and William had elocution lessons so that they could talk properly. I would say he had those lessons from the age of 8 until he was 12.'

It wasn't all lessons and artistic pursuits for the young McGeoch. As with any lad, he enjoyed a variety of pastimes. He loved nothing more than to go fishing, either with his dad or with his mates. John was somebody who made friends easily and was immensely popular with his peers. Annie remembers that her front door was forever being knocked on, his pals asking if John could come out to play. He was also uncannily intuitive as a youngster and would want to include the children who didn't find making friends easy. This was something that would stay with him throughout his life – he was a giver and a carer. How much of that was simply his nature and how much could be attributed to the fact that he had such secure foundations at home? He had been blessed, and it was something he never forgot. He recognised the debt he owed his parents and in every way he was a considerate son.

Once John picked up the guitar properly, he never looked back, and although he carried on with the piano it was clear where his passion lay. He became proficient rapidly and before long wanted to upgrade from his little wooden guitar to something a bit more tasty. At 15 he convinced his parents to buy him a red Commodore electric guitar that he had seen in a second-hand store for £25. He paid his parents back a pound a week from the money he earned doing his paper round. The Commodore would be his go-to instrument and only electric for the best part of the following seven years.

It was during his early teens that John got involved with martial arts, learning Wing Chun and yet again showing real promise. He moved up the ladder quickly and developed his general fitness to the point where he could do the splits upside down with his back against the wall. He also had a tall bag of sand in his bedroom which he would practise his kicks and punches on.

Even at such a tender age he was something of a Renaissance boy. He was as happy reading as he was roundhouse kicking or developing his creative pursuits. In his artwork he was moving into using other mediums such as watercolours and acrylics. John also loved the music that was all around him in the late sixties and early seventies – the sound of the guitar-heavy bands and artists like Led Zeppelin, Deep Purple and Rory Gallagher, not to mention the songwriting genius that had been The Beatles. As he became more comfortable with the guitar he would seek out opportunities to play with like-minded people, who like him wanted to express themselves and experience the magic of performing music to an audience. He got his chance when he joined a band with some older kids, 2d Sparklers, a standard covers act that went on to change its name to Slugband. Greenock garden fêtes would never be the same again!

No sooner had he started on his first foray into music than his parents took the decision to leave Greenock behind and move south of the border and to the place where all great stories start: Essex! Goodmayes is actually recognised as a part of Greater London, again no bad thing, but to all intents and purposes it really is more Essex in its location. It was here that the McGeochs took over the management of a local high street store, Trident, which sold electrical items, and where they had a large flat above the shop.

The Essex/east London of the early 1970s that the McGeochs

relocated to was not the land of dreams that it is now, as extolled by a famous reality TV show. This was a tough and rough place, with – like Greenock – plenty of decent working-class people, but certainly not lacking in villains. This was the era when football terrace violence was at its height and there were still remnants of the mods' and rockers' battles. Coming down from Greenock to a place like Goodmayes, John would have been pretty exotic. Luckily, he was more than able to take care of himself and adapted to his new surroundings quickly. His friendliness, humour and ability to get on ensured he wasn't ostracised. Naturally, he gravitated towards people who, like himself, loved the music of the day and shared a new passion: motorbikes.

John enrolled at Redbridge Technical College at 16. Joe Barry remembers how he first met John: 'I met him on the bus because we both went to Redbridge Technical College. That must have been around 1972. We got chatting and he started hanging out with [us] – we were into playing the guitar and we all had motorbikes. John played a bit of guitar, but he wasn't that good or at least I didn't think he was that good. I mean, he was better than me, but everyone was!'

It was at this time that John started attending guitar lessons at Loughton Tech, where Mark Knopfler (yes, of Dire Straits) was a lecturer in English and also ran a Saturday morning guitar class which John joined. Dave Barker, another of John's friends, recalls those days: 'John turned up in my art class. We just sort of palled up and there was a girl in the class called Ronnie and she was into music. So, basically, it was me, John and Ronnie. John and I had things in common – both of us had our hair long and were growing scruffy beards!'

As his mum remembers, John was never shy of work. From his time growing up in Greenock and also down in Goodmayes, he always had a job. 'He worked in a carpet shop on Green Lane in the school holidays. He really didn't like the smell of the shop at all. He got a job on the night shift at the Sunblest factory. His job was putting cherries on the top of cakes! They came along on a conveyor belt and he had to stand there and put them on the top of these iced cakes. He asked, "When does this stop?" and was told, "When the cherries run out!" They just kept coming and coming and he told me that he'd had a go at eating them or putting two on top of the cakes, but the cherries never ran out! He also got a job in Woolworths in Ilford, where he more

John during his long-haired college days, 1973.
McGeoch family archive

or less swept the floor and folded up cardboard boxes. He worked in a tailor's as a Saturday boy and also worked in one in Greenock as well, which sold the modern fashion of the time. The tailor's in Ilford was actually the first job he got when we moved down here. He was never idle; as a schoolboy he always had a job. He wasn't frightened of work.'

Another friend, Ciaran Harte, himself a keen guitarist and later member of the bands Glass and Religious Overdose, also taught John some pieces on the guitar. Ciaran remembers, 'We jammed a lot and that was what we did. John was a much better guitar player than I was. He was taught piano as a kid up in Greenock.'

The young Scot maintained his love of language and reading, although as remembered by Joe Barry, 'I wrote poetry, but I think John always thought that was a bit wet! You've got to remember how young we were, and I think he was more concerned with appearing hard, you know – we were all wearing leather jackets. I think he was just embracing his masculinity.' Perhaps this was age or perhaps there were deeper things at play as John was always aware of his emotions – even in his earliest days he was a sensitive kid. John did find a constructive outlet for harnessing and channelling his emotions and masculinity by continuing to practise martial arts. This was the heyday of kung fu movies and every kid wanted to be like Bruce Lee. 'He was an emotional guy, a bit neurotic at times. He'd get into states about things and he had a temper on him. He would just blow up about things. Look, I loved the guy, but he had his demons.' As Joe would accept, we all have our demons and hang-ups, it's just how they manifest that differs from person to person.

As John's mother explains, he continued his studies at Thurrock in Essex, doing a foundation in art prior to enrolling at Manchester Polytechnic for his degree. 'He was granted a two-year scholarship at Grays Technical College. Usually, it would only be a one-year provision but because he was doing so well, he was offered two years. The teachers at Redbridge College put him forward for that.'

Ciaran Harte looks back on those early days: 'We were just sort of drinking chums. When John came down [from Scotland] we played quite a bit, then when he went to Grays Thurrock College to study art we used to meet up most days and play a bit of guitar as I was studying at Rush Green, which was on the way. We were all fairly intelligent people with similar interests and outlooks. It was mainly about drinking and trying to get off with birds. The music side was a common interest for all of us.'

Dave Barker remembers what John was into at the time. 'When he first turned up from Scotland, he liked Deep Purple and Rory Gallagher, and why not? People wouldn't necessarily say it, but Rory Gallagher and Ritchie Blackmore would have been an influence on him at that point. He might have got rid of the influence later on, but he had it. It's fair to say he went on to find his own voice, but so did those guys.'

Around 1974 John, Joe and a few mates got jobs at the local psychiatric hospital in Goodmayes, famously known as being where the former world boxing champion Frank Bruno was taken after being sectioned. Joe Barry remembers, 'We all did nursing at the psychiatric hospital – motorcyclist musicians who were nurses! I think as a group we were all touched by that and it was something John would eventually go back to. He was into it.' Although not involved himself, Ciaran recalls those days: 'He'd finished his foundation at Grays Thurrock and, as I remember, he'd taken a year out to work at Goodmayes Psychiatric Hospital. Which is another common thread, really, as Joe, John and a guy called Steve Dunphy all took jobs as untrained psychiatric nurses. It was like a gap year job. Crazy, really. Interesting though that John went into the nursing after PiL and all that stuff.'

It was something that was a natural fit for John, recognising the vulnerabilities in others and the desire within himself to be able to offer support and do something positive for marginalised people. John was also gifted with a natural empathy for the emotional states of others. At this stage in his young life it was never going to be a direction he would immediately want to take beyond earning a few quid; he was already focused on his first big independent decision.

TWO

FRIENDS OF MINE

Moving to Manchester to study fine art, and the first meeting with Howard Devoto

---

In 1976 when I was in art school in Manchester, punk rock happened and I was an avid devotee of all that. Devotoee/Devoto is the word, really; because when Howard left the Buzzcocks he was looking for someone else to work with; through a series of lucky breaks I was introduced to him as a guitarist and we started working together.

Guitarist magazine (November 1985)

BY 1975 JOHN was ready to strike out alone and move away from the family, to Manchester, where he was accepted to study fine art at the polytechnic. His ambition at the time was to become a successful painter and he had diligently built his portfolio prior to making the move. In many ways he couldn't have made a better choice. Manchester was a city still haunted by its industrial past, but with the necessary attributes to go on and become (in the late seventies through the nineties) a hub for music, literature, art and scenes within scenes. Manchester had a rich cultural and musical heritage long before punk took root, spawning bands like The Hollies and Van Der Graaf Generator to name but two. The gigging scene was entrenched in its backstreet pubs and clubs and in the many established venues within the city.

Even after the sixties had been and gone, Mancunians were exposed to the biggest and most exciting acts around. The Who, Fleetwood Mac, the Stones and Bowie all regularly played there. There were several scenes that had been established as the seventies got under way, from the bohemian acts associated with the city's streets to the pub rock scene. Many cultural movements and experiments begin within the university setting and Manchester was no different. Unbeknownst to John, Manchester was attracting like-minded youngsters who, in just a few short years, would reshape not only the city but the cultural landscape of the north of England and beyond.

Of John's first day at the poly, fellow fine art student and friend Liddy Papageorgiou recalls: 'We met at Medlock [Fine Art Centre]. The first day, we were all put into this big studio to draw whatever we saw, and most people were drawing a view outside of the window or something. Standing right in front of me was John, so I decided to draw him from the back. The reason was, he was wearing this jumper that obviously his mum had washed and it had really shrunk and she had hung it on the line to dry, so the sides of the jumper were sticking out from where the pegs had held it on the washing line. I've still got that drawing. I just remember thinking, "Gosh, you know, anybody who can wear that and carry it without being embarrassed is going to be a friend of mine!" He was like that, John, completely confident.' Of the set-up and how they settled into the course, Liddy explains, 'The thing about those days is, it was art for art's sake. You're thrown into a studio and you're given paint and then you're also shown a library and told, "If you want to research anything, go to the library." Obviously, he liked all the abstract expressionists like Jackson Pollock, we all did in those days.' John and Liddy hit it off in a big way and would go on to share accommodation for the next five years or so, including later in London. As she explains of their first home together, 'John and I were at art school together, living in a ghastly place. So, we both just thought, "We've got to get away from here and find somewhere else!"'

John and Liddy ended up moving to a flat on the Wilmslow Road in Rusholme, directly above Cowlishaw's fish shop. It was here that John met Malcolm Garrett, a man who was to find recognition designing album sleeves for the likes of Buzzcocks, Simple Minds and Duran Duran. He also started at the polytechnic in 1975. 'I met him through a friend of mine, David Atherton, who was studying printmaking and I took a room in the house David was living in. Within a month of living there, John and a very good friend of his, Liddy, who was also studying fine art, moved into the same house as us. From there John and I became mates and we started hanging out.' David Atherton remembers the set-up of the house that John came to call home for the next couple of years: 'I had one room downstairs which was a smallish room. Above me Malcolm had a small room and then the big rooms towards the road. Fellow student Trevor had one downstairs and John had the one at the top. He had quite a large room in the flat and that was how we lived for several years.'

Of the house in Rusholme, Liddy remembers, 'We moved to the house that Malcolm lived in above a fish shop, and it stank so badly of fish! We just never even locked the door – we never got burgled or anything, nobody ever came in. It was a grotesque place, but it was just so much fun.'

John and Malcolm struck up a really close friendship helped by their shared similar interests, notably music. Little would he realise at the time, but Malcolm would prove instrumental in pushing John in the right direction, despite John's less than favourable initial response. 'I introduced John to punk. I played him [Buzzcocks'] *Spiral Scratch* and I remember distinctly him saying, "Ah it's fucking rubbish!" I played it again ten minutes later and he said, "Actually it's quite good!" It was so left-field and out of the blue, and on the first listen he was quite critical of the musicianship, but after he came back to it, he realised it was about the attitude.'

As Malcolm would explain to me, it was amazing how little you had to do to stand out in Manchester in 1976. Tight trousers and short hair were enough to mark you out as a freak, a threat or somebody to be avoided. John revelled in it; he'd always had a side to him that liked to push the boundaries and, more than that, he was a young man who wasn't going to be told what to do, what to wear or how to act. He had a natural flamboyance and appreciation for the finer things in life that went hand in hand with his artistic pursuits, his love of good (and not so good) wine and his quick wit. He had a sharp sense of humour to go with a sharp sense of style that was all his own, an air of grandiosity but not wrapped up in pomposity – every inch the young artist.

John was enjoying the freedom of being a student in Manchester, where he could start to express himself and assert his independence. He took to his studies with a discipline and drive that were matched by his enjoyment of the bars and gigs the city had to offer. Malcolm remembers one of the nights out they shared. 'We went together to see Can when they came to play the student union in Manchester. I can remember, and this is when you sat down at gigs, I was a little worse for wear on drink. I'd drunk a lot. I was by no means a non-drinker, but I didn't tend to get drunk but that day I did. I can remember the band came on late and we were all sat in the auditorium which was basically like a big gym, so you sat there, and I started banging a can of beer on the floor and the whole audience were banging cans of beer. Then I got quite ill, so as we stood up to leave, I went to the toilet to throw up and John, being lovely, came in, picked me up and carried me home as we only lived a quarter of a mile down the road from there. So, it was that kind of relationship.'

As he was beginning to appreciate, it was a great time to be a young man with aspirations and with the charisma and talent to back it up. However John hadn't really done much musically, outside of entertaining his housemates with the guitar, since making the move from London. As Liddy recalls, 'He always had a guitar, and it was the extension of his arm. I mean, he spoke through his guitar. Whenever we were at home, he was always sitting with it. He'd talk to you and add colour to what he was saying by notes on the guitar, he was so much of a musician.' Equally John loved to paint – he loved the freedom that it allowed him, translating to canvas the creative expression that found outlets in all areas of his life, from his sense of humour to his choice of clothes. As Liddy explains, 'He loved painting. He had this thing which was very uncomplicated – he was so present, he wasn't neurotic about painting like a lot of people can be. He'd just get his paints and dive in and paint, experiment with shapes, materials and marks that he made in the most genius way. He was very present, somehow, and I think his music was the same; his paintings really were brilliant, fab.' David remembers, 'John came as a mature student. So, he'd had quite a lot of experience of both painting and life before he came to Manchester. His work was abstract, in the truest sense of the word, and I think he probably did what he needed to do, and he knew exactly what the tutors wanted. So, he was able to play the system quite well while he got on with the things he was more interested in – which were probably music and socialising.'

He'd brought his trusty, if slightly battered, Commodore with him, but he wasn't looking for a project to sink his burgeoning skills into... yet. John was reunited with an old friend in Manchester when Ciaran Harte decided to come up and study there. 'I got to know John a lot more when I went off to Brighton Polytechnic and promptly got kicked out after a year. Then from around '75 to '76 I was at Manchester Uni when John was at the poly up there. John was living with Malcolm Garrett above Cowlishaw's, which was godawful. It was like *The Young Ones*' flat. I used to go there every Sunday and we would just drink and jam all day. That's really where I got to know John properly.' Liddy remembers fondly how much fun they all had when Ciaran came over and recalls those occasions vividly: 'Ciaran was an amazing guitarist and he used to come over at the weekend. I mean, he was amazing, he used to play like Jimi Hendrix. They used to play all day and all night in this room in Rusholme and it was just bloody great. We had a tape player and we used to do loops. Ciaran would play like Hendrix and John used to dance around him with his guitar, picking like he did, and of course the electricity would go out because the meter was in the room of the conventional guy who used to come and collect the rents so we couldn't just go and put money in the meter – we didn't have the money anyway. So, we just used to sit in the dark playing music. Occasionally, because there were always other people around, somebody would get too stoned and fall asleep and John, being the prankster, would arrange this person's breathing to come out of a recorder or something and then put in the loop and they'd play guitar over the snores!'

It would be down to David to gather the rent money from the housemates, and Liddy looks back on how John would wind him up. 'The hilarious thing was when we shared the house with Malcolm, and John and I had a huge room together, he had half and I had half. David was the self-appointed gatherer of rents who lived downstairs – also an art student. He was kind of conventional and well... he was convinced that John and I were having it off! Every Friday morning he'd come to collect the rent and obviously the door would be locked so

John would say, "Wait, wait, wait!" and we'd both quickly strip to the waist and put a naked shoulder round the door and say, "Yes?" and you could tell that this guy was just dying to come into the room to see what was going on. Next Friday, same thing, and John would put a naked leg out and give him the rent! He was such a prankster.'

His flatmates knew he was a talented musician. They'd all appreciated his ability to learn and perform songs from a wide variety of bands and styles. At this point, however, his thoughts were very much centred around getting his degree and seeing how far that might take him. As with his guitar playing, his ability as a painter was clear and he had gained admiration for his conceptual pieces. Malcolm Garrett says, 'John was somebody who whenever he turned his attention to doing something, two things: he would devote all his time and energy to doing it, and he would want to be the best at it that he could possibly be. So, in coming to Manchester to study fine art, he wanted to be the best painter. He had sort of given up playing guitar – he had it, but he wasn't really doing that much with it. The same was true, I think, of martial arts. He'd given up, but I once saw him demonstrate how good he was in the kitchen. There was a fly buzzing around and John just shot his hand out and caught the fly in mid-air and I was like, "What the fuck?!" He let it go and then he shot his hand out and caught it again!'

John's diligence and drive to be the best was something noticed by another friend from the poly who was studying on the same course as John, Roger Cleghorn. 'We were in a block [fine art] away from the rest – design and textiles – a factory unit next to the Mancunian Way called Medlock Fine Art Centre. So, we were *artists*, we weren't designers! We thought a lot of ourselves, I think – too much of ourselves. We always used to say that whatever John did, he'd give it 100 per cent. He'd throw himself into whatever it was wholeheartedly and excel. He was excellent at his martial arts. I'm not sure if he was a black belt, but he was really good at it.'

John must have been quite the character to be around, and it is little surprise that his company was sought out by those who came to know him in student land. Ciaran recalls the 'Sunday specials' that he and John would partake in. 'I was in Manchester from October '75 to June '76 and that was when we'd do our jamming. I was into tape recorders at that point, so I'd set up my Sony TC-377, we'd rig that through his hi-fi system in his flat, get drunk and just leave it on echo while we played.'

Manchester itself was on the cusp of something. Culturally there was a current of change, similar to that affecting large cities up and down the country, but it would have particular resonance in Manchester. John was witness to something special – he was in the right place at the right time. There seemed something predestined about it. One major precursor of this change was an event so steeped in folklore that it is easy to overplay its role in what was to come. Afterwards, Manchester would never be the same. And though it was something that John himself didn't witness, it would, indirectly, change his life forever too.

Pete Shelley and Howard Devoto, who had met while at Bolton Technical College, were switched on to what was starting to go off in London with the advent of punk, and had already been getting their own band together, Buzzcocks. They made a point of travelling down south in 1976 to go and watch the Sex Pistols perform and had the nous to approach their manager, Malcolm McLaren, and book the band to appear at the Lesser Free Trade Hall in Manchester. The fourth of June 1976 is a date that neither punk aficionados nor those in attendance will ever forget. This was perhaps the single most important event that really kick-started the careers of a host of young Mancunians/Salfordians, including Ian Curtis, Peter Hook, Steven Morrissey and one Mick Hucknall (apparently!). The aura of myth surrounding the Pistols' first appearance in Manchester is such that those who claim to have been there are not always believed. For the first time, these aspiring young talents were exposed to what had begun to spark a real power surge of musical creativity in the capital. Buzzcocks had intended to support the Pistols that evening, but found themselves short on actual musicians as the band underwent something of a change in line-up. They did support Johnny Rotten and his cohort on their second Manchester date, however, less than two months later, and the rest is most certainly history.

Of that first Pistols gig at the Lesser Free Trade Hall, Peter Hook recalls, 'The oddest thing about it was that it was shit. It sounded shit. The support band were a heavy metal group that played *Nantucket*

Sleighride by Mountain in its entirety for twenty-five minutes, so everybody was bored fucking shitless by these long-haired wankers. *Nantucket Sleighride* is a great record, yeah, but the fact that they played it – maybe they were ahead of their time in terms of tribute bands, but everyone was bored. For us it was just like, "Look, fuck off, if we'd wanted to hear that we'd go and see Mountain!" because Mountain were still touring. Then the Sex Pistols came on and they sounded awful and they told everybody just to "Fuck off!" and we were like, "Oh, my fucking God! I could do that; I could sound this shit and tell everybody to fuck off. I could do that!"

'It was a revelation, because before, musicians had seemed like Jimmy Page, John Paul Jones, Santana – completely untouchable, and you couldn't even consider yourself to be in the same room as them at a concert, never mind trying to make music like they did. The Sex Pistols and punk, it just looked like you could do it. We formed a band, me and Barney [Bernard Sumner], as we walked out the door. He had a guitar, but I didn't have a musical bone in my body. That was the effect it had on you. It made me form a band and I'd never even considered it! It was nuts, it was a nuts reaction.

'Ironically, when you listen to the bootleg, the Sex Pistols are actually quite good – rock'n'roll and a bit like Eddie and the Hot Rods – but that night they sounded fucking dreadful! It was like Malcolm McLaren had gone, "Fucking turn everything up!" and everything was just feeding back. There was forty-three people there, because Pete Shelley had told me how many tickets he'd sold. If you see those very famous pictures, you can see the back of everybody's heads – that's the only shot, there were no shots from the stage out. [...] It inspired us for a really strange reason and in some ways, sometimes you think that maybe Manchester was ready to be inspired and it was almost like a collision. As a football fan who was a bit of a yob at that time, the fact that they had a fight at every gig, we were like, "Yeah, that's fucking right!" You didn't get many fights at Deep Purple concerts or Led Zeppelin or Santana or David Bowie concerts. You went to see the Sex Pistols and there were battles going off, we thought it was great.

'It sort of backfired on you when you became a group, particularly the spitting. Yeah, it was very inspiring and for all the wrong reasons and it became like an avalanche then – all over the country. The bad thing about punk was it was very nihilistic and aggressive. We were like bad teenagers, but it gave [us] post-punk bands like Siouxsie and the Banshees, Joy Division, Killing Joke, PiL – that ilk of bands inspired a lot of great music after punk, and that wave was very inspiring. Those years from 1980 to 1988, because it all changed with acid house and it became a much more cosmopolitan thing, but up until then you look at the groups – it was a fantastic period of music that was inspired by, if you're going to be honest, one of the worst periods of music because most of punk was pretty shit, wasn't it?'

By this point McGeoch was well and truly immersed in the pub rock/punk scene in Manchester. Bands were regularly coming to play, making it very much the place to be outside of London. Buzzcocks were the figureheads, but by the start of 1977 and almost as soon as *Spiral Scratch* had been released, Devoto walked, claiming he wasn't really that mad on punk rock. It was a bold move, as *Spiral Scratch* was very much a seminal release of the era and firmly put Manchester and the band itself on the map. People were taking notice, the power was shifting from Liverpool across the M62, something was going on. As Barry Adamson recalls, 'For me, the world changed quite a bit with the emergence of Buzzcocks and the EP *Spiral Scratch*. I'd always been all about rock and soul and a combination of the two – I could love a Stooges record as much as a James Brown record. It [*Spiral Scratch*] was something relatable. They dropped the EP, which I went to buy from a record shop in Stockport. The guy who ran the shop turned out to be Paul Morley and I remember thinking that this guy was really talking eloquently about the record but, you know, he's not very punk – he's got long hair!'

Liddy remembers another musical explosion which, along with punk, was offering the youth of cities like London, Manchester and Birmingham not just an introduction to new and experimental sounds, but a sense of unity and respect for different identities against the backdrop of rising far-right activity. It brought white punks together with their black counterparts, largely first- or second-generation sons and daughters of immigrants from the West Indies. This crossover was as relevant and important as punk and was something McGeoch lapped up. 'Reggae and dub was a huge, and I mean huge, part of the scene in Manchester. We were seeing bands all the time at the Band on the Wall club. Apart from Burning Spear and Steel Pulse, who were properly famous, we saw loads of other cool bands. John loved them. We would also go to illegal clubs to listen to DJs "toast and scratch". One club we used to go to was over in Moss Side, a rough and semi-derelict neighbourhood, after hours, like 2 a.m. to 7 a.m. It was a boarded-up factory and the only way in was from the slightly less boarded-up factory next door, up a fire escape and over onto the roof! It was heaving and unless I had John with me, I felt nervous to go there. He just made friends with everybody and the rhythms and complex beat of the music really affected him and were reflected in the subsequent weekend jam sessions.'

Other young Mancunians (Salfordians, Leythers, Wiganers included) were following in the footsteps of what Buzzcocks had caught on to with punk, and the city started to hothouse a host of innovative and credible acts to let London know they weren't the only game in town. These were bands like The Drones, The Fall, Slaughter and the Dogs and Warsaw (later to find cult status as Joy Division). It's impossible to overstate just how significant a role Tony Wilson of Granada Television played, with shows like *So It Goes*, in shining a light on what was going on in and around Manchester culturally and, in particular, in its music scene. Wilson was in attendance at the Lesser Free Trade Hall gig and, as with so many others that night, his life would never be the same again. He is often quoted as saying that bands such as the Pistols and Joy Division were on stage because they had 'no fucking choice', and I think the same is true of Wilson himself. He knew that this burst of new music was crucial and needed to be heard widely. Manchester needed to be felt. It wasn't just Wilson who was showcasing a new movement in the north-west. John Peel at BBC Radio 1 was also impressed by the records that were finding their way onto his desk, and he more than championed the sound, helping it to gain momentum and greater exposure.

By 1976 and 1977 many people were experiencing a sense of desperation and a feeling of hopelessness. The economy was stuttering and in so many ways there had been stagnation culturally. The charts were awash with twee and superficial hits that could never speak to a frustrated generation. Whether McGeoch felt this way is unclear;

probably not. Here was a man of keen intelligence, studying for his degree and geared for success in whatever form that might take. He was far from being one of the disenfranchised, without work or hope for the future. Yet what was going on musically was as important to him as it was to any other person in their late teens or early twenties. One of the main reasons punk took off was that the Britain of the mid to late seventies was a dull and boring place to be. So much can come out of having nothing to do and feeling intense frustration and boredom. Boredom is largely eradicated from society these days, with technological advances ensuring that we are stimulated 24/7, whether we want to be or not. Without boredom I doubt punk could have ignited, and even if it had, it wouldn't have had the impact it did.

Manchester was reimagining itself through the youth who were raised there, or simply passing through. Its flavour was its own – culturally it could never be like London and nor would it aim to be. After the capital, it was widely acknowledged as the most significant city in the UK for punk and later post-punk, and the cultural flagbearer for the north of England. Liverpool would find its own voice later. Bands coming up and playing in Manchester were exposing John and his contemporaries to something that would have seemed inconceivable just a year or two before punk emerged. As Malcolm Garrett relates, 'Early in '77 we were going to the Electric Circus. We saw The Clash on the White Riot tour, The Ramones, The Jam, Buzzcocks. There was a gay bar called the Ranch just off Piccadilly Gardens and we'd go there on a Friday night and after the Electric Circus on a Sunday night. We'd go there because gay bars were the only place you could go and feel safe, because punks were as much outsiders as the gay community was. Literally at that time you could get beaten up for being a punk – all it would take was to bump into the wrong person on the way home on a Friday night and violence could ensue.'

David Atherton recalls going to gigs with John and one meeting in particular that would become a full-blown collaboration years down the line, unbeknownst to either party. 'John and I saw Siouxsie and the Banshees at Rafters and I remember him talking to Siouxsie after the show. There were so many groups that we saw at the various little clubs in Manchester. After seeing the bands we'd stagger via the back way to Rusholme and go and have an Indian at, I think it was called the Plaza, which was a really grim Indian restaurant where you'd just get a plate of slosh with tons of rice.'

Of the burgeoning punk scene in Manchester, David adds, 'To Mancunians punk bands were things like Buzzcocks, like Slaughter and the Dogs or Iggy Pop. The Clash were like a London pub band to Mancunians, and another thing was the myth of the conflict between punks and anybody else simply wasn't true, or rather not from the punks. Punks were often incredibly peaceful – they might have been anarchic, but they were not violent. The media created this war between punks and skinheads or Teddy boys and that started the violence really. When we went to places like Rafters or the Ranch, there was no kit or uniform for punks. Punks didn't go around in tartan trousers, braces and strange haircuts based on some Mohican style. Punks would wear anything. From straight-legged trousers to bin bags to storm trooper uniform. The "look" was created or manufactured by the media – before that point it simply didn't exist. It was just a time of complete freedom. It was great because you no longer had to listen to prog rock or wear flares – they had well had their day by 1976. The punk stuff was just such a breath of fresh air.'

Roger Cleghorn looks back on the impact of punk at the time, specifically for the youth in and around Manchester. 'It was a great time and I kind of knew John a bit through the course, and we'd see each other out and about at punk gigs. At the time there were very few of us going to those places, so you'd see the same faces. You'd see Malcolm [Garrett] there and find out he was at the poly and then there was the connection with all of our various girlfriends as well. One of the great things about punk was that people were scared of it. There was always that edge, that danger of going to a Pistols gig or going to see Buzzcocks or even, God forbid, Slaughter and the Dogs in Manchester. It was that wonderful underground feeling.'

Naturally funds were tight for the young group of friends and meals could become something of a luxury. As Liddy explains, 'He was such a fantastic cook and it was the same as with his painting and music, breaking all the rules. He was very, very kind and generous and he was always including friends in things and sharing stuff. I remember we were so hungry as students, always hungry, because we mismanaged our money and spent it all on going out and by Sunday night you haven't eaten for two days. I remember one time that we went through all our pockets, bags and the sofa and got together as much money as we could, which I think came to about 3p or something. So, he went out and came back with a small packet of crisps which I think were roast beef flavour and we sat there next to each other on the sofa with our eyes closed completely sucking on these crisps imagining that we were eating proper food! That's what he'd do, just bonkers.'

The lack of funds only added to the charm and haphazardness of the time. The sense of fun and optimism of being young, of being creative and making the most of it was something they all felt, and John in particular. As Liddy says, 'It was just this world of creativity where everybody was busy. Malcolm was busy, as were we all, and it was bloody great. John was my best friend – I love him to bits and always, always loved him to bits. He was very inclusive, and I remember people would come up to him and he'd give everybody time and talk to everyone. He was very kind-hearted and, you know, he had his Achilles heel, but he was just a very good person.' David is in agreement and goes further: 'Everybody was the same. The same in that we had no money, but also in that everybody worked like Trojans. When we were working at college, we would be there from nine in the morning until nine at night and then we'd go on to the student bar and then on to The Conti [club] or wherever. We worked incredibly hard and loved what we were doing, it wasn't a chore. Malcolm would just talk music all day and all night and do very little work himself, but then as soon as his assessments approached, he'd drop a load of speed and work solidly for four days without any sleep. He would come up with the best results imaginable. John worked in a similar kind of way, perhaps not being able to manage his intake as much as Malcolm could. They were just fantastic times.'

The fun they shared wasn't just about music, art and partying. Even the odd near miss with household appliances could have the friends in stitches. As David relates, 'We never had any money, so whatever we did have went on Boddingtons and records. One day before we went to college John wanted to iron one of his white shirts. He liked his white shirts. I was the only person in the flat with an iron, but this thing was ancient. It had belonged to my grandfather and was probably one of the first electric irons that had been invented. Basically it had no plug attached. What it did have was two wires which I would have to pop into the three-prong plug socket and then quickly put a socket from another appliance in so that the wires stayed in place. So, I had showed this to John and after I'd left for college he decided he wanted to iron a shirt. I came home that day at around lunchtime, which was unusual for me, but when I got in I found Liddy pouring water over this gaping, burnt hole in the carpet with clouds of steam rising. What had happened was John had plugged it in, as I had shown him, gone off and left the iron to heat up, and forgotten all about it. The iron had somehow either fallen over or had already been left flat on the carpet and it burned through the material of the carpet, the underlay, then the wooden floorboard and fallen through the floor into the ceiling of the room below! As it had done so it had yanked the wires from the plug socket, thankfully. All you could do was laugh – it was absolutely hilarious.'

In March 1977, Malcolm and John decided to host a party at their flat. There may have been a bit of gamesmanship on Malcolm's part in using the occasion to introduce John to Howard Devoto. Howard was, by now, toying with the idea of getting back into the saddle and doing something with music again. 'I met John relatively early, April of 1977, three months after I had left Buzzcocks. We were introduced a long time before Magazine started coming together. It was Malcolm who said to me, "The guy I share a house with can play all the guitar parts to *Marquee Moon*," and that made me think that he would be somebody worth knowing. I was vaguely thinking of getting involved in another band at the time and I had a couple of ideas for songs. It was just going to be something, not punk really, as indicated by the advert I placed for musicians "to play fast and slow music."'

Malcolm explains: 'John had decided to put the guitar to one side while he studied fine art. He'd been in rock bands before coming to Manchester. The thing was that it was obvious, it was just obvious to anybody, when he picked up the guitar and he decided to play it – as he might have done when we were just sat around watching television – that he was really fucking good! Normally when your flatmate picks up the guitar there comes a point where you just say, "Will you shut up?" It was obvious that John had mastered the instrument. After I introduced him to Buzzcocks with the *Spiral Scratch* EP, we hosted a party in the flat. Howard Devoto had left Buzzcocks, I'd met Howard and I'd met Richard Boon [who was managing Buzzcocks] through Linder [Sterling]. She had seen Buzzcocks and become closely acquainted with Howard and did some of the early handbills for the band before I arrived, but she wasn't so interested in graphic design. She introduced me to Howard and Richard and as I was into graphic design, I ended up designing and working with her, using her montage and illustrations. I knew that Howard had left Buzzcocks and was toying with the idea of forming another band. I had said to Howard, "You need John, you need this guitarist!" Famously, or infamously, John and I organised this party for a Saturday night and it was at this party that Howard, Richard and Linder all came – and with Howard, Pete Shelley came along. It was the first time that I'd met Pete and it was also the first time that Howard met John. Howard decided that they should try out playing together and then the week after John went to Howard's house and Magazine was formed, with Barry [Adamson] joining them soon after. I remember Pete Shelley sitting on John's bed half the night at the party, playing songs on John's acoustic guitar, and the following week I went to see Buzzcocks for the first time at the Band on the Wall.'

David recalls the party atmosphere: 'The flat was known for having great parties, we really had a good time. I think it may have been someone's 21st birthday party that we had there, and Malcolm was dressed in all white and John was dressed as Noël Coward – he loved Noël Coward. So, there he was, wandering around in his silk dressing gown with a cigarette holder with his hair all slicked back. I remember Buzzcocks being around and playing about – we'd discovered black lights and we had them everywhere. I know that the people in the shop below knew we'd had a party at the weekend because all the plaster had fallen off their ceiling and into the shop. The halcyon days of student life and being in Manchester!'

Roger Cleghorn adds that the feeling in Manchester, and the sparks of creativity that were flying in all directions, created a 'can do' attitude, of wanting to try something new. 'Manchester had a feel of its own back then which was very different. The art and the music scene, hooking up with people like Malcolm on the design side and punk being what it was. It all just came together, and it really was a

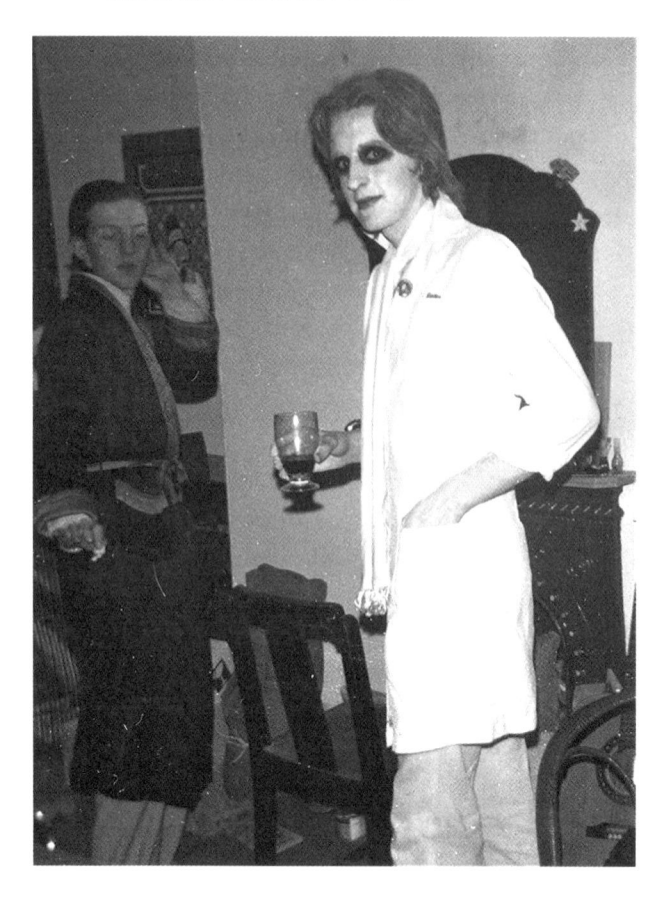

John, left, dressed as Noël Coward with Malcolm Garrett at their Manchester house party, 1976.
Malcolm Garrett archive

beautiful conflating of everything, it was great. At the time you don't necessarily think that. You're just with your friends, then a mate joins a band and the next thing you know they're signed to a label and in the *NME* and *Melody Maker* and that kind of thing. Hindsight is always different, but it was a fantastic opportunity. An opportunity that a lot of people grasped.'

THREE

SECONDHAND INSIGHT
The formation, rise and fall of Magazine

The reason Magazine originally came together was to record 'Shot by Both Sides'. Howard had written that song and another two songs and was looking for someone to work with him and bounce ideas off of – which was me. Originally we were going to use a couple of members of the Buzzcocks and me on guitar and record it as a one-off.

International Musician and Recording World (April 1981)

BY THE SUMMER of 1977 there was enough motivation for Howard to kick on with his concept for a new band. With John in tow, albeit away in London earning some cash in the holidays, it was decided that placing an advert looking for musicians to play 'fast and slow music' should be the next move – an ad was placed at the Virgin store. Jon Webster had recently been put in charge of the shop when Howard turned up, note in hand. 'Howard came into the shop and said, "Do you mind if I put this up?" and that was the notice for musicians. I wish I'd kept that! We were all surprised that he'd left Buzzcocks, but it was an artistic decision. I don't think he was comfortable in that set-up. I didn't know him that well, but the thing about Howard is he's always wanted to plough his own furrow. It was a shock, definitely a shock. Howard put the ad up and I think someone nicked it actually and he had to come back and put another one up. You can imagine some punk seeing that, looking for a souvenir and thinking, "I'll have that, thank you very much!"'

Paul Morley takes up the story of how a new sound and identity was emerging in Manchester: 'When I started writing for the *NME*, which I did in '76, the first piece I ever had in was Buzzcocks. A few months later I had a piece in about this Manchester scene which had started to develop, with obviously Howard Devoto, The Fall had started by then, and Warsaw had started by then. There was a wonderful big picture taken by Kevin Cummins of Howard Devoto and Linder for the *NME* in '77, I think. Suddenly there was a scene and so I was a very enthusiastic supporter of Buzzcocks, and then that seismic shift when Howard left Buzzcocks – and then there was Magazine. [...] One of the things I loved about Howard was that this strange intellectual element had emerged within it all, which sort of catered to my taste – having read certain things, having thought certain things and for it having a seriousness attached to it. It all seemed incredibly important, and it also seemed important because local music and local musicians were getting national exposure. Even though we'd had that before with your 10ccs, Herman's Hermits and Sad Café – they never really seemed "Manchester", they never sang in a Manchester accent and they didn't sing about Manchester things. Suddenly there were these groups who sang about local things in local accents and it was extraordinary, and I recognise the significance of that even now.

'Howard leaving Buzzcocks was a huge moment, and in a way it felt a bit like Mick Jagger leaving the Stones – it was like a huge transformation taking place in something that had only just happened. I remember Howard telling me that it felt like he was "running out of breath" and that he "couldn't pack all those words into songs any more". He felt he needed to try something else, so the materialisation of Magazine was already like folklore even then. You had the ads going up in the Virgin store and these other musicians appearing packed around Howard.'

Enter Barry Adamson, who had recently acquired a bass guitar (with two strings) from a friend. 'I was given this bass that only had two strings, so I decided at the weekend I'd go into town and buy the other two strings. By this point Buzzcocks had already broken up and

I was in the Virgin store and I saw this advert that Howard Devoto had put up. So, I said to my friend Willie, 'I'm going to answer that ad!' He knew we had the punk chutzpah to do something like that. You were encouraged – it was a very different sort of scene and very doable and DIY. I bought the strings and, as I didn't have an amplifier, I sat on the bed and used the wooden frame to get a sort of amplification as it reverberated. So, I practised on the bass – I knew some chords on guitar but didn't know my way around a bass. I went the next day to meet Howard and all I'd really learnt was the low E note, which I kept playing, and then Howard showed me "The Light Pours Out of Me" and I was very nervous of course. Howard reassured me that it wasn't really an audition, it was more about seeing where it might go. I played this low note that I'd been practising all night, and it worked... it just fit. I think he may have shown me "Shot by Both Sides" and "Touch and Go". I was able to follow a rhythm so that was OK, and I was in and that was it! Very quickly we were rehearsing. At this point John was away, but Howard told me about this guy and how they'd put together "The Light Pours Out of Me" and that he would be coming back from London and just what an amazing guitarist he was. This was August '77 and that was it then. We got together and went to Martin Jackson's house, who was recruited to play drums, and got into it.'

As Howard notes, 'I didn't see an awful lot of him [John] after our introduction, as I remember. Then in the summer, when I was ready to move forward with the idea of the band and met Barry and Martin Jackson, I then auditioned with them.' (John at this point was in London.) 'I felt then that there is a basis of a band starting here. I called John and asked him if he could come back to Manchester.' Though the initial contact with McGeoch had been brief, it had been productive. John was able to work with the outlines and come up with dynamic parts that would help create and shape the sound that became Magazine. Bob Dickinson was brought in on keyboards.

Howard reflects, 'It wasn't an idealised aesthetic, it was more practical than that – I was an opportunity for John. John had the skills and yes, he had the sort of personality that I felt I could rub along with OK. My take at the time was let's see how it goes, because he would then have to meet Barry, Martin and Bob Dickinson and how is everybody going to get along? You have to feel your way in with things.'

It's fair to say that playing with Howard was a major opportunity for the young guitarist, as it was for Barry and Martin and to a lesser degree Bob Dickinson, who wasn't really into the punk scene. Among the small but discerning circles of Manchester's music scene, Howard had an identity all his own, a following and a cachet due to Buzzcocks. His involvement with Buzzcocks had not only shown that he could write and perform but that he possessed the intelligence and drive to also manage band affairs. He had proved his credentials when getting the Pistols to perform in Manchester and handling general managerial duties before Richard Boon took over. All of which would give him a degree of seniority within the new set-up.

At this point, it was unclear whether Magazine would be a long-term project or would simply try to record an EP with the material Howard already had, based on ideas from his time with Buzzcocks – namely what would become 'Shot by Both Sides'. Barry was a shrewd acquisition, as he would rapidly develop as a bassist and musician. He was a natural, and the style he developed would become the blueprint bass sound of the post-punk era. Martin Jackson on drums was all-in on punk at the time. He was solid and right for where the band were moving initially, although ultimately reluctant to grow as both a player and bandmate as the sound changed. Bob perhaps was the odd one out, more drawn towards classical playing, and was never going to be a long-term fit for the band. The major issue would be his dislike of performing live.

John returned from London to meet up with Howard's new recruits and start laying down tracks for what would eventually become the band's debut album. Barry has fond memories of his first introduction to John. 'John breezed into a rehearsal room, everybody was being very polite around each other and all of a sudden this guy comes steaming into rehearsal tripping over everything and being very clumsy but in an affable and charming way. It kind of cut through the feeling we had of being around Howard and being on our best behaviour and feeling slightly awkward. John arriving was a total breath of fresh air, and then he plugged his guitar in and all of a sudden you were witnessing somebody who could not only push the boundaries of what playing the guitar was about, but also somebody who had this strange combination of styles which I had never heard before and that was very exciting.'

John was only really known to Howard up to this point and his initial playing with the band certainly didn't disappoint. Along with Barry's distinctive playing on 'The Light Pours Out of Me', John elevated the song to classic status, which was solidified by Howard's foreboding vocals. Howard recalls the input John had on making the song what it was: 'I remember one point where "The Light Pours Out of Me" was an idea for a song that was in its very early stages. We'd got the drums and an idea of the bass, my guitar bits in the verses and the chorus. We presented it to John when he'd returned from London to Manchester and I am sure on the spot he said, "Ah, well I've got this," and showed us what would become the two guitar solos in the last third of the song – the "shiny light solos" as I always think of them. John came up with those, more or less, there and then, and they fitted so well that I felt, "Right, wow, we could really truck with this." Those particular bits always seemed a bit [Television's] Tom Verlaine-like to me – there is something about the tone of the guitar that reminded me a bit of "Guiding Light". I knew it was good.'

The writing process moved on very quickly and John was a crucial part of that. He was bursting with creativity and had been playing the guitar long enough to translate those ideas into sound. Working with Howard clearly triggered something inside, and it became apparent pretty quickly that Magazine were going to be more than a flash in the pan and that there was something here worth pursuing.

Things were changing in John's personal life too. Shortly before meeting Howard for the first time he had started dating a fellow Manchester Poly student, Janet Pickford. 'He was studying fine art at Medlock and I was on a different course but did a subsidiary subject over at Medlock. The next thing I know, I kept finding him popping up at my department looking for advice on how to make things. So, I kept running away. "Oh God, it's that short Scottish guy again!"' Despite the initial reluctance on her part, the two became an item and Janet became familiar with the guys in Magazine. All the while he was busy throwing himself into Magazine, it is worth remembering that he was still working for his degree.

John and his girlfriend Janet.
McGeoch family archive

The band began the early rehearsals in a basement in Chorlton-cum-Hardy. Ideas would be bounced around, with Howard having final say, although Barry notes that John established himself in the writing stakes early on. 'John was very innovative. He would come up with stuff on the spot and also at home. He would show me something he was working on and ask my opinion. The writer side of him was pretty pushy, and I think we all were to an extent, which may be one of the reasons Magazine ended, really. From the earliest days I feel that John had quite a secure position from the writing side of things, and of course the band being guitar-led, he was privy to having his ideas heard. The idea of writing and performing the songs was the ultimate for him.'

The band were working hard, galvanising each other, and there was already a bit of a buzz stirring about Devoto's latest project. It wouldn't be long before record labels came sniffing about. Bands with much less pedigree were being signed to deals, simply for owning instruments, so the musicianship and writing skills within the band were not going to go unnoticed. They sent off their early demos to several companies, including Virgin Records. Confidence in the camp was high and Virgin, having expressed interest, followed up on this, making the move official when Simon Draper signed them up to a deal.

'I was managing director at Virgin and head of A&R and signed Magazine to the label and all the acts in the seventies and most in the eighties also, but Magazine in particular was my project. I was aware of Pete Shelley and Howard Devoto through Buzzcocks, so when I heard that Howard had formed a band I was very interested indeed. I attached my allegiance, if you like, rather more to Magazine than the Sex Pistols, who were a harder group to deal with, and in a way Magazine appealed more to me because they were more intellectual, very cerebral and very impressive.'

On the inner workings of how bands were signed to Virgin, Simon explains, 'Richard Branson left all the A&R decisions very largely to me, especially during that period. The company was run by me and I was in charge of artwork and A&R and so I had to carry the staff with me, but they were all like-minded. The people we hired, almost by definition, had similar taste. Sometimes I had to persuade people, for instance when I signed Japan – not that many people in the company were convinced, but they rapidly came round to it. The company were totally behind Magazine. I didn't have to do a lot of persuading where they were concerned.'

A lot had been achieved by the band in a very short space of time, and before they had even performed live. The band's debut came on the closing night of the Electric Circus in Manchester on 2 October 1977. The band had borrowed equipment from Buzzcocks, and John was still using his old Commodore. It was more by chance than design that this was Magazine's first gig; there hadn't been a lot of preparation for it, other than the previous few months of general rehearsing and working on songs. Nevertheless, it was the necessary next step in the evolution of the band. Shortly after this Magazine performed at another cult venue, Rafters, also in Manchester. This was much more of a 'proper' debut and something more considered than their first attempt. These were the places you had to be playing if you were going to be taken seriously in the city and within the scene. These were the venues that John himself frequented, and where, alongside the likes of Malcolm Garrett, he had witnessed some of the best and most exciting new acts around. The band performed a short set and the buzz of hearing songs like 'Shot by Both Sides' and 'The Light Pours Out of Me' for the first time must have been incredible. Here was yet another exciting local act bursting onto the scene, with a well-known frontman and a unique style. John was made for moments like this. He was laying it down in rehearsal, he'd impressed his flatmates, but this was him offering up what he had to a wider audience. On stage, in total command of his own performance, from the start he held those who witnessed him live in the palm of his hand. Magazine and McGeoch had arrived.

Of the Rafters gig, Roger Cleghorn remembers one particular concern John had prior to taking to the stage. 'In the very early days when Magazine played at Rafters, which was the second gig, I think, I was John's guitar roadie and bodyguard – I've got no idea why! Where the bodyguard thing came from, I couldn't tell you. I was a friend and John just said, "Come down and look after the guitars for me, set them up and make sure they're in tune." Then it became this guitar roadie/bodyguard which has always been hilarious to me. I can remember when they were doing the soundcheck in the afternoon and Richard Boon and Pete Shelley were there, just checking in and seeing how everything was going. John took me to one side and said, "Look, tonight if – and I don't know whether he will – but if Pete tries to get up on stage to play "Shot by Both Sides" with us, you've got to chuck him off the stage." Fortunately, he never did. I remember being crouched down at the side of the stage really scared that he might, and I would have to try and do that, because Pete Shelley was quite popular in Manchester at the time. [...] Clearly it was a worry for John. I still don't know why John would need a bodyguard because he could take care of himself, thank you very much.'

Paul Morley remembers the gig and that even from the very outset, the new group had a distinctive feel: 'I remember the first time I saw Magazine, which I think was at Rafters, and at the time we couldn't quite believe it, because they were so different from Buzzcocks – if only because they had a keyboard player.'

Peter Hook, himself on the cusp of making music history as part of Joy Division and later New Order (starting off under the name Warsaw), remembers the band's ambivalent if appreciative opinion of Magazine. 'They actually stole our drummer, the bastards! We were very, very annoyed. Ian Curtis had lined Martin Jackson up to join us as Warsaw and, for some reason, and I don't really remember how it happened, but we'd met, talked about it and he was due to join us, but he fucked off and joined Magazine! So, we were very upset at the time with Howard Devoto. We knew Howard quite well. We were very working class whereas Howard and Pete Shelley were middle class without a shadow of a doubt. There was a bit of an awkward fit with us – I think we had the chips on our shoulder, shall we say. We did rub along which was quite nice, and we became friends, if you like, as well as adversaries. The competition was always there, with playing. Every band had to be very competitive and Magazine were our competition. I was very impressed, and whenever I'm DJing, playing mostly dance music, I think to myself that I could just slip "Shot by Both Sides" in there and it would sound great. A great record.'

John would never have been content within the musical constraints of a punk band. He was far too gifted a guitarist for that, and although he enjoyed the scene and the bands he'd seen, he realised that musically he would need a bigger and better vehicle not just to grow and expand his own abilities, but to appeal to a broader audience. The newly emerging post-punk acts were geared up for that. They had taken the breaks that punk had given them, as Keith Levene comments. 'With punk it was like, what doors have we smashed down? Maybe we're still stuck in the building but let's find out. Cynically you could say punk lowered the bar, but in another way, you could say it actually made music a free market and broke down barriers about being drop-dead gorgeously good looking. It just opened the entry to everybody. It was all new and you can't take that for granted.'

It is hard to pinpoint just what kind of crowd Magazine were going after, perhaps sweeping up those who got punk and just realised, as the guys themselves did, that it would only take you so far. Ultimately, however, the music would dictate the direction.

The stage was set for Magazine to get the material they already had down on tape. The band knew they held a trump card with 'Shot by Both Sides' but they were equally confident about the strength of their other material. Given the right production, they knew they could create an unforgettable debut. Before that, however, the first tough decision the fledgling band had to make was to find a replacement for Bob Dickinson. As talented as he was, and as much as he was enjoying being a member of Magazine, the fit just wasn't right. The band had to spread its wings. They needed somebody as adept out on tour as in a rehearsal or studio setting. Somebody who could blend rock with the quirkier elements of what the band aspired to.

Having signed to Virgin, and thanks to an advance, John was able to purchase the tools of the trade. He opted for a Yamaha SG-1000. Some may consider this an unusual choice, but no doubt John had thought about it carefully. Howard remembers John buying the guitar: 'I think he had already played that specific guitar at the shop where it was purchased, A1 Guitars. He knew exactly what he wanted [...] – possibly knowing that we would be signing a deal and able to invest in equipment.' Shortly afterwards John had his MXR Flanger pedal adapted, as Howard remembers, 'so that it could be mounted on the microphone stand. Having it on the floor and operating it could be quite difficult, so he had it adapted to manipulate it on the mic stand.'

With Bob relieved of his duties, the band entered the studio to record their calling-card single, 'Shot by Both Sides', with Mick Glossop producing. The record was released in January 1978 and people immediately paid attention. If ever you wanted a debut single to spell out what you were about then this was it. It was a perfect debut for John also, who immediately received praise and recognition for his work on the track. It was a big deal to receive a response like this – near universal approval. The expectations for its follow-up and a full-length LP were heightened. So well received was the single that a short tour was arranged prior to setting about recording the album. As Howard remembers, 'We'd done at least two tours prior to the release of *Real Life*, coinciding with our first two singles. We were certainly getting more used to it by that point.'

'Shot by Both Sides' was a pivotal release, not just for Magazine but for the direction that edgy, guitar-driven music would be carving out in the months and years ahead, following in the footsteps of punk. Paul Morley looks back on its significance, both personally and for new

MAGAZINE

24 January
100 CLUB, London
25 January
SANDPIPERS, Nottingham
26 January
RAFTERS, Manchester
27 January
ERICS, Liverpool
30 January
NASHVILLE, London
31 January
BARBARELLAS, Birmingham
1 February
F CLUB, Leeds

A flyer for Magazine's first tour, 1978.
Andrew Krivine archive

Manchester-based music: 'I remember very early on being so keen to review "Shot by Both Sides" for the *NME* singles page. It was the first time I'd ever reviewed the singles for the *NME*, and I remember to this day the opening line, "Hero you come at last!" Even though it had probably only taken about three months for it to happen, it felt like we'd been waiting forever. Then there was this extraordinary-sounding record that sounded so immense and so not local and so not like Buzzcocks, and yet had come out of Manchester with these new Manchester musicians of which John was a part – despite not being from Manchester. He was very much from out of the local scene.'

Exploring the dynamic at play between what was evolving in Manchester and the reaction to it in the capital, Morley adds, 'There was a view down at the *NME* in London, where I was writing about these new Manchester bands, that I was exaggerating or making it up. Which could have been true – when you're saying Joy Division are like The Velvet Underground, and Magazine are incredibly important in terms of coming after Roxy Music and those sort of groups. It could have been perceived that you were just supporting your pals and there was a suspicion that that's what I was doing, but the funny thing was that it was actually true. They were records that stood out. Because of Malcolm Garrett, because of Linder and Peter Saville, they all looked like they were international and timeless. They didn't look provincial, regional or local. There was always, even then, that slight condescension towards local music. The first piece I did on Buzzcocks for *NME* – the headline referred to cloth caps, whippets and clogs. There definitely was a condescension. I remember then that Greil Marcus in America responded to "Shot by Both Sides" and that gave it a certain, if you like, more official stamp than simply being reviewed by local writers saying that it was an astounding piece of music and one of the greatest modern records that you're going to hear. Suddenly it was getting confirmation from outside the local world.'

The quest to replace Bob Dickinson on keyboards was fulfilled when Dave Formula joined the band, having been recommended by former flatmate and friend Martin Hannett to watch a Magazine performance on TV. 'I started going to rehearsals in Chorlton-cum-Hardy, south Manchester, following a meeting with Howard, and that was where I got to see John and hear what he could do. I found both John and Barry to be very interesting and exciting musicians. You would hear John and it was like "What?!" It was so different and very innovative.'

John and Dave formed an understanding early on, both recognising the talents and creative capabilities in the other. As with any new set-up it would take time to truly blossom, but the band were on course to establish a more cohesive framework for what would become *Real Life.* Dave recalls, 'I hit it off with John musically very quickly. With myself being that bit older than John and with us all having our own particular influences, which the best bands tend to, but we shared the same important influences that met and made it cohesive.'

One of the interesting aspects of Formula joining – at that point still going under his birth name Tomlinson – was an overhaul of equipment. Up until then Dave had favoured his Hammond organ as well as a Fender Rhodes, which were fine instruments in their own right and a staple of the northern soul scene of which Formula had been a part. Dave purchased a Yamaha organ and notes, of one of his initial introductions to the band, 'When I first met John and Barry, they had H&H

transistor amps, and walking into the rehearsal room I bit the inside of my cheek and thought, "Christ, why are they using those?!" I suggested to John that he upgrade to Fender or Marshall and see how he got on with those, and he opted for a Marshall Twin. The difference was like night and day. It just really improved the sound and fortunately both John and Barry upgraded before we recorded *Real Life*.'

John, centre, with Magazine, 1978.
Adrian Boot

Following the release of 'Shot by Both Sides', the band had been asked to appear on *Top of the Pops*. This was something that, initially, Howard was not keen on and knocked back, but he accepted at the second time of asking. There would undoubtedly have been a degree of expectation from Virgin that singles should be promoted as much as possible, and this was at a time when shows like *TOTP* were pivotal and gave groups exposure to wider audiences. The man who would go on to produce the forthcoming LP, John Leckie, remembers the television broadcast, which he watched with the band in between recording sessions for the album. 'When we were at Ridge Farm we would go into the dining room where the family was, and they would serve us our evening meal at seven o'clock. There was a television in the television lounge, but Frank Andrews' mother, or it may have been grandmother, would sit and watch *Coronation Street*. I said to Frank, "Hey, the guys are on *Top of the Pops* tonight," because they had recorded it the day before, I think, and I said, "Can we watch it?" and he said, "I'll have to ask my mum," and he asked his mum and she said no! "No, you can't watch *Top of the Pops* even if you're on it – I'm watching *Coronation Street*!" We did, I think he begged her, and we stood at the back while she sat there knitting with her cup of tea, and as soon as the band had finished, she switched it over to *Coronation Street*!'

The performance itself was not without incident, as Barry explains. 'I remember a very interesting thing happening early on when we played *Top of the Pops* and John takes the solo on "Shot by Both Sides" and I had the idea to play the main riff on the bass underneath, which would creep up as a melody which I would keep going. I don't know why, but it caught the cameraman's ear and as John is playing the first bar, he switches the camera from John over to me. Afterwards John fucking lost it with me and confronted me about it: "Fucking hell, what's going on? The camera switched to you." Not that it was my fault – I just thought it was a good idea at the time. In hindsight I wonder if it was me trying to steal a bit of the limelight, or at least John saw it that way. That made me realise that there was a line that you shouldn't cross, and woe betide you if you did.'

This, however, by no means marked the beginnings of tensions within the camp – it was more a case of the bandmates laying claim to their own contributions and wishing to be recognised. To this point Barry adds, 'What was great about those early days of Magazine was that we were influencing each other. We all had those bands and musicians we were into from Alice Cooper to The Stooges. You could see from the way that we looked at each other and it was like, "Oh, what are you doing? Yeah, I'll have a bit of that." John would chop some guitar, but it was never contrived, and it was all part of us inspiring each other. There was still a healthy dose of competition within the band and, like all of us, John was out to impress. You had to respect the music you were a part of and not overstep the mark; you recognised that if John was doing a solo or Dave was laying something down... you accepted that this stuff was fucking good and you wouldn't try and play over anything.'

One of the things that was clear from the start was that, at least from the perspective of the press, this was very much Howard's band. The attention was focused on him as band leader and as a recognised character who had been heavily involved with the Manchester punk scene. The trouble with this, however, was that the music itself risked being overlooked. This was something that would hang over the band for its duration and play a part in its demise, leading ultimately to McGeoch's decision to move on. Listening to *Real Life*, *Secondhand Daylight* or *The Correct Use of Soap* in 2022 is a very different experience, and when framed within the context of the achievements of each individual member... well, hindsight is a wonderful thing.

I don't think the image of Magazine was contrived at all, as Howard himself asserts, but there was and perhaps always has been an uneasy relationship between the press and artists who don't necessarily toe the line. People who, in one way or another, aren't hell bent on selling their souls for silver and to appease the masses. The material was strong, but the personalities within the band were equally so. They had started as they meant to go on; it was a case of who might blink first.

Despite the acclaim for 'Shot by Both Sides', this was not reflected in the charts, where it reached only 41. Simon Draper reflects on the group's debut single, the press and perception of both Howard and Magazine. 'I couldn't believe "Shot by Both Sides" wasn't a Top Ten hit – fantastic track. The fact that when they got on *Top of the Pops* it actually went down, and how do you explain that? Howard did alienate a lot of journalists and maybe he alienated the broader pop audience with his performance on the show.'

Paul Morley takes up the point and explains just how significant the *Top of the Pops* performance was, and not just in the short term. 'For me, the great moment when Magazine perished was that *Top of the Pops* performance of "Shot by Both Sides". Howard had decided he would try something unusual and try and present himself as some sort of pale ghost almost, and come in from the side. It should have been an incredibly important moment for the band. I remember it being one of the few times where a record that had been on *Top of the Pops* actually went down [the charts] the week after. It was as if it was too much: too much information, too much content, too much power to come through *Top of the Pops*. It could also have been the case that Howard failed to transfer the individual power he had on stage to a TV studio and came across as frail and unconvincing. The momentum the band had been building by signing to Virgin, the enthusiasm of the press and the response they were getting seemed to just crash into a wall because of that performance.'

Regardless, and particularly since the addition of Formula, this was never going to be a brief blaze of glory. By now the band were fully committed to knuckling down and putting in the necessary time and effort to create an LP worthy of their talent. Simon Draper set about putting some structure in place for the new group. 'Most of the dealings with the band were really through Howard, who I don't believe was represented then. So, we introduced the group to Andrew Graham-Stewart because he was involved with Virgin. He'd been managing Tangerine Dream and he was capable.' Graham-Stewart took over managerial duties for the band for the immediate future. Andrew recalls those early introductions with the band. 'When you've got a raw band – Magazine at that point had hardly played live – and therefore they didn't have the sort of infrastructure and knowledge to get out of their home town essentially. So, for any record company, investing many thousands of pounds et cetera, they need to know somebody has got experience of touring, dealing with record companies and marketing. Somebody with the experience to take them to the next level. Simon told me that I needed to listen to this [band] – I went up to Manchester, saw them rehearse and was very impressed, to put it mildly.'

John had, by now, left the flat he was sharing with Malcolm

Garrett and moved in with Janet. 'He lived near one end of Claremont Road and I lived at the other, in Whalley Range. Eventually he decided to come and move in with me. I lived with my best friend who was going out with John's best friend [Joe Barry].' Of the move, Janet remembers, 'We were quite poor students, so when he moved in with me, we didn't get a taxi. He put all his stuff in this big suitcase, and we walked along Claremont Road and it was really heavy, so I turned to him and said, "What the hell have you got in there?" I made him open the suitcase, and every time we came to a bin I said, "You're going to have to chuck something out." So, out came the white platform shoes and other weird items that were far from punk. He did like to make himself feel taller! I said, "You're not bringing them! If you think I'm carrying those all the way home, you've got another thing coming and I wouldn't be going out with you if you wore them anyway!" By the time we got to my place his case was only half full.'

Janet was giving John something he needed – the grounding and dose of reality that could have been hard to maintain given what was going on with the band. In Janet, John had found somebody he could respect and be himself around, but also somebody who wouldn't take any old shit. Janet reflects on how important his image was to him in those early days. 'He was trying to get his look right, so I was cutting his hair. We went a bit wild and off-piste with it. He was keen to get his image right.'

With a settled personal life, if not hairstyle, John and the band set about entering the studio to begin recording the LP that would become *Real Life*. Getting John Leckie to produce the album was no small feat; with his impressive track record he was certainly fit for the task. Simon Draper explains the role he and the label had in deciding the direction the group were to take. 'I actually dealt with Howard directly. This was something we were used to. By that I mean finding bands that had a strong sense of their own identity. I felt very much like a facilitator, really. In 1973 I was 23; by 1978 I was a bit more experienced and had done quite a lot of stuff. I still treated the artists as being quite capable of making their own decisions, particularly with things like artwork and producers. We would suggest people, so I suggested Mick Glossop, who was chief engineer at The Manor and produced the first single, 'Shot by Both Sides', and I suggested John

Leckie, who'd worked with XTC and who was somebody I liked very much and was very good at what he did.'

The album was largely recorded at Ridge Farm, with mixing and loose ends completed at Abbey Road. John Leckie recalls the recording process: 'I never rehearsed with the band, I never went up to Manchester and I don't think I ever went to a gig. So, I can't remember how we met face to face, but I did the single "Touch and Go" and "Goldfinger", which I think came out after "Shot by Both Sides" [and] before the album. I'm sure we did it at Sound Technique Studio, which is in Chelsea. Sound Technique is a little studio that was mainly used for folk bands – Fairport Convention, Nick Drake did all his records there, and Joe Boyd used it a lot. In those days Virgin would send me the demo – I'm presuming there was a demo for "Touch and Go" – and they'd ask me if I was interested and, if I was, then to be at Sound Technique Studio next Wednesday. So, we recorded it and "Goldfinger" and then it was a case of we love it, the band love you, so go in and do the album.

'I've no recollection of rehearsing or going to a gig until later, because normally you'd go into a rehearsal room and rehearse and even do demos before you do the real thing, but I don't remember that with Magazine, but to be honest I don't remember that with a lot of bands back then – it was all very much a case of go in there and get it done quick. So, I went to Ridge Farm Studio, which actually wasn't a studio. Ridge Farm, which is near Guildford, became a studio, but at the time it was a rehearsal barn. It was a barn attached to an old house and there were two brothers – Frank Andrews, who ran the house, and Tony Andrew's who ran a PA company called Turbosound. The house ran as a bed and breakfast, so you basically got bed and breakfast and an evening meal, along with a barn to rehearse in. The thing was, you could take a mobile studio, which was a 24-track with a mixing desk, on the back of a truck. Virgin had two of them and The Rolling Stones had one. The *Real Life* album was done at Ridge Farm Studio with a Virgin mobile. It was just me, the mobile and the band. We just got down to it and recorded for twelve to fourteen hours a day. We'd start at, say, eleven in the morning and carry on until two or three in the morning, or until we dropped, really. You'd get up the next day and do it all over again.

'I guess it would have taken a week to ten days from start to finish. The last track, "Parade", was recorded at Abbey Road, studio 3. They came in and said they wanted to do another song – I'm pretty certain that was the only track done in its entirety at Abbey Road. There might have been overdubs, keyboards and vocals done there, but most of it was done at Ridge Farm.

'What I remember about John McGeoch is very often he would go home, or that he wasn't there because he was doing his art degree in Manchester. To some extent it was a little odd not having the guitarist, but Dave Formula had so many keyboards that often I didn't notice because there was always keyboards to work on or vocals to keep me busy. It's very much a keyboard album. I mean it's fantastic, I'm really proud of it because I've always thought that it never goes out of date, it always sounds like a modern record – it always sounds like it's a new album that was recorded a month ago, very modern, and I don't know why that is. Probably the keyboards, the sound and Howard's vocals. Magazine are held in great esteem by so many artists – Simple Minds for example were in awe of Magazine. Charlie Burchill was very much imitating John McGeoch, if you listen to *Reel to Real Cacophony* and *Empires and Dance*, in that he didn't want the guitar to sound like a normal guitar – he didn't want American rock. At the time, everybody was kind of against that bluesy or Jimi Hendrix American rock style. He adored McGeoch and the sound he had.'

The band powered through the album. They were already well rehearsed and had gigged enough to realise the material was strong. John's contribution, not just in performing but in composition, was to the fore. Songs like "Shot by Both Sides", "The Light Pours Out of Me", "Burst", "My Mind Ain't So Open" (which had been the B-side of "Shot by Both Sides" but didn't feature on the album) and "Recoil" – the latter two being very punk in attitude – had McGeoch's mark all over them. As noted earlier by Adamson, John was keen to be at the forefront of writing material. He wasn't shy in putting his ideas across and, as Howard recalls, when putting together material for Magazine's fourth studio album, and the first without John, *Magic, Murder and the Weather*, 'It was at the point when it came to writing the next album that I *really* started to appreciate just what John had brought to Magazine.'

Real Life was released in June 1978, five months after the release of 'Shot by Both Sides' and 'Touch and Go' in April. As with the first single, the response from the critics was positive. It is hard to see how the band could have put together a stronger statement of intent for Magazine than *Real Life.* People were listening, and John's playing was not lost on a young guitar fanatic in Manchester who would go on to form one of the most important bands of the 1980s, Johnny Marr. 'Like everyone else who noticed John McGeoch, it was because of "Shot by Both Sides" and then "The Light Pours Out of Me". I absolutely loved Magazine and I really liked what all the band members were doing – all of them. I liked the words, the arrangements, the drumming, bass playing, keyboards – everything about them. I thought they were great, but being a 15-year-old guitar fan, I was particularly interested in John McGeoch's guitar playing. Like all great groups, all the parts fit together really well. What he was doing was clever, but most importantly it was appropriate, with really interesting attitude. That word "arch" comes to mind – he uses a lot of halftone runs, and there's a considered conceptual mind at play there. You really hear it in *The Correct Use of Soap* and riffs like "Because You're Frightened" – it shows someone who was doing something very deliberate and it is also someone who was very of the times.'

John Leckie has fond memories of the album and its enduring appeal, in particular John's contribution. 'All the parts he plays on *Real Life* I thought were really imaginative and inventive, like no one had done those things before. It was totally modern and, dare I say it, the opposite of Eric Clapton or an American blues-based type guitarist – that was all out the window. Then again, John played a Yamaha SG, which Bill Nelson from Be-Bop Deluxe switched to from Gibson and Fender, and then Stuart Adamson [of Skids and later Big Country] also played the same guitar. Everyone loved it because it was really solid, it stayed in tune and was reliable and it wasn't American – it was a Japanese guitar and those players really knew what they were doing. They were forward lead guitarists; they weren't a rhythm strumming in the background. So, with John's guitar I always remember thinking, he knows what he's doing because he's playing a Yamaha SG. There was never a problem, there was never a search for sound – there was never a lot of time wasted fiddling around with amplifiers

A flyer for Magazine's first album, 1978.
Andrew Krivine archive

and different pedals. John had it, he plugged in and he was ready to go. The flanger was a big thing for the time, but he never overdid it. He was strong and upfront – "Shot by Both Sides" and some of those others like "Recoil" and "Motorcade" are really great. Of course, "The Light Pours Out of Me" – it's funny because it's not the best-sounding song on the record, but it's the most atmospheric, which everyone loves.'

To coincide with the album's release, the band embarked on their biggest tour to date. Andrew Graham-Stewart recalls the live performances. 'I tended to watch them every single night, either from the front of the stage or in the audience. They were an astonishingly dynamic band. It was just impossible, if one were working with them, to be anything other than a fan.' Of John in particular and his stage presence and mood prior to shows he adds, 'John was always in good humour before a gig and got on well with everybody. I think he was also that gifted a guitarist, that even if he was nervous before a show, it wouldn't be apparent on stage and as soon as he was on the stage, he was in his element.'

In the midst of his commitments with Magazine, John completed his degree in fine art. As remembered by Janet, 'It was the end of his second year and beginning of his third year at the polytechnic that Magazine started taking off. For his last year he was hardly at the poly as he was busy touring or down in London, or somewhere recording. He still managed to come out with a first, and I really don't know how he managed it. If I was stuck for ideas with my artwork, he'd give me suggestions. He was very good at whatever he did and put his mind to. He was a genius, always very creative. He had so many interests. He loved his painting, photography, reading and cooking.' John's inherent creativity and belief in what he was doing is expanded upon by Liddy when she says, 'As far as painting goes, he had respect for everything, but he also had a great ability to not be tied down by it. Even with all the threats of the tutors saying, "If you don't turn up blah blah." I used to cover for him a lot, but he didn't really care, you know, because he had a bigger dream. He knew there was more, always.'

John earned a first class degree with honours, one of only six awarded that academic year. It says a lot for the man that, as well as recording an album and writing material, he could excel in his studies. Despite all the excitement of what was happening musically and socially for John, he never wavered in his determination to complete what he had started in moving to Manchester in the first place. Fellow art student and friend Roger Cleghorn has this to say of John and certain parallels between his painting and aspects of his personality. 'I had one of John's paintings which he gave me. His paintings were a bit like him – angry, abstract expressionist. That's how I remember them. I couldn't tell you now what they looked like, but I just remember that feeling from them. John's show at the end of the course – I can't remember people talking about John's paintings or passing comment on them, but I just remember the anger, and there was a power to them. There was obviously him inside them, but for all that they were clearly well liked because he got a first. There was an energy there inside John which often came out as being spiky, and he was driven, he had to believe in himself. Maybe that was just a front.'

With his degree under his belt, he was free to dive headlong into the world of touring and recording, determined to make Magazine as successful as they could be – all on their own terms. The tour, which ran throughout July 1978, took the band nationwide, culminating in a performance at the Lyceum in London on the 30th. It was hotly anticipated and successful, and attracted the occasional dose of controversy connected to the punk scene, which by now was essentially over anyway.

Richard Jobson, who would go on to form The Armoury Show with McGeoch, remembers his then band Skids supporting Magazine and his thoughts on how significant their debut album was. 'They were signed to Virgin and so were we, and therefore they were keen for us to play with Magazine. We played with them in Glasgow up above the Apollo theatre. They were amazing. We played with them again a few nights later at the Lyceum in London and they were equally amazing. *Real Life* was an extraordinary album – everything you wanted punk to be, redefined, you know, *Real Life* did it. It really was one of the great albums of our generation.'

Magazine had kicked into gear, and with the next LP, what remained of the punk influence would be subtle at best. What had become clear by now was how much of an understanding had developed between John and Dave. They almost intertwined as a twin lead, as it were, and were able to push each other further musically than they had gone before. It was something John revelled in. Barry was hardly sitting on the sidelines – he was more than holding his own and giving solidity and groove to the free form expression that both John and Dave revelled in as performers.

As Dave remembers, 'Listening to John's improvisations and bits of playing in rehearsals or between recording, or waiting for something to happen – it was very atonal at times and quite early on I found out that Eric Dolphy and John Coltrane were among John's influences. It was great to find out that we shared an interest in and appreciation of jazz.' Dave elaborates, 'When he wasn't just playing standard Magazine riffs, when he was just messing about and practising, there was something very different and special about his approach to the guitar. So, for me bringing in the synthesiser, piano or organ, it felt like a really interesting thing to be able to offer to the band, given what they already had going on.' Barry had noticed the chemistry between the two and what they were able to bring out of one another. 'I think rubbing up against Dave Formula, or me in support, it brought out another character to his playing. He very rapidly put an identity together that people were quick to try and copy. It was that perfect balance of being sympathetic to what the song requires but having the imagination and ability to utilise a bit of flair when required, and add colours to the canvas which would make somebody listening go… "Woah" at the right moment. John had that in his back pocket and could do it at will and it was just his way, I think, of him saying, I know who I am and remember who I am.'

Another element that John brought to the band and *Real Life* was his ability to play the sax. As Howard relates, 'John's sax playing, which he mentioned to me when I met him, came in useful.' Dave, also a keen jazz fan, noted, 'I think John thought of himself, given he played a bit of sax, as using certain techniques of sax playing and applying it to the guitar. The freer jazz element of Dolphy really appealed to him, that there aren't any right notes to play as such, provided it benefits the music, which I think influenced his own guitar solos. If it worked that was what mattered – it might take five notes to get back to the basis of where the chord was but that didn't matter. He definitely had a very open mind and you can hear it throughout his playing. Some of those runs he does just stop you in your tracks, but it works.' Having an open mind and being familiar with another instrument could only open new avenues for the band as it grew. As Dave confirms, 'I got the impression he'd been playing the sax for a while and it was something he liked to mess about with and enabled him to come up with unusual ideas. He used it on *Real Life* but also on the song "Twenty Years Ago".'

John the lesser-known sax player, 1979.
Dave Formula

By this time Barry had moved in with John and Janet in the house on Mayfield Road, which as Janet recalls became known as the 'music house'. Of this time Barry says, 'I remember John coming into my room and tripping over something, looking almost regal in his dressing gown, holding a big bulbous glass of wine, hair flopping over one eye and me thinking, "Ooh, it's Lord Hoo-Ha." We would joke about this sort of shit. That said though, there was definitely a legacy of the regal Scots about him.' Barry goes on, 'It was observed by a friend of mine that I appeared to be a bit doting on John and hanging on to his every word. I don't see it that way, we were just like schoolmates, really, and there was a lot of give and take. There was a security to the relationship that he would feel comfortable enough to have a go at me at times and likewise I could do the same with John. I always felt, however, that there was a kind of fragility to his ego. John was brilliant and you had to give him praise and deservedly so, but he definitely needed that recognition. It was the same if we were walking down the street and people would look or nudge each other, and John would turn to me as if to say, I've got this, should the question be asked (which it wasn't), "Are you the guys from Magazine?" John would adopt a sort of royalty to himself and say yes, we are. So, at that stage for us as two young guys, it was a laugh, and it wasn't a big deal.'

Joining them at Mayfield Road was his friend Roger, now thankfully relieved of his bodyguard duties. 'For all of the stuff we love about it, the seventies weren't great. Places like Leeds, where I'm from, and Manchester weren't particularly nice places to live. The housing, the infrastructure wasn't great by any means. Where we lived, Whalley Range, was a red-light area. I remember when they were trying to catch the Yorkshire Ripper, just walking out of the house to go to the kebab shop or off-licence, you'd walk a couple of hundred yards and literally on every street corner there would be a police car with a couple of policemen in – watching for the Ripper because it was a red-light area and they thought they might catch him. That same area has now been gentrified.'

Despite all the progress the band were making, there were difficulties emerging. Martin Jackson was increasingly being viewed as a bad fit, or perhaps less adaptable to the breakthrough the band were on the cusp of making. Jackson was more drawn to the punkier elements, and the tensions between himself, Dave and the band's manager, Andrew Graham-Stewart, were heading to one conclusion: time for a change. Jackson left the group more on his own terms than being fired, as had happened with Bob Dickinson. The band were now left with the task of finding a replacement, and somebody they would regard as an upgrade. They were non-committal at this point, knowing that it wasn't a decision that needed to be rushed, but they did need somebody to fulfil their touring duties supporting Patti Smith. The band recruited Paul Spencer for what would have been a momentous opportunity for McGeoch and the band to take their music to new audiences. The tour was gruelling. The band returned to England and guested on *The Old Grey Whistle Test.* Paul was relieved of his duties and John ultimately had the biggest hand in finding the long-term successor to Martin Jackson.

McGeoch returned to his old stomping ground at Manchester Poly, where he saw and introduced himself to John Doyle. 'I was playing in a band called Idiot Rouge at the time and we got a final gig at the Manchester Poly freshers' ball. Our main songwriter was going off to university himself, so we played the gig and John McGeoch just happened to be there. He approached me afterwards and asked me if I wanted to audition for the band. I was gobsmacked, really. Obviously I had heard of Magazine and knew that they were more than a punk band, but I didn't know a great deal about them. I was working in motor insurance at the time and I phoned in sick on the Monday, had the audition, handed in my notice on the Wednesday and by Friday I was playing with the band in Munich on German TV. I've condensed that story, I'm sure, but it really did seem to come together very quickly. [...] I didn't have a kit at the time, so I was just trying to learn *Real Life* by tapping it out on my knees. They'd given me the song "Give Me Everything" to learn and I think that swung it for me. On reflection, I don't think I was that different from what they had had with Martin Jackson – I just put my own slant on it. It was a case of raised eyebrows and nods of approval and I was in.'

Barry recalls the effect Doyle had: 'John Doyle coming in was like the glue which made everything stick for Magazine. He brought the rock and funk elements to the drums and I was trying to avoid all labelling and create a style which was my own. I was trying, as we all were, to keep to a melting pot of originality.' Of his early days in the band and of McGeoch in particular, Doyle notes, 'John was very technical and always searching for something and willing to try out new effects. He was such a one-off, and such a skilled guitarist that he was reinventing his approach constantly, always looking for something new. He didn't want to sound like anybody else.'

The band now had all the tools at their disposal to move forward without interruption; the personalities fit and the proficiency had been enhanced with the arrival of Formula and Doyle. Another UK tour followed. The band recorded and released the single 'Give Me Everything' towards the end of 1978, an indication of what was to come. The attitude of the press towards the band was changing somewhat, and Howard was just starting to show some degree of mistrust of journalists – something that would become a pattern for the band. In reality, the response to the band following *Real Life* had been favourable. It had started to get a bit more personal when some sections of the music media had questioned Howard's attitude and ability to perform live. Undeterred, by early 1979 the band were rehearsing and recording what would become their second LP. John again took a leading role in writing, but Dave, who by now was well bedded in, naturally wanted to showcase his own ideas more than on the previous record, which had really been a baptism of fire for him.

By this time, John and Janet had moved down to London, where the band would also be recording. As Janet says, 'Shortly after Magazine signed to Virgin, John and I moved to a flat in Holland Park. We moved in with Liddy and her husband Steve. I don't think we even paid any bloody rent!'

The band had wanted the film score composer John Barry as an arranger for the new album. Virgin approached Barry, who was living in the States at the time as a tax exile, and although he would have been prepared to do it, it would have meant the band recording Stateside, which at that point Virgin were not prepared to subsidise. Tony Visconti was considered, but ultimately the band went to Colin Thurston, who had worked alongside Visconti on Bowie's *Heroes* and Iggy Pop's *Lust for Life.* It was the perfect compromise, and while we can only imagine what an album involving John Barry may have sounded like, the band were in safe hands with Colin.

Magazine took up residence at Good Earth Studios in Soho to record the tracks that became *Secondhand Daylight*. The album was a new defining chapter and a clean break in many ways from its predecessor. As Howard recalls, it 'was more focused, it was more "taking no prisoners"… we were able to go somewhere further with songs like "Feed the Enemy", "Back to Nature" and "Permafrost" than we'd been able to on the first album.' Reflecting on *Real Life*, he admits, '"Recoil" and "Shot by Both Sides" were both pretty fast and punky. There aren't many vestiges of punk by the time we get to *Secondhand Daylight*.'

The process would ultimately prove to be a frustrating one for McGeoch; the approach was markedly different, and his guitar influence is not as apparent as on *Real Life*. That said, it did bring out another side of the man as far as arrangements were concerned, and he composed 'The Thin Air' on keyboards. As Howard explains, 'John felt squeezed [on *Secondhand Daylight*], which I wasn't aware of and I can't recall how I came to learn about it. Dave certainly became more prominent on that album, and the guitar less so. Having said that, "The Thin Air", which was John's piece, didn't feature guitar on it anyway and I think that is one of the songs that makes people think of it as a keyboard album. His working title for that song was "From Toe to Crown" and the piece that you hear is very much as John came up with it.'

The album certainly saw Dave putting more of his stamp on the band. As Howard reveals: 'The creative input and the layering of the sound is what makes *Secondhand Daylight* what it is, it isn't about the mix. Dave liked to layer things and use different keyboards all on the same piece, whereas a lot of the time for John it would be one guitar part that he would put down. It's almost compositional, really. John had "Rhythm of Cruelty", for example, on the album, in my opinion one of his very best riffs.'

Barry Adamson has fonder recollections of the album and John's contribution. 'What was great about Magazine was, for me and my development as a musician, playing with McGeoch, John Doyle and Dave Formula there was an attitude of "keep up with us". The songs would always dictate how you would play, and I was very fortunate to be in a position that I could express myself. I am especially proud of *Secondhand Daylight* – the writing was superb, as shown with a song like "Back to Nature". The absolute highlight of that album for me personally would be John's solo on "Permafrost", which I was privy to, being in the room of the mobile studio at the time with John Doyle when McGeoch performed it. It was just the most staggering thing that I have ever witnessed in a recording studio. The way he controlled the feedback, with Colin Thurston switching in the harmoniser, bending the strings and going out of tune on purpose – you just feel like you are on top of your game at moments like that. For me that album is the sound of Magazine.'

John's notes for the flanger pedal on 'Permafrost', 1979.

As Dave relates, 'Magazine were very democratic when it came to composition and general ideas. Musically we'd all be heard, and we'd always be willing to try out others' ideas, as we respected one another and wanted to make it work. It was all very amiable. Working in that positive and confident environment helps to move things along. The only no-go area was with lyrics – that was Howard's domain and thankfully so, because he was very good at what he did. Howard always had a notebook on his lap, and bits of things that you said would end up in lyrics.' John Doyle shared this view of the way the band wrote and recorded material. 'You were given room in Magazine to come up with your own ideas. It was very creative and fruitful – you were encouraged with guidance, as opposed to a sledgehammer. I've worked in other bands where it has been "you must do it like this", which can be pretty restrictive. Magazine was the polar opposite of that. There was a belief in each other and what we could all bring to the plate.'

Regardless of how McGeoch felt during or after the release of *Secondhand Daylight*, what can't be questioned is the level of commitment and effort that went into it. The band had learned from their previous experience of recording an LP and had all been changed in some way by their experience of the European tour. It is a truism that the follow-up to the debut is always more difficult, yet at this point the band had fresh impetus with the arrival of John Doyle, and from a willingness to adopt more experimental sounds and approaches to the whole process. Released in March 1979, *Secondhand Daylight*'s reviews were less than flattering in the main. Was it that people just weren't ready for a more sophisticated and keyboard-infused progression? Was it, as Martin Jackson had felt when leaving the band, that they were losing what made them special by changing direction? I think the former is probably true; *Secondhand Daylight* is a classic of the era. The lyrics and arrangements are more intense, more challenging. More is expected of the listener, but perhaps the pay-off in the long term is greater. John's playing had incorporated the use of guitar synths, which, when thrown into the mix of Formula's keyboard work, has you second-guessing just what you might be listening to at any point. Magazine were pushing on and seeking out new expressions of their collective identities. The band were poised for acclaim, but when it didn't come the disappointment was hard to conceal, as Dave explains when reflecting on the critics' response to the album.

'We'd worked really hard on *Secondhand Daylight* and received mainly less than complimentary reviews at the time, which in hindsight perhaps helped *The Correct Use of Soap* to be realised, but nonetheless felt unnecessarily harsh.' Howard is pragmatic about the failure of the album to achieve recognition. 'I've always felt its [downfall] came down to two things – its gatefold sleeve [which in those days had connotations of Pink Floyd] and I'm afraid "The Thin Air", which I felt, even when John presented it to us, again there was a hint of Pink Floyd about it... and you weren't supposed to go there. It was the era of Johnny Rotten's "I hate Pink Floyd" T-shirt. So, I put a lot of the negative reaction down to those two factors.'

Paul Morley, one of the album's detractors at the time, remarks, 'I gave it a bad review. I suppose what was happening was textures and sounds that were coming through that were surprising – it was quite a radical shift. In hindsight I've become much more a fan of it. Their sound had shifted, or I felt that it had, from post-punk to new wave – whatever that meant. At the time you just thought, "Oh dear, what are they doing?" It seems weird to say it, but it felt like another earthquake had happened. It was only a year since the release of *Real Life*, but back then a year felt like a long time and it did have that "proggier" edge to it. Taken out of that context and appreciating it for what it is, it is a great album. Then it was only a year until the next album, and again another change in direction which caught you off guard – there again, that seemed to be what Howard was up to.'

Of the album's disappointing reception, Andrew Graham-Stewart states, 'I don't think that *Secondhand Daylight* had the equivalent standout for the potentially commercially attractive track, or tracks, as the two or three on *Real Life*. *Secondhand Daylight*'s integrity is as an album. It is difficult to take things out of the context of the album. *Real Life* had two or three songs which could be taken in isolation and had huge commercial potential. I think the next track, and this was after my time, that I felt had huge potential was "A Song from Under the Floorboards".'

Despite the disappointment, the band hit the road for their biggest tour to date. They gigged round the UK and took in Europe again. His friend Dave Barker recalls catching up with John when Magazine came to play at the University of Essex. 'That was really good, because they didn't have all their mates hanging about with them, so we had plenty of time to just sit and have a yak. At London gigs, it would always be a case of, "Oh yeah, how you doing? Oh, I've just got to speak to this person, or do this interview," which is understandable.'

The *Secondhand Daylight* tour, for which the band teamed up with support act Simple Minds, was well received by the audiences who flocked to see them. Regardless of record sales, the interest was there. The band weren't playing to empty halls, and to that extent, it was a success. Michael Jobson remembers that tour and how he came to meet John and just how significant that would eventually become. 'I loved him; he was more like my brother than Richard was. I was only 14. I ran away from home, not by design – I went to see them play [...] and I just followed them for almost a week. I went to introduce myself to him as Richard's brother and his hospitality towards me was the greatest, really. I only went there expecting to see the gig and ended up backstage after the show and then on to the hotel where he bought me drinks and I slept on the floor in his room. That was it – he was my hero from then on, really. They had the police out looking for me. When I got home, I got a bit of a roasting. It's funny to think that I ended up working with John a few years later.'

Prior to parting ways with Magazine, in July 1979, Andrew Graham-Stewart was aware of some of the issues that would ultimately result in John leaving the band. 'John was a very different character to Howard. John liked to party, as most musicians of that age do, but he was no hellraiser. He was incredibly professional on the road, very driven, and I think he was frustrated by Howard not liking touring – the drudgery of touring. Howard found touring a struggle, whereas John was in his element. There was the buzz of the performance, it was an adventure. Howard held back and retreated, whereas John knew that touring was an essential component of getting the exposure the band would need.'

Raf Edmonds came in and took over tour managing duties before taking over full managerial control of the band, although finances and artistic direction remained Devoto's domain. Howard acknowledged that Magazine were seen as his band, and after all, it was his creation to begin with. Raf was able to take the band to the States for their first tour of the 'promised land'. This was an opportunity to be seized, as Dave reflects: 'We'd arrive in New York, have two or three days off to acclimatise, then have a couple of rehearsals and then it was a pretty heavy schedule. The first time in America was just a fantastic adventure. The reception to the band was really good and we enjoyed every minute.' Dave and John would room together, and he remembers a certain near miss in Philadelphia. 'New York was electric, it had the edgy feel to it, but we never had a problem there.

I remember one incident in Philadelphia, however, when we were both wearing those black kung fu slippers. John and I used to go out together, if we had the time, wherever we were – maybe go to an art gallery or a museum. So, we are walking through Philadelphia with our kung fu footwear on, and these two guys came towards us and assumed a martial arts position, saying, "Come on, let's do it," and they really wanted to have a go at us. I suppose we probably stood out a bit and might have had a bit of make-up on. We were able to blag our way out of it, thankfully.'

John must have felt liked he'd arrived; this was where he wanted to be and this was the sign he needed that, despite his dissatisfaction with the album, Magazine were still on the right path and making inroads. Although this wasn't reflected financially. The band were struggling, and supporting themselves in a new country was proving harder than it should have been for a band with a rapidly expanding record label behind them. As Dave relates, 'The experience was great, but we were dependent on the gig money while there – it was a bit hand to mouth, really. We had a bit of money from Virgin, but it was a bit precarious, even having enough money to travel from town to town. The gigs themselves though were held in some really interesting venues, from big clubs to smaller clubs, to the occasional bar. One of the gigs was held in two houses converted to make a club, and we were supported by a really brilliant band called The Bloodless Pharaohs, who were an early incarnation of Stray Cats – they were exceptional.' The tour went coast to coast and the reaction from audiences was highly encouraging. John was finding satisfaction and, despite the financial difficulties, could see that progress was being made. The experience would prove invaluable, as the first European tour had done for *Secondhand Daylight*. Exposed to new elements of underground music and style, the bandmates had their minds opened to different possibilities that would inspire the direction the new LP would take.

Although the creative dynamic remained essentially the same, there was a collective push to give John more space to express himself than on *Secondhand Daylight*, as Howard confirms. 'There was a definite feeling that we needed more guitar, it needed to be featured more. So, we went into it with that idea. As an album it's very consistent and a number of the songs started to take form when I wasn't even there. The band had a few writing rehearsals, so I wasn't even sure how a few of the songs began.'

The bandmates were more than prepared to assert themselves, even more than on the previous record, and John's guitar would be to the fore. The approach, the sound, was – simply put – an energised and savvier version of his previous contribution. There is a ferocity and explosiveness, almost an urgency about his playing on what would become *The Correct Use of Soap.* The highlights would include some of his very best playing to date. Songs such as 'Because You're Frightened' and 'Philadelphia' are as much McGeoch classics as they are Magazine's. With *Secondhand Daylight* the sound of John's guitar had been pushed down, no doubt about it, and that sacrifice was not without its own merits, but it could at times be hard to differentiate between guitar and keyboards; even the guitar parts sounded synth-laden. McGeoch's talents should have always been used to their full advantage. His rhythm and lead parts on *The Correct Use of Soap* are what give the album its flavour, and Howard's writing was again second to none.

On the relationship between his lyrics and John's intuitiveness, Howard comments, 'John again impressed me with "You Never Knew Me", which was kind of my song. I just had a few chords and melody, but not very much going, really, so I put it to the band – "Have we got something here?" – and it was John that picked up on my vocal melody and put that guitar part that goes through the verse, echoing the melody, and he stitched a song, as it were, together there and then. Suddenly there was the song, there was enough to get us most of the way there. It was another point in the writing process where he really impressed me.'

Martin Hannett had been called in to produce the album, which as Barry recalls wasn't without its problems. To his mind, the end product suffered. 'There was never a conscious idea with what we were doing, everything just happened as it happened. I never really liked the sounds or ideas in *The Correct Use of Soap.* It became more of a Martin Hannett-controlled project and moved away from the sort of Bowie- and Iggy-inspired world that I felt best represented what we were doing, but it was something that was out of my control. I was starting to lose a bit of ground by then. I think that was going on for John back then too. You just felt like you had given it everything you could, especially with *Secondhand Daylight*, and with a song like "Under the Floorboards", I still expected that we would have taken over the world.'

Without doubt there were tensions within the band by this point. Some of these had been exposed more obviously while on tour in America. Though great as an experience, the management issues and the financial constraints had begun to weigh heavy on Howard. John, on the other hand, was solely focused on pushing ahead regardless, and felt that Devoto should seize the opportunities that were finally within the band's grasp. That would signify the beginning of the end, the end of a viable working relationship between John and Howard and also, eventually, the end of Magazine. John felt that Howard wasn't putting enough into the promotion of Magazine, a band that had been his creation, after all. With *The Correct Use of Soap*, John was putting himself in the shop window, even if only subconsciously, and he was also making moves for the band to have much more of a say over their direction, which would only add to the growing friction between himself and Howard.

One of the things John pushed through was with credits, as John Doyle explains: 'It was John's drive that got all the tracks to be evenly distributed, percentage wise, for the publishing on *The Correct Use of Soap*. It was John that pushed to make it an equal split five ways. That was John.' Howard could have perceived this as his band – or more specifically John – turning on him to some extent. It created a situation where Howard retreated inwards, possibly questioning the direction the band were heading in. As he puts it, 'John could be quite arrogant, although I am sure you will find people who will say that about me too!' And reflecting on the decline in their relationship, he accepts the part that the previous tour had played. 'It's more on the road that tensions are exposed. You're under a lot more pressure, rammed together and seeing a lot more of each other.'

As the recording for the album stepped up, it was clear that not everybody was convinced by Martin Hannett. Certain shortcomings in his abilities were exposed, such as always requiring a sound engineer to be present, and he also seemed to want more

A poster for Magazine's third album, 1980.
Andrew Krivine archive

control over the arrangements than they were used to conceding. Hannett was a larger-than-life character, a completely different personality to John Leckie or Colin Thurston. Dave was very familiar with Martin and his peculiarities, having lived with him, but for those in the group who didn't have that frame of reference, the process was possibly not as harmonious or enjoyable as it could have been. That being said, those tensions are sometimes needed to create something exceptional, and upon its release in May 1980 the album was widely lauded. John's frustration was really about his feeling that Howard didn't push himself, or the band, when the material was strong. Howard's relationship with the press had never been conventional – as with his lyrics, he was a hard man to pin down but journalists took this as arrogance and would lash out. This prejudice had hung over Magazine since the start, when Howard was disliked for appearing 'too intellectual' or aloof. As Dave states, 'Part of the problem was that Howard was considered difficult by many of the journalists at the time. He challenged them and I don't think they liked that. It was as though they had the attitude of, "You're the musicians, play the music, and who the fuck does Howard think he is with all the Dostoevsky quotes? That's our job." That attitude from the journalists held us back, I think.'

One way or another, McGeoch likely knew this would be his last hurrah with the band. He wasn't prepared to sit about and just wait for the recognition he craved, but as Janet puts it, 'John himself wasn't commercial and he wasn't interested in gaining big commercial success. He did want to be successful and wanted it for the obvious reasons – because he was good and wanted to be on the winning side, so to speak, but he wouldn't sell his soul.' Which is perhaps evidenced best by the fact that he had remained loyal to the ideals of Magazine, despite the lack of commercial success.

He hadn't quit after the first album when he had gained instant praise for his playing on the future classics 'Shot by Both Sides' and 'The Light Pours Out of Me', when even at that early juncture he would have had suitors. John had desperately wanted Magazine to get their break and become the band they should have been. John wasn't alone in feeling beaten up by the experience and Barry was becoming just as frustrated by the lack of recognition. The cracks were starting to become more pronounced and John's relationship with Howard was becoming more fraught, and at times explosive. The pair were reaching a point where continuing to work together was just going to become a drain on them both. John was never the sort to mince his words, although much of what he truly felt would have been bottled up while he considered his own aspirations and options. He was open to new possibilities.

Prior to the full album release, the band put out the singles 'A Song from Under the Floorboards', 'Thank You (Falettinme Be Mice Elf Agin)' and 'Upside Down'. John Doyle reflects on the commercial aspect of *The Correct Use of Soap*. 'As I saw it, commercial success wasn't the sole drive of the band, or rather there was never a desire to be a commercial-sounding band. I never felt that motivated the band or galvanised us to be creative. Look at the single covers for *The Correct Use of Soap* – plain cardboard with very sparse graphics, and we released one a month. Talk about commercial suicide. John probably felt more hampered by the lack of success, but privately.'

It is hard to encapsulate what a career-defining album like *The Correct Use of Soap* means at the time of release, when it is all new and fresh. It was McGeoch's favourite Magazine album, as it was for most of the band. Listening to it in 2022, informed by the direction each artist involved would take later and what would be in store for Magazine, puts it more fully into perspective. Hearing it in 1980 though, as Johnny Marr explains, was everything.

'I understand that not all the members of Magazine are happy with *The Correct Use of Soap*, but I think it's a real work of genius. If you're a music freak, as I was at 17 with my girlfriend, and one of your favourite bands puts that out and it really delivers every song, both musically and lyrically, you really appreciate it. It sounded like nothing else. I was working in a clothes shop in town at the time, and I used to play it at least twice a day, if not three times a day. It was the soundtrack to the customers coming into the shop! There's not been anything like it. There are bands who have been influenced by The Smiths, The Cure and New Order but that third Magazine album can't be copied. In that way they remind me of Roxy Music, I think, in that it is so definitive. It's a statement in itself.' Marr acknowledges why McGeoch might have had to move away from the band, however. 'I would totally understand if John McGeoch felt like Magazine had come as far as they could artistically or personally, or whatever it is that happens to bands. Then he gets that opportunity to create something new with another group of people, that's something that I understand and it's something that I've done myself.'

Andrew Graham-Stewart sees that there was a path readily available for John – should he wish to pursue it. 'I can well imagine that John was seeing opportunities outside of Magazine which were very attractive. Given how superb he was as a guitar player, he was naturally being courted by various people. Anybody of his standing in the guitar world would not be lacking opportunities.'

It wasn't just among upcoming artists in the UK that *The Correct Use of Soap* had an impact. Over on the north-west coast of America a young Mark McLaughlin, better known as Mark Arm of Seattle grunge pioneers Mudhoney, got to hear just what McGeoch and Magazine were about. 'There was a small radio station around 1979 that later called themselves "the rock of the eighties", a local station high up on the FM dial. They sort of played new wave with a bit of The Kinks and Bruce Springsteen to kind of ease people in. They didn't play punk rock at all; you wouldn't hear the Sex Pistols or The Damned or anything like that – you might hear Buzzcocks. Around the time of *The Correct Use of Soap* they were playing songs from that record, which led to me buying it and then the two previous ones and I just really, really got into all the records – loved them. Eventually, in 1980, I went to college in rural Oregon and wormed my way into the radio station and that's when Virgin serviced that station as well, and I've got to say when *Play* showed up, looking at the credits and not seeing John's name on there – my heart sank.'

Jonny Greenwood of Radiohead looks back at just how seminal *The Correct Use of Soap* was in his own musical journey, having been exposed to the album at a young age. 'I heard *The Correct Use of Soap* when I was about 10 or 11 – it was my sister's record, and I played it constantly. "Sweetheart Contract" was my favourite – it still sounds so good. I love that McGeoch played everything in the service of the song – not to grandstand. On this song, his feel, and the sound of his guitar, is just so fluid and musical. He rightly gets credited for the strange sounds and melodies he created, but the subtle stuff is also great. It's telling that, in early Radiohead interviews, I'd always forget his name when praising Magazine: I always admired that he was a band member, rather than a soloist. The records were more important than the players to me.' Greenwood adds, 'They were ambitious writers – lyrically as well as musically – and occupied an odd space between punk and keyboard-driven music. The songs were well written and arranged thoughtfully – never ponderous or pretentious. It's hard to be all those things. Put simply, the songs were short and interesting. It was a lesson in not being boring.'

―――――――――――――――――

FOUR

STRANGE DAYS
A brief flirtation with the emerging New Romantic movement courtesy of Visage

---

Oh yeah, Visage, of course! That's a sort of hobby. Quite a pleasurable one though. We were just a bunch of friends who said, 'Let's make an album and sell it to a record company.'

International Musician and Recording World (April 1981)

JUST UNDER A year before *The Correct Use of Soap* – and with John, Dave and Barry living in London – certain possibilities were created and doors opened that would impact on the future of the band. John had begun frequenting the clubs and bars, where a different sound was developing. The New Romantic era was in its infancy, and a different type of dance music from across the pond and Europe was gaining ground on the dance floors. This was the world of cocaine, hedonism and, to some degree, style over substance. A culture where being seen was just as important – if not more so – as being heard.

The Blitz club was the playground of a certain Peter Anselm Egan, otherwise known as Rusty Egan, who had until recently been the drummer with the band Rich Kids (which featured former Sex Pistol Glen Matlock, Steve New and Midge Ure), and more recently Skids. Rusty had got to know John and the guys from the band prior to leaving

Rich Kids. As he puts it, 'Magazine released the debut single "Shot by Both Sides", and as with our guitarist, Steve New, I was blown away by it.' Rusty was DJing at Billy's club and then the Blitz, where he would drop songs like 'Parade' and 'Permafrost'. By the end of 1979, Rusty had left Skids, who he had been drumming for on tour. Along with Midge Ure, he started putting Visage together and invited John down to the recording sessions. Rusty recalls, 'On "The Dancer" John played sax and said he would ask Dave and Barry if they were up for a jam.' As Dave Formula recalls, 'We both saw Visage as a bit of a side issue, and something to have a go at and see if anything came of it. It was Rusty and Midge Ure who were in the driving seat with that, and it was never a conflict with what we were doing with Magazine. It actually proved to be somewhat lucrative in the end.'

Rusty met up with Billy Currie at the Blitz, and along with John and co. decided to have a go at making music, as and when time and other commitments would allow. As Rusty remembers of that meeting, 'We stepped outside for a photo with Steven Strange taken by Sheila

John, second from left, with Visage outside the Blitz club, London, 1979.
Sheila Rock/Shutterstock

Rock. Shortly after, John, Dave and Barry all met Boy George, Kirk Brandon, Phil Lynott, Midge Ure, Siobhan from Bananarama, Marco from Adam and the Ants and Richard Burgess of Landscape. It was very social, there were loads of odd and wonderful people about.'

It was also at this point that a certain somebody who would prove instrumental in John's next big career move would show an interest in John and his availability, while Rusty was pushing through with the concept that would become Visage. Rusty explains: 'Steven Severin was interested in John for the Banshees. I made my move and grabbed him for Visage first, along with Dave and Barry. Midge returned with Phil Lynott's management and record producer Martin Rushent had offered his studios, which gave us a place to record and everyone agreed to one-sixth of everything, even if we toured. That never quite worked out, as John had moved on by then.'

Rusty's enthusiasm was like a breath of fresh air to John, and it gave him the chance to properly evaluate his options. Barry had his own feelings about the project. 'We started to go to the Blitz together, John, Dave and I. We'd be hanging out with Rusty Egan, and Steve Strange was on the door. There was a bit of a hustle and bustle around this whole New Romantics scene; we were kind of on the fringes of it really – not being a New Romantic band ourselves. Dave and John got involved quite quickly, whereas I sort of held back a bit really. Dave talked me into going along to some studio and playing on a B-side as I recall, "Train". It didn't play out well for me in Visage, really. We were sought after, and Midge Ure and Rusty kind of knew that we could provide the meat around the bones that were the ideas they had, and that Steve Strange would be put "puppet like" at the front. I was involved enough to be a part of it until the money started to be made, of course! Looking back, it was a difficult time for me – my own addictions had started to surface and I wasn't really looking out for myself. I kept what I felt was a healthy distance from what I perceived as being too mainstream and uncool – at that time it was all about what was cool.'

For John it was much more about widening his own network, of becoming known to other influential artists and movers within the industry. There was the prospect of making a few quid and giving himself a bit of space after being purely focused on Magazine.

So, with John, Dave and Barry involved, only Howard and John Doyle were left behind in what was becoming a more fractured outfit. Howard didn't overthink the Visage project, but comments, 'I didn't think it was the greatest thing to be involved in, but in truth I don't really remember hearing Visage and I certainly don't remember them gigging. John liked the club scene.' John did enjoy elements within the scene – he was sociable and willing to try new things, but always with one eye on the opportunities it might present to work with new people.

I don't think anybody could have foreseen how successful that first Visage album would go on to become, how massive a song like 'Fade to Grey' would be. It did, however, prove to be a very financially successful venture for John. It enabled him to enjoy the finer things – not that he was obsessed by material wealth, but at the same time he aspired to live comfortably and do things he loved. He was ever keen to explore new experiences, to test the waters and immerse himself in culture, and to have his finger on the pulse of what was happening. It was natural to him to be inquisitive and open to new possibilities, something that manifested musically as well as domestically. John enjoyed good food and expensive wines and became quite knowledgeable about those things. Most people of that age and in those times wouldn't have had a clue about Merlot or Shiraz, but John knew his stuff.

Did John see Visage as anything more than a chance to be creative with new people and make a few quid? I doubt it. It was never going to be a long-term fit. John was an artist, somebody who had the ability to extend his talents to a wide range of pursuits, musical or otherwise, but that said, he was a guitarist first and foremost. That was how he'd shot to recognition and that was what people wanted from him.

———————————————

FIVE

HAPPY HOUSE

John leaves Magazine and joins up with Siouxsie and the Banshees

---

The Banshees asked me to play with them because they liked my guitar playing. They could have got a session player – some nameless person who was proficient. But I wrote my own guitar parts on the early Banshees stuff – 'Happy House' was the first. I wrote the guitar part for that – the song was written, more or less, but I added my guitar part.

International Musician and Recording World (April 1981)

BY EARLY 1980 Siouxsie Sioux and Steven Severin were ready to start thinking about recording their follow-up album to *Join Hands*. The only stumbling block was that they still hadn't found a replacement for guitarist John McKay, following his (and drummer Kenny Morris's) disappearing act mid-tour while in Scotland the year before. Robert Smith of The Cure had filled in and worked tirelessly, both as part of the support act and on stage as a fill-in for the Banshees. The band had recruited Budgie from The Slits to complete the tour and found that his tribal, percussive style merged well with their evolving sound. The band began developing material that was already in an embryonic stage, with lyrics and ideas for composition already in place. They weren't sure what direction they wanted to take when it came to recording, but they did audition exhaustively to try to find the right fit on guitar.

McGeoch appeared on the Banshees' radar, as Siouxsie recalls: 'I remember us really, really desperate to find a guitarist and we'd been auditioning, and it was so soul destroying not finding anyone that had a spark. Of course, "Shot by Both Sides" – that song and really the sound of the guitar – was just something which said we have to see if this guy is available.' As Siouxsie remembers, he wasn't somebody they knew well enough to simply call upon, as they had with Robert Smith. 'We didn't know him [socially], really. Although we all lived in London, we all toured so much back then that there was very little down time.'

Bassist and co-founder of the band, Steven Severin, was very aware of what a player like McGeoch could contribute and shared Siouxsie's admiration for his work with Magazine. 'I'd seen Magazine on TV doing "Motorcade" and "The Light Pours Out of Me". Midway through "The Light" I knew he was the one for us and suggested to Siouxsie and Nils, our manager, that we try to approach him. Details are a bit foggy but it is certainly true that the initial meeting was brokered by Steve Strange.'

It wouldn't be as hard as they may have imagined to persuade John to make the move. He was unhappy with how he felt Magazine had stagnated. His relationship with Howard was effectively over and he needed a new direction to showcase his talent – something he had desperately hoped *The Correct Use of Soap* would provide. His eyes had been opened to life outside the band, courtesy of his work with Visage, but the reality was that creatively it wouldn't be the right platform for a player of his dexterity and talent. John needed recognition as a player, he needed to be pushed and he needed stimulation. Until an approach for his services was made, however, he wouldn't simply quit. For all the tension between Howard and John and the frustrations that they all felt, John was loyal, and he was proud of the music they'd made. He would have been acutely aware that whichever direction he decided to take, it could be the make or break moment in his career. His status as one of the most significant players around meant his stock was high and he wouldn't be short of offers.

Siouxsie recalls exactly where and when the first meeting with

John took place. 'I first met John on 2 January 1980 in his local pub in Notting Hill. A few days later we started rehearsals and by the 13th we were doing demos of four songs at Polydor in Stratford Place.'

Steven Severin remembers how John felt at the time and how the move worked for all concerned. 'John was ready. He talked about how he wanted to get into more "picking" things on guitar like "Floorboards", like "Happy House". He said he felt constrained by the ever-present keyboards in Magazine and that they were hitting a brick wall where commercial success was concerned. He'd already done "moonlighting" work for Visage so we could sense he was restless. We met him just before Christmas 1979 and did first rehearsals early in the New Year.'

John was proud to show his potential new collaborators how pleased he was with how *The Correct Use of Soap* sounded and also, as Budgie recalls, how it looked. 'When I met John... I remember he came in proudly presenting this package, *The Correct Use of Soap*, the colour of the cardboard and the printing of it. He was so proud of it. So proud of *The Correct Use of Soap*, and "A Song from Under the Floorboards" was the song. I got it, but I didn't get it from the music. I got it from the whole picture.' The feelers were subsequently put out and John was invited into the Banshees fold, along with former Sex Pistol Steve Jones, to lay down some guitar parts. This in itself would be John's audition.

As Siouxsie relates, 'For *Kaleidoscope*, Steve Jones came along. At that time we weren't sure if it was going to be a "band band" that stuck together or whether it was just going to be a case of every time we wanted to record, we'd use different people who were available and at a loose end at that time. We quickly realised that to actually go ahead and write material and have ideas to bounce off and have things that start from nothing and just evolve is much better, especially with John who was just so fluid musically and also flexible... He could do something on a piano or an organ; he was just very versatile and open, which made the writing process really easy.'

The material was strong, as was the determination within the band to come back with an album stronger than anything they had done previously. Given the recent disruption to the line-up, the sense of betrayal at what had happened was still acute. Budgie was now *the* drummer, and it would be up to John to showcase his credentials. As Siouxsie remembers of that time, 'With *Kaleidoscope*, the songs were pretty much written, and people were able to add and contribute, and he did add, he didn't just fill in space where there was space, you know, he did add to it.'

Former Magazine manager Andrew Graham-Stewart makes an important observation – something that would have been as true for John's work on *Kaleidoscope* as it would have been for any of his future recording endeavours. 'Once you get into that market [session work], it's not just the band members who will be talking about him – it's the producers and the engineers in the studio. They'll all be talking about this amazing guy, who did all this great stuff in one take. His reputation would grow exponentially courtesy of his studio work.'

Siouxsie offers insight from her own diaries, starting from when John began laying down tracks with the band, commencing with the first four songs on 13 January 1980 in Stratford Place:

Happy House and its B-side Drop Dead, Hybrid & Desert Kisses.

23rd January recording at Phil Manzanera's studio for a day. Technical gremlins so nothing much achieved bar a work-out.

February 4th, 5th & 7th recording and mix of Happy House at Surrey Sound with Nigel Gray.

Cut of Happy House on 11th.

February 13th with Severin for another writing session at Chappells.

25th back to Manzanera's studio for 3 days. Christine, Desert Kisses and Hybrid.

28th Feb – 13th March press, promotion and video for Happy House.

14th – 19th rehearsals for 7 UK dates 20th – 28th March.

April 10th – 12th back at Chappells with Severin for more writing.

April 27th record Eve White/Black & Tenant at Polydor with Severin.

May 13th – 30th final recording, compiling and mixing of *Kaleidoscope* at Surrey Sound with Nigel.

John finishes on the 20th May (to go off on tour?) He did odd days at the studio. Steve Jones records his guitars in one day on Clockface, Paradise Place and Skin on the 28th.

JOHN WAS ABLE to take the bones of the songs and elevate them to something truly original and enduring (the iconic 'Happy House' went on to become a dance sample hit many years later). He understood what they were trying to do – the fit was right. John's contribution to the recording of *Kaleidoscope* is indisputable. In every sense this was a special record. In particular, the guitar parts were clever and catchy without ever trying too hard. They'd harnessed an energy, a loyal following and were well on their way to establishing themselves as *the* standout band of what came out of punk. They were developing that hard-to-realise combination of underground 'cool' with hit single potential, which naturally they wanted. This suited John perfectly; he didn't want to be involved in anything obscure or lacking the key ingredients to make it successful – he'd already had his experience of that.

As it became clear both musically and personally that there was something worth pursuing here, John would have been eyeing a permanent role in the band. Here was a group who had torn up the rule book with their first two albums, setting a high standard of creative expression and going all out to make an impact. Siouxsie was a force of nature, a tireless performer and with a vocal style unlike any other. Admired and adored equally by men and women, she was driven by a desire to push the envelope as far as possible; her status as a legend and icon would cement itself very quickly. Steven Severin knew how to complement and cut through the riffs with a style that, like Barry Adamson's, was very much his own. Budgie was arguably the most original, intuitive drummer around. There was something about his playing that felt like it had jumped out of legendary jazz drummer Phil Seamen's record collection and formed an 'Afro rock' hybrid – he really added something so vital to the band. With such talent and with each part integral to the sound, the guitarist couldn't be anything less than exceptional. If this was going to work, if the band were going to really make it, then there could be little room for error. John McGeoch had impressed the Banshees – perhaps even exceeded their expectations – and would be asked to join, but first there was the matter of the tour commitments he already had with Magazine.

These were his mates, in particular Dave and Barry. He wasn't about to just up and leave them in the lurch with gigs pencilled in and fast approaching – besides, there would be contractual obligations to be fulfilled. It was agreed that he would return to the Banshees afterwards and become a fully fledged member. Siouxsie and the boys had got their man. Simon Draper explains the situation for labels and artists at Virgin at that time. 'Basically, we wanted people to sign exclusively to us. We were using industry-standard contracts which we would then negotiate, so we were flexible on certain things. We were very flexible in giving artists artistic freedom, but in terms of actually securing their exclusive recording rights we would be very loath to feed those to anyone else. John would have been signed to Virgin as a member of Magazine, but if he went solo we would have retained the rights to his solo records. When he left Magazine, as he did to join Siouxsie, we would have just accepted that. Siouxsie and the Banshees had their own career which we couldn't interfere with; had he made a solo album we may well have had a different attitude. If by that point Magazine was in the process of disintegration anyway, which I think it was, then there is not much you can do about that.'

Leaving something you'd given so much to and something that had also given you so much back was never going to be easy. In John's case it represented the end of an era: the student days of flat sharing with Malcolm, jamming with Howard, and Pete Shelley playing guitar at the foot of his bed. These would have been precious memories to John – strong bonds had been formed and, of course, Janet had been there the whole time watching the band evolve. John agonised about whether to leave, and then about how to break the news to his bandmates. Much like ending a marriage, this would not be an easy conversation.

There were also changes for John and Janet in their living arrangements as they moved down the road to Ladbroke Grove, to house share with friend and Members frontman Nicky Tesco. He recalls, 'He hadn't long joined, or he was being enticed to join, the Banshees when we started living together. I'm thinking it was around 1979 that we all moved into the house, just off Portobello. It was a massive house that myself and my then girlfriend, Annie, found purely by chance. Janet and John were living up the road on Kensington Park Road in Notting Hill. We socialised quite a lot and we were actually there one night and Richard Jobson was there, his brother Michael was there, friends and girlfriends all doing what young people involved in rock music around Portobello Road did at that time. Some guys turned up wanting to come in, and it wasn't a party, it was just friends having a good time. Jobbo was like, "Fuck off," and these guys went off and came back and threw a scaffolding pole, which hit John in the face. This led to John having some scars on his lower face. The guys legged it and I'm not surprised they did, because there were quite a lot of very tough, very angry people chasing them up the road. I don't include myself in that, by the way, for two reasons: I'm not particularly tough and I'm not very good at running!'

Richard Jobson recalls the night – and the other side of John that was provoked due to the attack. 'John was no pushover, and he had a temper. Everybody talks about the John McGeoch smile, which was one of the most charming things about him, but he definitely had a temper. I remember these guys came to the door and wanted to come in and he said, "No, you can't come in." Then they smashed a scaffolding pole through the window. Me and John ran out to take them on, assuming that the others inside had followed us down – but they hadn't! I thought, "Shit, I'm in trouble here." I was expecting John to be a bit of a wimp, but he wasn't, he got stuck right in and set about them and we fought them off. John actually got scars that night from the pole through the window. He was a tough little fucker! He would be the same on stage years later, when if something went off in the crowd and I jumped down to steam in, he'd drop his guitar and come and help me out. Very different from Russell [Webb] and John Doyle, who weren't fighters; they just aren't those type of people. John had your back.' A change of address may have been welcome at that point!

So, John and Janet moved in with Nicky and other friends from the music business. As Nicky explains, 'My then girlfriend and I were kicked out of our place and I believe John and Janet were having to leave theirs. My girlfriend came across this house which was being rented out by this elderly Egyptian couple and it had about four or five floors and the rent was great. We obviously needed to find people, so we had John and Janet on the ground floor in a big room which was probably once a living room. We had another guy who was like the local coke dealer, but he was actually working at a record distributor, in one of the back rooms. Then on the next floor up there was this massive kitchen and living room and then further up there were more bedrooms. So, another two couples, me and Annie and a young woman who worked at Virgin records. We all knew each other and were all really good friends.'

John in his famous Lewis Leathers jacket, 1980.
Virginia Turbett

This will have been a happy time for the housemates – they were young people living in a great city, having a laugh, supporting one another through the insanity of 'the industry' and being creative. Having Nicky there was as much a support to John as it was to Nicky. Both knew what being involved in bands was like; they knew the highs but equally they understood the pitfalls of touring and then the comedown of finishing and returning home. 'The house became this place of creativity, fun and happiness. I think for a lot of us it really was an incredibly happy period. Because the kitchen was so big, we did the classic orphans' Christmas one year. This really long table was just surrounded by, not just the people who lived in the house, but people we knew in London who didn't have family to go to. Everybody chipped in for everything – you can imagine for all the smoke-ables, all the food-ables and all the drink-ables. It was brilliant, it was a party that went on for about three days!' Everything was gelling at just the right time – both in John's personal and professional life – to produce what many would regard as his creative peak.

Siouxsie reflects on John's contribution to the band he would join and change forever. 'The three albums John was involved with [*Kaleidoscope*, *Juju*, *A Kiss in the Dreamhouse*] are albums that are really at the top of the Banshees' game, I think. We all found each other at the right time. He was at a loose end, as I think he'd left, or was leaving, Magazine by then and maybe started his work with Visage. So, he was just looking to fill in the gaps that had appeared. He was just very open, very fluid and very easy to work with.'

Budgie says of the *Kaleidoscope* sessions, 'With *Kaleidoscope*, quite a few of the tracks were already written in the publisher's studio, with limited bits of equipment. "Red Light" was the first and there's no guitar on that. John came down and started adding parts – I think it would be tracks like "Desert Kisses" and other songs, where you can hear John picking up like a sitar guitar sound.' John got a writing credit on the album for the song 'Trophy', a jarring riff, but it's perhaps for his work on 'Christine' that his contribution on *Kaleidoscope* was most felt. Something akin to the opening of The Beatles' 'A Hard Day's Night', it was a chord and tuning that McGeoch created, but which has remained stubbornly elusive for those who try to replicate it. As far as original guitar parts go, it's up there – just as with 'Shot by Both

Sides', John had struck the sweet spot early on with the band. The single was released on 30 May 1980 by Polydor and peaked at 22 in the British singles chart. The album's other single was 'Happy House', which had been released in March and done slightly better, reaching number 17.

Paul Morley explores the shift in dynamic that McGeoch's collaboration with Sioux, Severin and Budgie brought to the group. 'Siouxsie and the Banshees had never really had a settled sense of anything other than Siouxsie and Steven at that point. At the time you wouldn't have been surprised to have seen it all fade away, but they clearly had a very strong internal sense of purpose. Truth was, it was exciting that John would suddenly wash up with Siouxsie and the Banshees. I loved the whole idea of the band because they just seemed so mysterious in their own way, but they also had hit singles. What was interesting is that John could work in that world and he could help them out with making hit singles. It was a time when that was a very difficult thing to do. They'd come out of punk and been so attached to it. Eventually they signed to a fairly ordinary label, but somehow still maintained this incredible otherness. From within all that John helped them build it up. Prior to that there was still a sense that it was possibly just a project that couldn't last very long. Somehow John was able to come in and help to lift it up to a different level of permanence. As a fan of John and a fan of everything he did and how he played and also a fan of Siouxsie and Steven – it was just a great moment. I suppose it's that idea as well of a new kind of collaboration that just made perfect sense. The kind of guitar player that Siouxsie needed would not have been superficially technically adept, yet they also needed someone who was. So, John was a paradox. He could play with a kind of traditional energy that wouldn't have disconcerted traditional rock fans, but he also had this more subversive element. John definitely lifted Siouxsie and the Banshees up into being a strong group that seemed to suddenly have a sense that they could be around for a long time. All the while, not sacrificing any of the more ethereal and askew elements of the group. John could somehow be in these groups that had a poetry about them and bring in guitar dynamics, but not destroy the poetic elements.'

John made his live debut with the Banshees on 19 March 1980, ironically in Manchester, at the Osbourne Club. The set list comprised 'Pulled to Bits', 'Happy House', 'Hybrid', 'Christine', 'Desert Kisses' and 'Drop Dead'/'Celebration'. For John Frusciante of Red Hot Chili Peppers, McGeoch was able to expand the Banshees' established sound and build upon the foundation of the previous incumbent, John McKay. 'As much as John McKay's playing tended to be within little boxes, he definitely created the framework which John McGeoch was able to explode within expressively. He was able to put all kinds of expression and creativity into that framework, and that really is a great feat when I think about McGeoch's contribution there. You see the basis of his playing, his style and his feeling of what he brings creatively – which you see in Magazine also. There is just something about that chemistry between him, Budgie, Severin and Siouxsie and it is one of those rare examples where somebody comes into a group that already has a sort of fixed limitation of what you can do and what you can't do and what the boundary lines are, and that he somehow figures out a way to put his creativity in that, as if those boundaries don't exist. It's a rare thing for somebody to be able to do, and when something that magic happens, I have a hard time attributing it merely to human beings. I feel as though it is something that comes from beyond, that you can't really prepare for or decide, yet for some cosmic reason it happens. What they did in the original Banshees line-up was already a big step to go from punk rock to that, and you see certain chord shapes that John McKay was doing which hadn't been done in punk. John McGeoch wound up doing really creative and inventive things with those same chords, and lots of other strange chords that nobody else had done. Creative guitar parts like this, and why I feel they are so creatively different, has to do with seeing them in the context of the bass part especially, and you see what McGeoch did alongside that and how he utilises the space between those two things and the difference between them. Generally, they are playing two completely different things and it's not as if one is following the other. Not that many groups have it, you know. Most groups tend to have it where one person is following another. In the McGeoch line-up with Siouxsie and what they were doing, it is like every member was in their own world and yet each part complements the other perfectly. When you take a guitar part that you think is particularly brilliant, it's really not just the guitar part – it's a drum part, it's a bass part and it's the magic of how those things connect to each other.'

John returned to Magazine buoyed by the experience of working with new people and keen to see how far they could go together. He knew that there was the job of the Magazine tour and, of course, breaking news of his departure to the band. As Howard recalls, the way it happened perhaps reflected the distance between the two and the realities of the music business. 'I heard it through our manager. I was hurt, actually, that John didn't tell me personally' – although Howard does concede that from a personal perspective his relationship with John was not a close one. 'In truth, I didn't feel I got on that well with John. I found him increasingly difficult to get on with, but perhaps it's not an untypical thing between the lead singer and guitarist to have a degree of discomfort.'

Barry reflects, 'I can see John walking out of a rehearsal at Lots Road and having a bit of tetchiness about him. It was more a case of being told, "John's left," and me being, "Yeah, don't tell me, I know."' It was a blow that would be felt by everyone in the band, but Barry recognises John's need to move on: 'I felt that John had a craving for success and the work with Visage showed him that there was life outside Magazine. I think there was a struggle within him in Magazine, and with the lack of success I could see his moods changing and I don't think it was anything more than, "Why am I not getting more recognition?" Like me, I think he thought *Real Life* would change the world, *Secondhand Daylight* would change the world. *The Correct Use of Soap* didn't change the world. So, what more can you do at that point? He was thirsty for validation in the mainstream, I think.'

Dave Formula is philosophical about John's exit: 'I think the tipping point for John came after we'd done *Soap* and there were lots of interviews and the reviews were good. We felt good about it and there was a great feeling within the band, but Howard made it clear that he didn't want to do interviews this time around. It was left to John and myself to take over that side of things, which neither of us really wanted to do because we knew that the journalists really wanted to speak with Howard rather than with us. Because this had the makings of the album that would push us forward and achieve more commercial success, I think that Howard not engaging frustrated John.

With Howard refusing to do the interviews I think John felt that Howard wasn't doing enough to make Magazine the success that it should be. Howard wanted success but wanted it on his terms, he wanted recognition and success on several levels but as I say, on his terms. Generally, you can't do it, unless you're very lucky, and there is a need to play the game, as it were. For John it just wasn't moving fast enough or going in the right direction.'

The implications for the band would only really be felt when it came to planning the next studio album. On John's contribution and importance to Magazine, Dave contends, 'I think, put a similar number of musicians together with diverse interests and you could end up with a mishmash. Yet somehow, between us, we were able to deal with it and use it creatively. I think that is why it was such a big blow when McGeoch left. Without overstretching the chemistry, something did break within the band when he left. Subsequently when we auditioned other guitarists it was just so hard to replace him; you couldn't replace him.'

The loss of John was a bitter pill to swallow. The others knew that trying to find somebody who could not only play as brilliantly as John but could also deliver the goods on stage as well as in the studio (and crucially could contribute so much to the writing of material) was going to be tough. Ultimately it proved impossible. According to Barry, 'You could feel the disappointment in the band. We were losing money and I was angry about its demise, but you could see it coming. John realised that it was over, and he knew he had to pursue another avenue to get to where he wanted to be.'

On his decision to join up with Siouxsie, Barry says, 'They were friends and they would be at parties together, Siouxsie would be there and Severin. They'd be talking with John all the time and it was almost like being at school, where they would say, "We've got this gang going on over here, why don't you join us?" He was perfect for that spot in the Banshees, but funnily enough, I think his playing was better in Magazine than it was in the Banshees. The way the guitar would be featured with them was very attractive. In Magazine John had to play a joint role with Dave, and of course there was a lot of admiration and mutual respect, but the limelight was being taken, whereas with just a guitar as the main attraction there wouldn't be that... it would be all

John. Siouxsie had a different edge to us, it was very pure and it was very cerebral and visceral. It was just a perfect fit for John and you would have to be seduced by it, you'd just have to be.'

The band had recognised that water was seeping in, but with John on the way out, the situation must have started to feel critical. Howard, by this point, was growing tired of the conflict. 'I was wondering how much longer I could cope with John. There may even have been a touch of relief when our manager phoned me to say he was leaving, there may have been a touch of relief in it.' If the status quo had ceased to be pleasurable for its commander in chief, then the issue of who would take John's slot in the band was not an immediate concern. Howard may have felt somewhat re-energised by clearing the decks and trying to arrest the rot that was setting in.

John played the dates he had committed to in the UK and Europe, while being clear he wouldn't be available to go out to the USA, Australia and New Zealand. When asked if there were attempts to persuade John to stay, Howard remarks, 'It was presented to us that John was leaving and at that point it's hard to say what we could have done to alter the fact he was off. We couldn't make our records any more successful than they were, not at that point – you still couldn't be sure how successful or otherwise *The Correct Use of Soap* was going to be. John left Magazine at the end of the European tour, so we were still to go to the States, Australia and New Zealand.' Howard adds, 'By the time *The Correct Use of Soap* came out I was in a very different mindset... I was backing off or low key as a frontman. I was told that John thought I was backing off from being so ambitious and I believe that had something to do with his thinking when deciding to leave.'

John was very fond of Dave Formula, and the thought of leaving him behind was one of the biggest wrenches in making the decision, but he couldn't allow sentiment to cloud his judgement. As Dave sees it, 'I think for John, and I say this as an ambitious person, he out-ambitioned me, and that's far from a criticism. You need that drive and perhaps I should have followed his example a little more in that respect. He knew his mind and he knew what he wanted to achieve. He wasn't ruthless at all, but he was quite cut and dried – "if it's not this then it must be that" kind of attitude. He knew he was talented, he knew he was original and he wasn't prepared to waste what he had.'

Steven Severin acknowledges the loyalty John showed to Magazine; while he wanted to fulfil his ambition of being a Banshee, he also wanted to part with the band on the best terms possible. 'It took six to nine months for John to extricate himself from Magazine, mainly because he wanted to fulfil his commitments to them properly. That's why John doesn't appear in the videos for "Happy House" or "Christine". The real key was doing some shows to support the release of "Happy House" in March 1980. He loved how it felt to be a Banshee on stage.'

McGeoch took to the stage with Magazine for the final time on 8 June 1980 at Festival of Fools, Amsterdam. What nobody would argue with is that Magazine had been a unique creative journey for them all. They had all brought everything they had to the party and John had been able to build a reputation through those albums and live performances. Johnny Marr could appreciate how special Magazine were and just how important an album such as *The Correct Use of Soap* had been to him, not just at the time, but throughout his career. 'Magazine were one of the few groups who moved forward from punk and really were what you might call progressive, in the true sense of the word. It's probably not a coincidence that the other two bands that immediately come to mind, who did the same thing, were Public Image and Siouxsie and the Banshees. That was before McGeoch had even joined those bands.' Of the Banshees, Marr claims: 'If the Banshees had come out last year, they'd be a modern group – a modern-sounding group.'

Howard recalls meeting up with John following his move to the Banshees. They were listening to the new Magazine album *Play*, a live recording from the previous tour. John had started the tour but had been replaced by Robin Simon, who now featured as the guitarist on the album. 'After we'd mixed the album *Play*, John came round to my place to listen to it and the two comments I remember him making were "John and Barry are really tight" and "Good guitaring." Which was a generous thing for him to say and, you know, at least half mean it!'

UPON HIS RETURN to the Banshees, the band made plans to play a few warm-up gigs under another name. As remembered by Murray 'Muzz' Mitchell, John's guitar tech throughout his time with the Banshees, 'When McGeoch joined, they organised some undercover-type gigs as

Janet and the Icebergs, which were little warm-up shows, because they had a booking at Leeds Futurama Festival – which was the big unveiling of McGeoch as a permanent member of the band. So, I was just there as a fan and a bit of a mate of Siouxsie and Steve's, and John had had a roadie in Magazine, so he needed somebody to tune his guitars. The manager turned to me and said, "Well, you used to be in a band, you do it!" That precipitated me being hired as a proper roadie with the band, as opposed to just tagging along, I guess. It was a very exciting prospect for a 19/20-year-old. I'd seen him play with Magazine and just thought he was an extraordinary guitar player.'

John made his 'official' live debut as a full-time Banshee on 13 September 1980 at Leeds Futurama Festival. The Banshees headlined on the Saturday night at Queens Hall, on the same bill as Echo and the Bunnymen, Soft Cell and U2. His joining the Banshees had caused a bit of a stir and expectations were high, especially following the success of *Kaleidoscope*. The timing was right and the trajectory that both John and the Banshees were on set the scene for something truly special. John slotted in seamlessly and his presence on stage gave the band an edge and a creative spark that made those performances so memorable. This was the best line-up they'd had; John was able to play the songs from the previous two albums perfectly and add his own flair. He showed just how honed he was on an appearance for the BBC, where the Banshees performed 'Tenant' and 'Israel'. His use of the flanger and his appreciation of the need for space to create an atmosphere were a joy to behold. Here was a man and a band on the cusp of something truly innovative and arguably without equal at that point among the groups of the day. But the best was yet to come, as Budgie reflects: 'John brought a lot to the table when he joined. There was a lot of stuff that I didn't have the skill set, at that point, to offer. I was still working on who I was as a player, whereas John was more established with who he was musically. He was moving through to a phase of real experimentation with what he knew and also how he didn't want to sound.' Regarding his own place within the band, Budgie adds, 'John made it easier because he was quite worldly. I still felt quite young. Siouxsie and Severin were definitely the London "scene".'

Siouxsie saw in McGeoch someone who had some of those same qualities that she possessed, in terms of standing your ground and not

John the Banshee playing at Stokvishal, the Netherlands, 1980.
Roy Tee

taking a backward step – the sort of attitude that suited the music they were creating together. 'He was very feisty, but I think in a good way. When you're in a band and you're somewhere public, quite often people just want to try their luck by pushing your buttons. Either they're fans or they've just got a chip on their shoulder. I'll never forget being in this bar and some guy kept trying to bum a cigarette, he just took my one cigarette that was lit to which I said, "Oi!" and he went to have a go at me and I pushed him. McGeoch was just like, "Are you having a go at my Siouxsie?" He went straight in there and just steamed in. Normally anyone else in the band would run a mile from any sort of trouble. McGeoch had your back if you needed it. He was very loyal, and he'd fight his corner with you.' Muzz confirms this when remembering John's strong personality and lack of tolerance for people taking liberties, either with himself or with his bandmates. 'He wouldn't take anything off anybody. He'd be the first to stand up and say, "Oi you, shut the fuck up." Definitely never a wallflower. They'd never had a henchman in the band before.'

John remained open to the possibilities of session work during this period and was invited to sit in and play guitar on some of the upcoming tracks for the Generation X album *Kiss Me Deadly*, which was released in January 1981. Billy Idol remembers, 'I had seen Magazine a couple of times, once at the Croydon Greyhound, and I'd met John but didn't know him that well. I was really super impressed by his playing because at that point when I saw him, which was when Howard had left Buzzcocks and formed Magazine, seeing someone like John who was really accomplished compared to a lot of other players in punk, he was something else. He was doing things that were so impressive, the textures – it was just obvious he was a cut above everybody in punk. Most people in punk rock at that time, they were still learning to play in a way. John already knew. He had his way of playing down already.

'So, when it came to the Gen X album *Kiss Me Deadly* we had already written the songs, but we had several players on some of the tracks – I played, we had Steve Jones, Danny Kustow and Steve New. There was a couple of songs where I played the guitar, but what we didn't want was power chords – we needed textures, somebody who could offer little hook lines and ways of helping to expand the feel of the song, the melody behind the singing. In particular, John was involved with "Heavens Inside" and "Poison". Both of these tracks were very empty, they just had me playing guitar – some basic chords and rhythm. What we didn't have was any lead or, as I say, textures or lines to add a dimension that wasn't there yet. So, on "Heavens Inside" he played this fantastic little lead line just behind the verse, and it was just like… wow! It was beautiful and a real eye-opener to us. I remember we all just looked at each other in the control room, amazed. I was kind of into things having a noise, a beautiful noise – we got him to use a bit of pedal on "Heavens Inside" and then at the end he'd play these harmonics, so it was like a little hook. What John was doing was beautiful and it really helped to create those songs and the melodies. His control was incredible. He could think out of the box, and that is how I would describe his playing. He'd give you something that I couldn't have remotely thought of, and what was great is you might give him a direction and he'd just take it to the nth degree and beyond what you were even asking, you know? He was so easy to work with, super professional and fun and he was delivering. John gave us what we were looking for in spades. It was the touches he gave that brought the tracks alive.'

Johnny Marr concurs with Idol's perception of McGeoch being ahead of the curve. 'One of the things I started to realise about John McGeoch and his peers, of which there were very few, and of which he was my favourite: when punk came along, he was already a very adept player. There were a handful of players at the time who couldn't hide the fact that they were already able to play Hendrix riffs and the whole repertoire and culture that the likes of McGeoch would have been very familiar with. Punk comes along and he wasn't going to pretend he couldn't play, so he managed to turn that artistic "big bang" into something so much more than just barre chord thrash. He wasn't pretending to be in some crap spitting punk band! What he was doing was conceptual.'

The Banshees set off on a two-week tour of America, the first time the group had performed there. The tour was the typical affair for many British bands of the time – having established a strong following at home and across Europe, the big test was in building a name for themselves in a country that isn't always as up to date culturally as is often assumed. The East Coast proved much more fruitful and enjoyable than out in California, where many of the venues were not entirely sold out or the audiences even aware of who the Banshees were or what they were about. Regardless, John had enjoyed his previous experience Stateside with Magazine and no doubt revelled in showing the rest of the band the ropes in 'familiar' surroundings. Siouxsie had flown out there prior to the tour, so she was under no illusions about what was likely in store for the band. As Budgie recalls of John and touring, 'It was a massive leap into the world of the Holiday Inn! You know, what does everybody do from arriving there until soundcheck and then what does everybody do from soundcheck until gig?

I'd never had the facility of a hotel room. I think John was definitely more aware of the possibilities of hotels and the lifestyle. I don't know if he became my teacher, as such, in lifestyle and if I think back, I wonder, "Were we very close?" We never had those lad-to-lad talks very much – he and Severin seemed to make that bond.'

Severin himself agrees: 'I clicked with John immediately. I know I have a spiritual bond with Scots in general but this was instantly easier than with either [former members] John McKay or Kenny Morris. We started to hang out together almost immediately. I felt it was my role to keep him interested, keep seducing him until he officially left Magazine. It worked both ways, though. Through John I met his London clan: Richard Jobson of Skids, Russell Webb of Zones, Billy Currie of Ultravox! I became involved in a broader social circle which was really healthy for me. The original Banshees had become so walled off by the time we split.'

Playing Space Invaders with a Banshees fan, 1980.
Peter Anderson

John carried on in the creative vein that had made *Kaleidoscope* such a thoroughly modern and catchy album. By the time the Banshees returned to the studio, they were set to unleash a record so ahead of the game that it would take the band, and John especially, to a creative zenith that neither could have anticipated.

John had always maintained a pretty simple set-up throughout his time with Magazine: the MXR 117 Flanger and the Marshalls. John was also working with Fender amps and, crucially for the trademark McGeoch sound of the early eighties, the Roland JC-120. The JC-120 was interesting when used in conjunction along with a Marshall Twin or Fender amp (offering stereo sound) in that its projection was crisp, icy – almost piercing. It would set the tone for a number of tracks that the Banshees would record in the lead-up to the new album. John was also into experimentation to construct the vision that Siouxsie would inspire through their shared appreciation of a cinematic quality – the space and images that can be manipulated with sound to add the right amount of drama and suspense. Siouxsie elaborates: 'I think – because possibly, from my point of view, I'm less technically musical – I probably try and explain what I want much more on a cinematic level, which I don't think anyone had done with him before. We always talked about film soundtracks or feelings that those sounds and colours give you. I always thought the Banshees sound was very much on a visual level. There's tension but there's something cinematic about it.' John understood perfectly what was required to enhance a given piece. This was his forte, being sensitive to the melody of the vocals and bringing the right amount of expressive playing to complement and elevate the sound.

The beauty of the relationships within the band was the ease with which ideas were translated into songs. So much of what went onto vinyl had been the result of soundchecks, studio rehearsals or just mucking about with chord progressions and a certain little innovative gadget. As Siouxsie explains, 'He had his own sound, he was curious, he wasn't set in his own ways. He was just really open to trying new things. Nigel Gray, who had his studio at Surrey Sound, worked with Godley & Creme a lot and they had this thing called a Gizmo which McGeoch used. I think he used it on "Into the Light". The Gizmo treats the strings like a bow by attaching to the bridge and it had wheels that moved and it's really distinctive, so it's got this symphonic sound to it.' One of John's traits in particular gained Siouxsie's admiration early on, and not just from a musicianship point of view. 'There was a mutual respect, because of him being who he was, and also what I respected about him was that he wasn't a yes man. If he disagreed about something, we'd have a row but then it would be resolved. I find quite a lot of people sulk if they don't get their own way, whereas he would actually voice it. Which I really respect and appreciate with anyone. I can't bear it when you don't know if you've pissed someone off or if they're saying yes to something and they don't really mean yes. He was upfront and I really appreciated that about him.'

John's friend and housemate Nicky Tesco remembers vividly John's time recording the new Banshees album: 'Music was just starting to become that little bit more interesting with post-punk. He'd left Magazine and there were a couple of offers on the table, but he'd started working with Sioux, Severin and Budgie and it was just like a magical combination. I remember when they were working on the track "Monitor" and he came home with a rough mix of it and usually, after being in the studio all day, you know, you have to decompress. So, you'd get home, crack a beer, smoke a couple of joints and have a listen to the mixes. So, John was like, "I've got a couple of mixes," and he played "Monitor" and I looked at him and I said, "I think you've just redefined rock music," and he thought I was being flippant. But I was deadly serious, because it was like nothing I'd heard before, it was so powerful. Those Banshees albums all stand up, they've not dated as so many of that era have.' A sentiment shared by Siouxsie herself when looking back on their output and on *Juju* in particular. 'It's aged well, there's a timelessness to it. With any music, regardless of what genre it is, if it's good then it's always going to be good. It's not going to be good just for that summer or that year.'

John Frusciante appreciates the subtlety of what McGeoch brought to guitar parts but equally just how progressive and intricate they really are when examined. 'Despite some of the apparent simplicity of McGeoch's playing, it's pretty complex, and some of those things are tricky to learn – almost every guitar part has a trick built into it and the fretboard is a very different world for someone like him. For him the neck is a big skeleton that he is able to work with, to connect one part of the bone structure to another part, and in ways that you might not have immediately perceived what the connection between those two bones is.'

Prior to recording the album, the band released the stand-alone single 'Israel' – their first 12-inch – in November 1980. It reached number 41 on the UK singles chart. It would lay down a significant marker for the direction the band were about to take with the new album. Siouxsie recognises the significance of 'Israel', not just at the time, but right throughout the band's career. '"Israel", I think, probably was the first song that started it, with us all starting from scratch as it were. Again, a lot of guitarists just love "Israel" – any guitarist since, whether with the Banshees or anyone, just wants to be able to play it and loves being able to play it.' Budgie shares warm memories of the song and its creation. 'I think it was a Christmas song! "We need to do one of those Christmas songs, that's what we should do!" John's part in that song – it's classic McGeoch isn't it?'

Severin could see that John was entering a phase of unbridled creativity, something which could only be beneficial to the band and the chilling yet beautiful new sound that was to define the coming album. 'By Christmas 1980 John had been with us (on and off) for a whole year. We'd just returned from our first US tour and had just released "Israel"; we felt like a really strong working unit again and were determined to make up the lost time from the fallout of the 1979 split. John would come round my place and we started working up ideas for *Juju*. Both "Spellbound" and "Arabian Knights" were started this way whilst most of the rest of the album would develop in rehearsal rooms with the whole band. John was really blossoming during this time, spinning off in unexpected and exciting ways, whether it be the "chaos noise" of "Voodoo Dolly" or the almost baroque sounds of the Gizmotron on "Into the Light". It was something to behold. Yes, there was drinking involved, occasionally a gram or three, but we were all pretty much in sync. You wouldn't have put money on John being the one who would escalate.'

Looking back on the McGeoch sound and the movement that had spawned it, Johnny Marr says, 'One of the really exciting and important things about the outcome of punk, and what is now known as post-punk, is that it was the start of a whole new thing. I've said this before, but for me punk wasn't the letter A in the new alphabet. Punk was the letter Z in the old lexicon and then after that it was a clean slate, but punk had set out some rules of what you shouldn't be, so blues riffing was out, extended off-the-cuff solos were out, distorted lead solos were out. What you were left with was a narrow set of parameters that definitely influenced me. You can hear that with John McGeoch. You take all that stuff away and you are only left with a few colours for your palette. There's not very much you can do with a clean sound. You can't hold a note and you can't play bluesy. So, what John McGeoch was doing is being very into the MXR Flanger, which he used masterfully. It was a deliberate modernism. The flanger is an interesting thing because it modulates the signal so that it wobbles, and the effect is psychedelic. That's something that I definitely get from McGeoch's playing, in the Banshees particularly. It's not psychedelic in the way of, "Oh so trippy, sixties man," or like Hendrix. It's psychedelic in the way like you've taken bad acid or been psychotic after three days of speed!'

Nigel Gray co-produced *Juju* with the rest of the band. The material came together pretty seamlessly and there was certainly a theme running throughout or overall 'concept' – that of a psychological thriller. The textures of the music, the lyrics and the vocals led to an album bursting with tension. John's creative flair was to the fore; he was experimenting with sound in new ways. As he had stated himself when joining the Banshees, he was moving into 'a picky phase' with his playing – he was challenging himself and challenging the other band members as musicians.

From a guitar fan's perspective especially, *Juju* is a phenomenal piece of work and, arguably, John's finest playing to date. The album absolutely secured his position within the band and demonstrated just what somebody that creative, that giving with ideas, could offer. It was a win-win. The Banshees gave him the freedom he required to be as creative as he liked and, in return, they got the best out of a virtuoso who would make the album so enduring.

Budgie looks back: 'We were all comfortable, we were even comfortable very early on going into the studio with very little idea of what we were going to do. We went in on *Juju* with a lot of stuff from soundchecks from the tours around Europe. The nucleus of the ideas that would become the songs was already in place. "Monitor", if I remember, came in the studio with John playing, and I got the beat going and it was pretty much a live take. We probably did it several

John, far right, in the studio with Siouxsie and the rest of the Banshees, 1981.
Ray Stevenson

times.' Budgie goes on to describe how 'Arabian Knights' was realised: 'I remember "Arabian Knights" coming together in the rehearsal room. I think Siouxsie had a little motif on guitar and the way she played it was in three-four – she certainly had the melody. It was John who suggested we switch it to four-four.' Siouxsie looks back on that time and the way songs were crafted: 'Quite often the writing was a result of trying to get sounds, and things would just happen, people would just join in, which is a great thing to have. Rather than being, right this is the song, and this is your bit, and this is your bit. Yes, we had the bare bones of things, but we were able to be very open in the studio as well.'

Certainly, the complex dynamics within the band were working, though there were issues bubbling with manager Nils Stevenson that would eventually come to a head while on tour in America. John Frusciante acknowledges the role that Nigel Gray's production had on the sound and feel of the record: 'The engineering's great on *Juju* and that's such a huge part of it as well. [John's] guitar tones are so wild, and Nigel Gray makes everything cohesive on that record. In my opinion the one that comes after that [*A Kiss in the Dreamhouse*], the production isn't as good, they produced it themselves. Without that element of the production being perfect it loses something. There are great guitar parts and great songs on there, but the production is really bad. Between studying the album and trying my best to learn the parts – despite the fact they are as caked in reverb as they are, and in what I consider in a production sense a really sloppy way – the guitar parts are very creative still but just a lot of wrong choices being made. The song "Melt" going to those acoustic guitars in the chorus, I just feel like there are simply a lot of bad choices. Like, the BBC sessions versions of those tunes sound a lot better than that record does and to hear them without so much reverb you can start to appreciate how good the songs were and what a negative effect on the chemistry the production had. Not to be putting stuff down. I mean, *Kaleidoscope* and *Juju* are just two of the best albums ever made by any group ever and you just can't discount the role of the production and the engineering in that.'

The production factor is something that Mark Arm picks up on: 'I've got to say, I'm much more into *Kaleidoscope* and *Juju* than *A Kiss in the Dreamhouse*. I never bought *A Kiss in the Dreamhouse*. I heard it at the time and I've listened to it again recently and to me that record – the production is so drenched in effects – it's hard to sink your teeth into. I mean, I know John uses a lot of effects but for me Siouxsie isn't as intense as she was on *Juju*, say for example on a song like "Head Cut". It just seems like they were trying to make more of a commercial move. I would have to try and get past the production on the album to really be able to appreciate individual songs from it. I mean, there was a whole thing in the eighties where production in general for all, or most, of what was commercial was terrible! By the mid-eighties hard rock bands had that terrible fucking snare sound and that was throughout every band.'

Siouxsie is justly proud of *Juju*. She says that one song in particular remains a personal favourite and recalls the part John played in that. 'I love the EBow on "Sin in My Heart". It's so simple, it's so powerful and strong and it just grinds and builds to this frenetic point that goes off into the stratosphere. It's that EBow, it's quite Frippy

[King Crimson's Robert Fripp] in a way; it is John playing with a new toy and making it something really special.'

Juju was released by Polydor on 6 June 1981. The album received wide acclaim domestically, from critics and fans alike. John, especially, was recognised for his performance on the album. The band put out two singles, 'Spellbound' and 'Arabian Knights' – released either side of the album, in May and July respectively. 'Spellbound' got as high as 22 on the UK singles chart, while 'Arabian Knights' got to 32. They had found the formula for achieving chart success while remaining interesting and not 'selling out'. Mark Arm recognises the special dynamic within the group that shone through on McGeoch's second album with the band. 'When John joins up with Siouxsie and the Banshees for *Kaleidoscope*, I feel like it's a really great collection of songs. *Juju* on the other hand is a cohesive album that was done by a band. There is a point of view, supposedly they'd played some of those songs on the road before they recorded them – you can tell they've been battle tested.'

Equipment wise, John's set-up with the Banshees was far from flash and hadn't expanded dramatically from his Magazine days. He had two of his trusty Yamaha SG-1000s in iconic McGeoch tobacco sunburst. The ever-present MXR Flanger pedal mounted to the mic stand with a remote foot switch and an MXR Dyna Comp pedal, which you can hear when John uses the big feedback squeal on 'Night Shift'. A Yamaha E1005 analogue delay with foot switch heard on 'Voodoo Dolly'. Amp wise, it was the Roland Jazz Chorus and Marshall MV50 combo. (Credit to Muzz Mitchell for that little list!)

Johnny Marr looks back on John's time as a Banshee: 'From the Banshees' point of view, what they got in McGeoch is somebody who was able to be as progressive as John McKay, but then take it into a wider place – that's what it sounds like to me. He was the perfect fit for them. It's uncanny, really, with how it all came about, that he was able to just pick up that baton that had been dropped when McKay left and build upon that sound that they'd already owned. That was dead cool for me, I have to say, that John – who was somebody I already really liked and was impressed by – left a band that I loved and went to join another band that I loved, and went on to make some really good albums. Put it this way, I can relate to it!'

Another prominent and highly influential guitarist who would go on to gain acclaim for his playing with Radiohead, Ed O'Brien, remembers how important John's contribution to the Banshees was to him growing up. 'I was aware of the music but not the person. I think it was about 1981 when I first heard "Spellbound" and I was bewitched by the whole track.' Of McGeoch's abilities he says, 'Firstly, his musicality – he was always serving the song. He was a total original – the way he played those fluid arpeggios then seamlessly moved into a rhythm part. The sound he produced was so visual... colours and scenes in his music... When you learn one of his parts you realise that there is a fluidity and elegance in the way those parts dance over the fretboard, and his groove was so good. For me, he and Johnny Marr were the masters of this.'

The band went out on tour to promote *Juju*'s release and overhauled their aesthetic, turning the experience into something which combined the sound with a highly visual production. As Siouxsie had recognised, especially since the addition of McGeoch, the Banshees were a band you interpreted on a multitude of layers. Be it the music,

A Siouxsie and the Banshees gig poster, 1981.
Andrew Krivine archive

be it the imagery that those sounds, lyrics and emotions evoked. There was a lot to unpack, and perhaps this has given rise to the difficulty in defining the Banshees' music. The 'goth' moniker seems lazy and reductive, when in reality there were so many tiers of influence and innovation that meant from album to album the band could reinvent themselves. Not only was it possible, but it was necessary to keep the ideas fresh and to continue to be on the cutting edge of true creativity.

Budgie appreciates how his own development as a performer coincided with the band being in constant evolution and mutual appreciation of one another. 'I was told very early on by the singer in a cabaret band – and he called me by my name – "Peter," he said, "look to the front and smile," which I thought was an awful thing to say or do, but I did it. What I found was it took me out of this world [head down] and put me in that world [the stage]. John was always paying the same compliment back. He was so attentive, and he's looking over his shoulder – watching where my left foot is. Perhaps it was because John and I had more varied experiences of playing. Severin was self-taught and coming at bass from a different place than anybody that John or I had played with, I think, be that Barry in John's case or Tessa [Pollitt, The Slits] in mine. Severin had this other approach to it, pummelling eights and not a lot of low end – there was no way that could happen, which gave a lot of room down there. Picking up on vocal cues and landing where Siouxsie needed it to land. It was never suggested it was all intuitive. There was a desperate need to find a commonality – we were realising this was something new, there was experience and there was lack of experience, but the two things were equally important in formulating something that became ours.'

On stage for the tour supporting *Juju*, Budgie says, 'We'd achieved something in *Juju* and we'd played it so much. The whole concept with *Juju*... we built a stage at every venue, the lights were underneath and the monitors had gone from the stage. All these concepts added up to really pushing the envelope for what could be achieved.' Of the live performances Siouxsie has happy memories: 'I just know it felt amazing on stage. We were all at some kind of peak at the same time.'

John, Budgie and Severin had their own pre-show rite of passage, as Budgie relates: 'We did have the ritual beforehand, when waiting for Siouxsie to come down from her room, of meeting quietly at the bar and all having the same drink. The vodka or the brandy – usually vodka. It's strange because a couple of years later I couldn't take a drink before going on stage. Very early we'd have a little drink, just one. Was it a bit of Dutch courage? I don't know.'

John and Janet by this point had bought their first house together in Cricklewood, north London. It was here that John had decided their set-up required a furry addition, as Janet explains: 'John loved animals. When we lived in Cricklewood we had a tortoise, two geese, a cat (which was mine anyway) and two dogs. John's favourite dog was an English bull terrier called Stephen. He found Stephen in a pet shop in Kentish Town and he came home saying, "I've just seen this puppy and I love him!" I told him, "No, I don't want a dog as you're away on tour all the time," and he said, "But I love him and I've got to have him!" So, off we went to get this dog and sure enough he was off on tour all the time.'

In between UK tour dates up and down the country, John and Janet got married on 9 September 1981 at Islington Town Hall. In

John and Janet's wedding day, 1981.
McGeoch family archive

attendance were the Banshees, close friends Russell Webb and Richard Jobson (along with his partner Mariella Frostrup) and Nicky Tesco. Janet says, 'We got on a flight with the Banshees to go to Berlin the day after we got married. I never went on tour with the band because I had a job and it wasn't my thing anyway, but we tied it in as a little honeymoon.'

It was during this time that Billy 'Chainsaw' Houlston, who ran the Banshees' fan club and sold the official band merchandise, got to know John. '*Juju* would have been when I really got to know John, because I did all of that tour – selling the merchandise with a company that I'd introduced the Banshees to from the *Kaleidoscope* days. I was always on the road. Really good days. They were phenomenal live at that point. There are certain songs that become standouts in the set because of the emotion that they generate with the audience and that ["Israel"] was always a particularly emotive one, especially because back then you still got skinheads objecting to it in the audience. There were often a few kerfuffles.' The skinhead element was a remnant of the band's punk origins, but something they all wanted to distance themselves from – so much so that Siouxsie would goad the audience to go after any far-right sympathisers in the venue. Similarly, John had mentioned on an American radio broadcast in California that he had actually jumped into the crowd to remove a swastika badge from one of the fans. Of the audience dynamic and the heckling of 'Israel' by some small, albeit vocal, quarters, Siouxsie proudly remembers how they set about tackling the issue and how the song was so much more than just a Christmas number. 'We were having to put up with skinheads and Sieg-Heiling. So, "Israel" was many things, but it was also a weapon against all of that. There were a few gigs, and one I remember in particular, where we just came off stage and came back on with our Star of David T-shirts and did "Israel" and, yeah, it was a good moment.'

After the recording of *Juju* had been completed John resumed some session work and contributed guitar parts to Ken Lockie's debut solo album, *The Impossible*. As Ken remembers, 'I signed with Virgin in 1978 and ran into John at their offices in Vernon Yard several times. Initially I was recording and touring with Cowboys International, and after touring Europe in 1980 was back in London. Virgin gave me studio time at The Manor and the Townhouse. I got John to come into sessions at the Townhouse. It was my idea to have him do it – I knew him and trusted his playing style. We hung out in clubs and at an apartment close by Vernon Yard where Virgin press officers were staying. The sessions went well. I think I had a producer at that point, Steve Hillage. The tracks he recorded on were already basically formed, so John did overdubs – rhythm and lead – whatever he came up with, we recorded.'

The *Juju* tour proper got under way in Europe in June and July. This was followed by a return to a more extensive run in the UK before the band headed off to the States for the second time, in October through to November. Muzz looks back with fondness on John's relationship with the road crew. 'He was kind of like everybody's favourite. He was very much a man's man, if you know what I mean. He'd always be more than happy drinking with the crew, go to bars with the crew – he was really like the middleman between crew and band, there were no airs about him at all. He was quite happy to go to a shit bar and play pool and everyone just admired him. There were times when he'd be at the back of the bus and he'd try and goad someone into sticking one on him – he was very handy at fending people off. He had the deepest admiration for the crew, absolutely. An awesome guitar player who could drink like fuck and fight like fuck. Proper chap! It was a bit extraordinary for the time, really.'

Muzz highlights one relationship in particular that John formed while on the American leg supporting *Juju*: 'It was very much a group thing and by the time we were on the second tour of America we were all on a bus together, with a minder! The minder had taken over the back lounge and would just sit there and dispense all sorts. He was spending all the tour money on stuff and John used to goad him all the time. He'd been Motörhead's minder and that's how he got hired for the Banshees. John got on particularly well with him – Mick Murphy was his name – and they took a total shine to each other. A few of the crew used to work for Motörhead and would flip-flop between the two bands. Mick particularly liked John because he could see the proper feller in him. John wasn't a lightweight, artsy-fartsy type at all – a real geezer!'

Mark Arm made a point of catching the *Juju* tour when the band came to Washington State. 'Siouxsie and the Banshees came through

Seattle, I want to say around the fall of '81, and I was starting my second year at college in rural Oregon. I took a Greyhound bus, which would normally be a three-hour drive, ended up as a six-hour trip, stayed with my friend that weekend and went to the show. They did an in-store and I went to that. The crazy thing is, the distance between the venue where they played and the in-store was around thirty minutes. It was way out in the suburbs, like the suburbs that I grew up in. I'm sure as they were driving to this store in Fucksville, they must have been thinking, "What are we doing, why are we still driving? Isn't there a record store closer to the venue?" – and there was! I remember going to that and I had all the records at the time, the only thing I didn't have was the "Israel" single – so I bought that in the store. Had them all sign it and when I came up to John I said, "I just want you to know I love your work in Magazine." He seemed really surprised that anyone here in Bumfuck, outer Washington State, knew anything about that. My recollection is that he was kind of humbly honoured – what I mean is that he was surprised by it and seemed really genuine. That was a super-cool moment for me.'

The American leg was not without its difficulties, and it was while out on the road that relationships within the band started to change. John and Steven had become friendly early on and had their own thing going on, while Siouxsie and Budgie had started spending more time in each other's company. As Budgie relates, 'Siouxsie and I were definitely splitting off. John always had a camera and it was an expensive camera. I'm going, "That's an expensive bit of kit," that he was carrying around and dropping. And the roller skates… Roller-skating around car parks and I'm thinking, we've got a gig tonight! It was kind of fun but there was something happening with John that was not part of the gang – he was finding another life. […] Similar things happened afterwards and that might be the difficulty of joining a tight unit. Where Siouxsie and Severin were an item prior to me joining, and after that Siouxsie and Nils were an item and I stepped in, and I became the next part of the puzzle, really. That's something I'm still trying to figure out – maybe I became the best enabler or the best co-dependent. That created a dynamic within our band.'

Dave Woods was involved with the group in an agent/tour manager role and the problems between him and Nils Stevenson, who

John and his ever-present camera, 1981.
Ray Stevenson

was the manager, were starting to surface. Both were friends of Siouxsie and Severin and had a history. Nils was having a hard time accepting that Siouxsie had moved on with her life following their relationship. Further to this Nils was developing a drug habit that was affecting how focused he was on business affairs. The combination of his infatuation with Siouxsie, his own dependencies and the fact that the band's popularity was growing exponentially meant they couldn't afford anything less than fully committed and serious management.

Siouxsie remembers the power shift that took place between Nils and Woods, specifically while out in America, and the role John played. 'He actually had a go at Nils when we were in the States. It almost came to blows, I do remember that.' On Woods' position at the time, Siouxsie recalls, 'Woods was our tour manager and kind of promoter, so he was connected with all that stuff around live dates.' Siouxsie had always maintained that heroin and the Banshees did not mix, ever. As much as there needed to be freedom to be individuals, to live your own lives as you saw fit, the idea of heroin being part of that was just an absolute no-go. Nils had history and, as things began to unravel, his own addiction to the drug became more apparent. The writing was on the wall for Nils; given the relationship that Sioux and Severin had with Woods, and with Nils's behaviour becoming more erratic and confrontational, the decision wouldn't be hard.

Budgie remembers one incident in particular that took place while on tour in New York, possibly the same incident as mentioned by Siouxsie. 'In New York, on a night out around Gramercy Park, I remember us coming back from probably Molly Malone's pub with a few drinks already on board. Nils was on another trip. I think he was into heroin, there was a lot of that going around as well and it laid waste to a couple of managers for sure, but John stood up to Nils, who was screaming and shouting, trying to get close to Siouxsie. He said, "Nils, you're out of order, you're out of control, you should go home," and he was ready to defend Siouxsie, he was taking control of the situation. So, he came from a different place. This was John from Greenock, I suppose, where fights could ensue any time, but that was the split between Nils and the band and John was central to that.'

Severin recalls the time and the shift in power between Nils and Dave Woods. 'By the New Year it had become obvious that we had to relieve Nils Stevenson of his managerial responsibilities. Siouxsie felt he was becoming too obsessed with her and rumours were circulating that Nils had a heroin problem. We had an obvious replacement in Dave Woods, who had been our booking agent since 1977 and in many ways was a de facto assistant manager. But Nils had been there from the very beginning, so this was never going to be a smooth transition.'

John wasn't just the guitarist in the band, he was also the guy who had an understanding of how bands should be run in order to protect the interests of the artists. He was somebody who, when pushed, would more than stand up to what he perceived as disrespectful and unacceptable behaviour. John recognised Siouxsie's stature as captain of the ship, so to speak, and perhaps had an old-school, gentlemanly response to shield her from certain negative influences and chancers. The Banshees were a family, and John himself would remark later on how Sioux would gee them up prior to gigs with chants, perhaps learned from observing crowds following her beloved Wolverhampton Wanderers. (Severin, being a Tottenham supporter, was maybe more prone to silence!) Unfortunately, here was a family which was not being taken care of properly. Between recording and touring, the band barely had time to draw breath. They had the potential to be very successful – to earn money, and, crucially, to make others wealthy. To say they were taken advantage of may be pushing it, but their needs as people and artists were probably not of paramount concern when tours were being organised. Dave Woods was an enthusiastic promoter-cum-agent, he kept them busy and kept the revenue coming, although how much the band saw is debatable. Even with the success of *Kaleidoscope* and *Juju* the band were far from minted. John's financial independence had really been as a result of Visage; the Banshees' income was simply keeping that topped up.

There was to be little respite for the band following the *Juju* tour. Nils was removed from the situation, Severin and John assumed more of a hands-on role from a business perspective, while Woods was promoted to fill the vacant band manager position. As Siouxsie explains, 'Dave was only meant to be a patch-up, because we needed someone to do the day-to-day stuff and it kind of made sense that he moved into that role.' Budgie wonders whether the removal of Nils, and Severin and John's interest in business matters, created a new dynamic which would ultimately prove too big a burden for the friendship between Severin and McGeoch to reconcile. 'We had an agent, Dave Woods, but at that point it was a case of John and Severin talking together and saying, "Do we just hand this back over or do we take more control of this?" Siouxsie and I didn't really care – I can't recall us having a discussion about it. So, I wonder, then – what happened? The two sides of the band... and when did Severin and John come undone?' Siouxsie recognises the savvy side of McGeoch, as he tried to get elements of the business side in order following Nils's spiral into addiction. 'When we got rid of Nils, John was very together. He recommended a lawyer to get involved and he was probably the most level-headed of us all to kind of navigate our way through it. He was probably a lot more helpful than anyone else.' As Severin himself relates, 'We had secret meetings with Polydor and Warner Chappell and John introduced us to an independent lawyer. All through January and February, I'd be on the back of John's motorbike zipping off to the West End – taking back control. In effect John and I managed the band until early March when we finally sacked Nils and Dave stepped up.'

John and Siouxsie backstage, 1981.
Ray Stevenson

The tour and the negative atmosphere had begun to take their toll on all of them. John in particular had found the experience exhausting. Being on tour and in each other's company for weeks on end is fine so long as it is going well but, as Siouxsie explains, 'When you're out on the road, and even if you get on really well with people, you can fall apart. It's like a marriage in a way. You can get irritable on the road – you're travelling, you're in no fixed place, it's exciting and all of that, but at the same time it's very testing and tiring. When you're younger you're a bit more able to live that lifestyle, but people have their ups and downs and their moods, as happens with anyone when you're with them 24/7.' There were factions within the group that were becoming more apparent, but which had formed during the recording of *Juju*. Budgie recalls, 'Severin and the guitarist always seemed to make that bond. That's why I probably gravitated to become Siouxsie's partner, you know, because I felt somebody needed to be the "token female pal", almost. I don't think I was that magnanimous – I don't think it was that much of a non-heterosexual gesture! I was certainly attracted to her. John was very private; I didn't know much about his world. When he married Jan we met the family but there was an established circle of people already around him and I just didn't have that. My world was the band, it was quite small. Maybe that, again, was another contributing factor to our little differences. The differences that maybe made us unable to understand things outside of the band, like family.'

Of John's circumstances upon joining the band back in 1980, Severin says, 'There was a different dynamic going on with John when he joined: he was engaged to be married and the three of us were single. He owned his home, whereas Siouxsie and I were renting, even though we had greater commercial reward from "Hong Kong Garden" and "The Scream". His publishing was owned by Virgin. He was obviously canny where money was concerned, and you could sense he was a bit of a maverick. All of that was never an issue for me because John didn't make one of it. Siouxsie and I thought, "Well, John has a house because we have put everything back into the band, especially after all the issues we've faced." Just keep working and things will even out.'

John coming from one established group straight into another, without the shared history that Siouxsie and Severin had, may have contributed to him feeling like an outsider – especially as the relationships and journey became more complex. John had a life firmly outside of the band; he was a married homeowner with friends and a lifestyle he enjoyed pursuing – which included substantial session recording commitments. By the time the band started to record the follow-up to *Juju*, it might be reasonable to ask whether John was questioning his role and whether he still felt as much a part of the band as he had done before. Siouxsie and Budgie had started their own creative experiment together during the recording of *Juju*, which would eventually become their side project The Creatures. As Siouxsie says, 'The first song that The Creatures ever did was "But Not Them". Me and Budgie felt that it was fine as it was, and John agreed. He said, "No, it doesn't need any guitar," so he was great in that his ego didn't get in the way of him having to play on everything, no matter what.'

The band wanted a clean slate, not just with a change in manager, but also with production. Nigel Gray had been fantastic and, in many ways, had helped educate the young musicians on how you set about recording and mixing an album. That had come at a price though, and one of the things that Gray had also introduced brought more negative elements into the recording process.

Greenock High School, 1967. John is second row, sixth from right.
McGeoch family archive

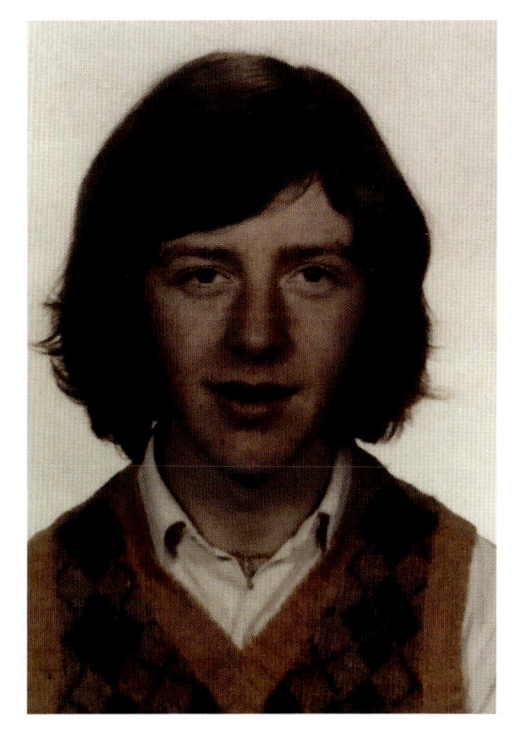

Teenage years, early 1970s.
McGeoch family archive

An early shoot for Magazine, 1978.
Adrian Boot

Magazine press shot, 1978.
Gered Mankowitz

With John Doyle and Dave Formula, 1978.
Dave Formula archive

Magazine on *Top of the Pops*, 2 February 1978.
BBC

With John Doyle, 1978.
Dave Formula

John D, John M and Dave doing phone interviews, 1980.
Howard Devoto archive

John during Magazine's UK tour, 1979.
Dave Formula

With Siouxsie Sioux, early 1980s.
Shutterstock

Out shopping while on tour, 1979.
Dave Formula

On stage with the Banshees, Paris, 1981.
Phillipe Carly

With Janet and Stephen, 1983.
McGeoch family archive

The Armoury Show, Rotterdam, 1983.
Roy Tee

John with Public Image Limited, 1986.
GEMA Images/IconicPix

Siouxsie and the Banshees, Amsterdam, 1981.
Roy Tee

With John Lydon and Allan Dias, 1990.
George Bodnar Archive/IconicPix

With mum Annie, 1988.
McGeoch family archive

John and Denise's wedding day, September 1988.
McGeoch family archive

Left: with Ronson, 1994.
McGeoch family archive

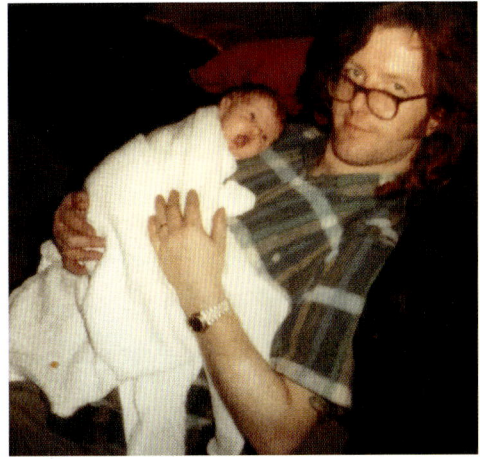

With daughter Emily, 1989.
McGeoch family archive

Left: on his trip to Nerja, Spain, September 1986.
McGeoch family archive

In the spotlight, 1978.
Dave Formula

As Budgie explains, 'Nigel Gray introduced the band to cocaine – he seemed to be in trouble with it by the time we met him. By the end of a session there was enough flaky stuff floating around in grooves on the desk or around the desk itself – it was kind of like a fun sport, and it was almost a gesture. Nigel turned the band on to it, although I don't think Siouxsie really got into it and I wasn't that bothered by it – I was more of a drinking drummer. Then there came the split: Siouxsie and I would have a bottle of wine whereas they would do a few lines.'

There was nothing unusual about a successful group in the eighties working in an environment where booze and coke were readily available. However, it was not an ideal recipe for prolonged creative output and, given the situation surrounding Nils's departure, a move away from a distracting culture of chemical candy would have seemed wise. Enter Mike Hedges, who the band got to know and immediately clicked with. John in particular found him to be a relaxed and positive influence, in and outside the studio. Hedges was brought in to be the engineer and to support the band, who would produce the album themselves at his recording space in Camden Town, Playground Studios. The band went off to tour Scandinavia in the spring and then entered the studio with Hedges in June 1982. Some of the material was pretty much there, like 'Fireworks', which had initially been recorded with Gray as part of the *Juju* sessions. It would get an overhaul when the band decided that to really elevate the track, live strings should be incorporated.

Other songs too had started to come together while over in Scandinavia. Budgie recalls how Greek tavernas in the Camden area influenced the sound of what would become *A Kiss in the Dreamhouse*. 'The difference on *A Kiss in the Dreamhouse* is that we had a song called "Melt" which stayed in waltz time. Using the bouzouki sound, we were in the Greek restaurants of Camden Town. The Greek influence wasn't just the bad wine and dodgy brandy, it was the culture and a bit of the music really [that] you heard in the restaurants. It was interesting because we were able to allow it to just be the way it was. Was it less powerful? There was a lot of joking going on.'

Siouxsie admits the atmosphere of the recording sessions for the album was different, but feels it was still productive. '*Juju* was something new, it was all new. By the time it came to *A Kiss in the*

Dreamhouse we'd done a few tours. In the studio it was still exciting, as we were working with Hedges who pushed the boat out there sonically as well. By then McGeoch was looking around a lot more – I think he was doing a lot more session work. There was a canny side to him as well of trying to get as much money as possible. There were a few blips but it was still a pleasant experience. I would say sometimes the drinking and the sessions went OTT, but generally I've still got fond memories of *A Kiss in the Dreamhouse* and I really love the album. It was a bit more disparate, as he would be going off to do other things, so the unit didn't feel as tight, but when he was there it was great.'

Thinking about those sessions now, Budgie believes all was not as well as it should have been, especially for John. 'Something happened in *A Kiss in the Dreamhouse* – it was the beginning of a pulling apart. By *Dreamhouse* it became a little less open, it seemed that John had developed his own habit by this point. We were no saints, there was a lot of amphetamine going around. The crew took amphetamine and that kept us going, and those sessions going, all night, so I could drink more or we could all put more marks on the bottle of Frascati in the fridge – it was quite pathetic. The coke started to get a little more serious, it put John in a kind of other camp. He'd be on the other side of the mixing desk, rather than on the side where the band were. He'd keep ducking down and then popping up again.'

On whether cocaine had a negative effect within the group, Siouxsie acknowledges, 'I think so, but not just with John. Personally it didn't really affect me. Obviously with what we know later on it was a bit more of a problem for him. It didn't seem a big deal then, but it was the beginning of something which took away from him, I think. It's a bit of a curse. It didn't seem it at the time – obviously hindsight is a wonderful thing. He'd have been better not to have been introduced to it, but I don't know how he could have avoided it, because it was rife everywhere. There are certain personalities that it just hooks into – it was his little "voodoo dolly", if you like.'

By this point there had also been a change in John and Severin's relationship, which may have increased his feelings of separation from the group. As Siouxsie admits, 'Severin and John had been really close. During the making of *A Kiss in the Dreamhouse* Robert [Smith] was about a lot. John wasn't spending the same amount of down time with us as he used to – he was involved in other projects and I think he may have bought a new house as well. John and Severin weren't getting on as well as they used to, I don't think.' Robert Smith and Severin were much closer by this point, hanging out in the studio and going out socialising together. John hadn't really experienced another guitarist being around the band like this before and one can only imagine it was adding to the tensions he was already feeling. On the developing coldness between Severin and John, proficiency may have also played a part, as Muzz explains. 'Severin was always struggling a bit to keep up with John. There was a bit of the "I want a few more pedals" type thing and maybe that was down to having a huge personality on the other side of the stage from him and that might have created a bit of a power struggle.'

Severin sees things differently and feels that perhaps the 'problems' while recording the follow-up to *Juju* were somewhat overblown. 'Tours of the Far East and Scandinavia were welcome distractions between sessions for *A Kiss in the Dreamhouse*, and contrary to reports there was no friction between us and John during the making of the album. Quite the opposite. We revelled in our hard-won freedom – it directly fed into the new material and the working process.'

With John using alcohol and coke much more by this point, we can only wonder whether it was just a case of rock'n'roll excess or a form of self-medication. Maybe a bit of both. As Janet remembers, John did find performing a strain. 'It was a combination of creativity and confidence. We all know that many creative minds have historically dabbled in drugs – it's not a new thing. I think all these things helped him initially, as I believe he suffered with his nerves before going on stage. I wasn't with him when he was on tour to keep an eye on him. He had free rein to do as he pleased and I think he did, on occasion, take it that little bit too far.' As Muzz remembers about life on the road, 'John just took everything that little bit further. He could always drink that bit more than everybody else, stay up longer, and there was just that bit of beast in him.'

When it came to how things were going in the studio, Peter Hook recalls dropping by one day to catch up with Siouxsie. 'I remember being in the studio with the band and Robert Smith was there as well and that was a bit frosty. I'm great friends with Siouxsie, so I went in to see her, I sat down and to be honest I'd never really got on with Robert because the rivalry with Joy Division was too immense, but John was lovely and you could tell he wasn't too happy with the set-up. I turned to Siouxsie and said, "You've got a fucking atmosphere here, haven't you, love?" She said, "Fucking tell me about it!" So, I just said, "Well, I'm not hanging about, I'm off!"' On the tensions within the camp, Budgie contends, 'John had this other world he inhabited with Visage and various things; we were not party to that. We were heads down, in the studio, and pretty much working through it all, even though the hours were ridiculous. It certainly seemed to be taking a toll on him – he was not the same John that we had on *Juju*.'

One incident in particular sticks out for Budgie as having possibly sown the seeds for irrevocable damage. 'I do remember the night that we had gone out to the Greek taverna down the street and John hadn't come with us because he wanted to do a mix. When we came back, it wasn't awful, but it was just somebody else's take on what we were doing. We'd never done that in the studio before. We only did that when we were all ready, when we all had our hands on faders. I suppose it was John's aspiration of being something more than just the guitarist in the band and part of the writing team, or was it, "Everybody's out and I can get stuck into the lines"? There's a bit of that maybe, but I don't know. Something had been pulled a little beyond the stretching point then. I'm not saying John had stepped over his personal mark, but there was something that happened to the relationship between him, Siouxsie and Severin, I think.'

Chainsaw Houlston feels that the impact of Visage's success may have inadvertently accelerated John's troubles within the band. 'John had earned a shedload of money with the Visage album. Back then records sold a lot more and you could make a lot of money off royalties alone. So, because of his financial situation, he was able to introduce the Banshees to expensive red wine! I remember that vividly. He got a taste for the finer things in life. It's the typical story, really, you make more money, you're able to get more drugs and more drink. Sadly, it was to his detriment really. Money wasn't the motivation for John, I don't think. The Visage thing just happened, and nobody could have guessed how successful that would become.'

By August the album was complete. The band again set about

booking an extensive tour which would begin in earnest with a UK festival date and a few warm-up gigs prior to the album's release. The band flew to Milan in mid-July for a show before returning to England to play Elephant Fayre at St Germans, Cornwall. The band were down to play on Saturday 31 July. Elephant Fayre proved to be John's last time on stage with the band in the UK. Severin remembers, 'We finished the album, and we were all really happy with the evolution from *Juju*. We celebrated with a one-off show down in Cornwall at the Elephant Fayre. I can distinctly recall the first signs that John was suffering, that he was falling behind, so to speak. We prepared for the "Slowdive" single video by getting Budgie's then girlfriend, Jeanette, to choreograph some dance moves for us, rehearsing two or three times a week throughout September. A dance video was the last thing anyone would expect and even though it was meant tongue in cheek, we were deadly serious about trying to get it right.' The rehearsing and recording of the video weren't without some difficulties though, as Severin explains. 'John just couldn't handle the rehearsals, sitting out often and regularly being out of breath. A few days later, on 7 October, we filmed the video. It was in a huge hangar in the Isle of Dogs, and we had a double-decker bus as a dressing room. It was mental and went on until 6 a.m. Brilliant fun. That's the last good memory before the trip to Madrid.'

The band's next date was in Madrid to play two shows, one on Friday 29 October and the other on Saturday 30th. They were then due to appear on *The Old Grey Whistle Test* for the BBC, before commencing the tour on 13 November at the Birmingham Odeon. Janet remembers the lead-up to Madrid: 'He was generally in a bad way for a few weeks, it wasn't sudden.' John didn't fly out with the band, but joined them later, as Muzz remembers: 'In what turned out to be his last gigs for the Banshees, we went to Madrid to play some club and he turned up to that and he was properly shot to bits. I think he'd kind of, I'm not sure exactly what had been going on, but from what I know he'd not been turning up to the studio when they were recording the album. I don't think he was enjoying what was going on in the studio, but basically he turned up in Madrid and he was in an awful state. The nice side of him was panicking because he realised he was not in a good state, you know, he was saying, "I think I'm having a bit of a fucking breakdown here." I remember at soundcheck he was actually struggling to remember guitar parts; he'd had a proper meltdown. I'd not been party or been invited to the studio, so I don't know the full story of what had been going on, but it was very sad to see him over in Madrid in no fit state to do a gig.'

Siouxsie looks back on Madrid, saying, 'I don't know what went on before the tour, whether we had some down time, which I doubt we did, because we recorded an album a year. So, whether it was a bit of burnout? The band were ready to go, always, and we had a crew that was the same. It was a very well-oiled machine. Now I come to think of it, the band were ultimately let down by its first two managers. After the touring of *Juju* had barely finished, we were caught up in the task of extricating ourselves from the first manager [Nils Stevenson], whose destructive behaviour was spiralling out of control. Given the tight schedule the band were on at the time, it's hardly surprising cracks started to appear as a result of this harmful distraction. The second manager [Dave Woods] would also let the band down six years later.'

Severin adds, 'No idea why Dave Woods had set up two shows at the Rock-Ola club in Madrid over Halloween. We flew over the night before the first show and John just seemed a bit tired, maybe a bit worse for wear but nothing drastic. Next day, I popped to his room and noticed he had brought with him a box of wine which was right by his bed. I guess that was the red flag for what would unfold.'

On John's general demeanour and behaviour in Madrid, Siouxsie noticed, 'He went downhill quite quickly. Bottom line is, I didn't really care what anyone got up to as long as the band wasn't put out or compromised and the audience wasn't let down, i.e. a show didn't happen because of someone else. I don't know how it got so bad so quick, but I think with the cocaine and then the alcohol, which I gather got worse when he left. When we were in Spain I seem to remember it was almost like every minute when he wasn't on stage you couldn't even talk to him, it was like he was drunk all the time from the moment he got up.'

Muzz had deep concerns for John's well-being: 'You knew something was seriously up, because he turned up with this mate that none of us had met before, a feller called Simon – just somebody from the real world. He brought this mate with him because he knew he was in pretty poor shape and he didn't make any attempt to hide it; he turned up and said, "Look, I'm really in a fucking bad state, you're going to have to help me out." He didn't try lying or hiding from it, but I don't know what the background to it was. I would imagine it was something deeply personal, but I wouldn't know. With regards to the whole thing in the studio, I believe they'd actually brought Robert Smith in because John hadn't been turning up. I think they were getting concerned that they were losing their guitar player. I think John might have been losing a bit of interest in it around this time, it had gone in a direction that wasn't for him. The way it was moving wasn't really for a guitarist of his stature – guitar playing is there to be featured and not just strumming in the background.'

John had been frustrated and had been exploring new projects, but he'd done session work throughout his time with the band. That in itself was nothing new. You can only speculate as to what other triggers there were, but John himself did acknowledge years later that he was just burned out. He'd been thrust into a situation with Magazine at a young age which had propelled him to a position he might never have imagined for himself. He'd gone to study art and ended up joining and leaving a band with three studio albums under his belt. He'd then jumped into the maelstrom that was Siouxsie and the Banshees, who had just started to get back on their feet and had a work ethic that would eventually push them all to the brink years later. John was trying to live a relatively normal life as a husband and homeowner – something had to give. It cruelly came to a head in Madrid. John may have developed a dependency on drink, he may have got caught up in the cocaine that was rampant, but above all else John was a professional. He took his craft seriously, he worked hard and he compensated for his own feelings of anxiety and perhaps insecurity – having seen his friendship with Severin deteriorate – by blocking it out with booze. It wasn't fun. Heavy drinking seldom is. You are doing it to escape something.

Budgie remembers an occasion that could be interpreted as John's cry for help – his recognition of something in someone else that he was going through himself. 'I was living in Stratford Villas, a little two-bedroom place. John turned up on my doorstep one morning. I'd never been visited by anyone in the band. John showed up and I don't know why, but to talk, I think. He said to me, "Budgie, you've got to watch your drinking," and I said, "Really?" I said, "Come on, John, you're one to talk!" Making light of it, throwing it back at him, and I don't know what happened after that. It just stuck in my mind, "Budgie, you've got to watch your drinking." I know, or I could fill in the gaps now with hindsight. He was right – I needed to be heeding some sound advice and I was never able to give him that. He was a little older and a little wiser, but he was aware, definitely.'

It's unclear who John was turning to at this point, who he was unburdening himself to. Just how aware was he of what was happening to him? Were there people close enough, people he could truly open his heart to and let it out? Was it a case of appearing to be coping for fear of appearing weak? Budgie considers this. 'To admit that you're not well was taken as a sign of weakness, I think. That requires a certain amount of maturity and an ability to cope with "I can't do it today, chaps" and feeling secure enough to say it. Maybe that was instilled in everybody– they [Siouxsie and Severin] had two people walk out on them for no good reason. Those two people probably rued the day they did it because they thought Siouxsie and Severin would come running after them. When they didn't, the plan had gone badly wrong, I believe. Maybe that sowed the seed... that we don't stop.'

The problems with excess weren't John's alone, as Muzz explains with regard to the lifestyle on tour. 'At that point his drinking didn't appear any worse than anybody else's. We were all having a lot of fun in those days. It was very much a culture of a lot of touring, and drinking went hand in hand with that. Sioux and Budgie were ferocious drinkers, so John was far from on his own in that respect.' Siouxsie admits that not just the culture surrounding the band but also the times were different, and things weren't as open. 'The drinking, seeing that as a problem, wasn't even considered because again, that was rife – everyone was drinking. There must have been signs, it must have been obvious – but again, when you're in the thick of it, it isn't. I think through those experiences you are able to do that, that's what experience is about and unfortunately you have to live through it by making the mistakes.'

Things took a severe turn for the worse in the hours leading up to the first show in Madrid, as Budgie recalls: 'All I heard was that, I think, he was given a stimulant to try and get him ready to go on stage. Woodsy was putting him in the shower and trying to get him awake and he was nervous, he was really shaky because maybe he was having withdrawal from the booze from the night before and he gave him a Valium or half a Valium. Mr Woods always had Valium. There was that, at the end of the night, the chance of a Valium. I never did understand it, downers and booze. I saw it in St Helens too much – go out for the night and drop a mandie or something, go to a bar, have a drink and go to sleep. That always seemed like a really shit idea of a night out to me. John could go quite quickly, and I never understood that about other drinkers anyway. He used to say I had hollow legs: "Where do you put it all?" That's what I heard and I don't know what kind of cocktail he was working off.'

Siouxsie is well aware of Woods' use of Valium. 'Dave Woods, when we first knew him, always had a Valium after his last drink to go to bed. It was sort of a running joke.' On finding out long after the event that John had been given a Valium, Siouxsie says, 'If I'd known Woods had given John a Valium, I would have gone ballistic. How is that ever going to help? I can see if you were going to go that route and somebody was intoxicated and can't get their act together, then I'd go the opposite way. If you're going to do something as stupid as that, do an amphetamine, not a bloody Valium.'

Woods' relationship with John wasn't without friction. They were never close, and Woods may have seen John as an annoyance, as he was keen to take an interest in the band's financial affairs. As Siouxsie herself acknowledges, 'The fact that Woods gave John a Valium – it could well have been malicious, but I think more stupid than anything. I don't know though. [...] So, Dave [Woods] was a friend as well. You know, it's been the complicated thing with us in that both those managers – it wasn't strictly business, as it were. So, it becomes very easy for stuff to not get dealt with, and just stuff being hidden, you know? That's the thing, because I think we all hated the music business per se and what that represented, which is why we probably went with people that we felt like we trusted – you know, they weren't the "Mr Twenty Percenters" kind of cold, trying to just get their percentage. Again, you put people in a certain [position] of trust and power and – more often than not – they fuck it up. It's a sad fact of life. When you're young and when the band first started, you think, "We're going to be equal partners forever and nothing is going to come between that," and of course, life! It never ends that way – the honeymoon period doesn't last long!'

John went with the band to the club, Rock-Ola on Calle de José Abascal, and what started as a struggle descended into an inability to follow the set list. John went into 'Cascade' when the others were getting into 'Spellbound'. Muzz remembers watching from the side of the stage as his friend and 'boss' fell apart in front of him in the most public of places for an artist to have their vulnerabilities exposed. 'He really, really struggled and it took his entire will to get through that gig.' Severin says of Madrid, 'The first show was a disaster and it was obvious that something was really wrong with John. The second night was hardly much better.'

Contrary to hearsay, nobody interviewed for this book recalls John collapsing on stage. On what happened following the show, Budgie says, 'I have no recollection of after the gig. I imagine if I'd been playing to character, I'd have ignored what was going on and had a few drinks and maybe too many drinks. I wouldn't have known what to say, or how to say it.' The following day the band spent some time in the city. As Budgie explains, 'I remember we were going out in the afternoon, we'd gone to a market. John had bought these plates. I probably still have mine, I think they had been fired in a kiln and enamelled with a symbol from the album *A Kiss in the Dreamhouse*. It was as if it was a token of appeasement. So, we all got these plates, and he was mortified. Drinker's remorse, I think they call it. Russell [Webb] was with us and he had the job of looking after John, hiding the evidence, which I found out later. I think even Dave Woods was trying his best to get John on the stage that night, which was the wrong thing probably. I mean, God, he bottomed out. I know the language now, but that was the first major fuck-up. We were just bemused on stage, you know, incredulous because John could play in his sleep – his hands would do it if his brain wasn't really engaged, so it was really out of character. I listen back and sometimes I know when there's a bit of sloppy playing going on. John's playing was so loose, so free around the beat and the groove and that's kind of what made it so exciting. He could be bang on when he's really slamming out the chords, on say, "Christine", but again with this lack of rigidity that no one could get afterwards.'

Of that second show, Budgie adds, 'All the crew were around us, somebody was looking after John. There was an icy kind of silence, an embarrassed kind of silence. An inability to just say, "Hey, shall we all just sit over there a minute and have a little talk about what happened last night?" We never did that. That was it, we flew back home.'

Siouxsie reflects on the first night in Madrid and difficulties that had arisen during the recording of *A Kiss in the Dreamhouse*. 'That one gig was the last straw that broke the camel's back. It was a gradual build-up and I think we weren't able to be adult about it, we weren't really adults yet. We thought we were, [despite] our naivety about the situation and maybe his too, of not being able to ask for help. Having that belligerence as well. In hindsight it's sad thinking he ended up behaving in a way that he would hate. He would have been horrified if he'd had seen himself do it, you know. It wasn't just that one gig, it was an accumulation of giving him chance after chance. Then with the last gig of him just playing a different song to everyone else on stage, it was like, "WHAT!" It was almost like he'd lost his mind for a while and there was a thing of trying to look after him and he'd hide bottles of stuff outside on the windowsill. Things had got bad. It was like we were having to babysit him, and we were just too young to deal with that – we've got our own shit to deal with! It sounds really callous, but it wasn't. It was like we were thinking, "What the fuck are you doing, John?" It's just so sad, really sad, that he got sucked into this. What a waste, what a real waste of his talent.'

When reflecting on how the Banshees' affairs were being handled, Siouxsie feels more could have been done to support them all. 'I do think it's the touring element that takes it out of you. I think at that time we were just doing it without questioning it. I think when you're on that kind of roll, you need someone who isn't in the band to just stand back. I'm not pointing any fingers, but whoever was supposedly looking after the band should have been able to just stand back and see what was happening. When you're in it, it's very hard to stand back and say, "Hey, I think if we took a bit of a break it would be great." I think our naivety in dealing with that situation, it's like being in a team and someone lets the team down – that's what it felt like. In hindsight it should have been handled a lot better. It was just left to us to police ourselves, really.'

Johnny Marr recognises what was happening to the Banshees, and the toll it was taking on John, as an all too familiar tale. 'It's part of being young and in a band, I guess, burning yourself out. It's the story of a lot of bands and it will be exactly the same now.' He adds, 'You can't ignore the creative excitement [that] joining a new group offers. It's something I experienced when I joined The The. It's a great musical adventure and by no means is it a doddle. You have to get in the studio and deliver and then you have to go out on tour and deliver. Nothing gets handed to you and, if anything, what's often forgotten in that scenario is, if it fucks up, everyone knows about it. So, it's great to talk about *Kaleidoscope*, *Juju* and *A Kiss in the Dreamhouse* and all the great stuff John did on those albums. It was a great collaboration, but no one did it for him. It takes application and then you go out, get on a bus, get four or five hours of sleep every night and maybe that's why it ended for him with the Banshees. The music they made, you know, it's really good stuff and good stuff takes hard work.'

John was spent; he'd given as much as he could by that point. He needed that space away from it all to rest and return as strong as he was when he first joined. The schedule couldn't allow for that, for any of them. There could be no passengers, and despite the 'all for one and one for all' attitude, the relationship had been damaged beyond repair. It's hard to know what would have happened if John hadn't fallen off the cliff in Madrid. Would he have left anyway?

Siouxsie wonders how John would have reacted had it been one of the other members of the band who went through what he did that night. 'Maybe he would have dealt with somebody in that situation better because he had worked in mental health. I remember him telling me about his work in the hospital [Goodmayes] and I think it had a big impact on him.' It is hard to see how the band could have taken a different approach. They had suffered the loss of two previous members at a pivotal point in their careers as artists and as a group. What had unfolded for John was not the same, but alarm bells would have been ringing. Was it a case of taking decisive action to save being let down in the longer term? Without the support of a mediator, either management or a person with influence to apply the brakes, what were they to do? The band would, at the time, have been of like mind about the situation, as Siouxsie explains. 'There's pride, and personally I would never cancel a show because I didn't feel like doing it. If you're committed to doing something, you do it, you don't fuck up. We all felt that way and I'm sure John did, but the situation was such – he did something that I know he would hate someone else doing.'

Whether John pulling out would have been enough to save his Banshees' career is debatable, but he clearly feared it would have looked like he was letting the others down. How much of a negative effect did the Valium have on the first night? It appears to have been significant, given that, despite being far from his best, the second show was much more proficient. The tension is palpable, however, and when listening back to a bootleg recording you can sense that here was a band just wanting to get the hell out of Madrid as soon as possible.

The band flew back to the UK the following day, and Budgie explains what happened next. 'It quickly went beyond just that gig for John. It was back home to Jan, and then he went to hospital, and I was never part of a discussion about John being fired from the band. It kind of absolves me, doesn't it? Gives me a little less feeling of guilt or consideration for John's situation. I probably would have just toed the line had I been involved in the decision and gone, "Yeah, you're probably right." Well, at that point I think it would have been the right decision to stop, just to stop – give John a rest and give us all a rest. The thing I can take from it is that we never learned the lesson. We continued and we saw another guitarist fail, and another guitarist, and individually we were falling apart at times, but we never stopped. We never gave ourselves space to take some rest.'

Of the return to England, Severin recalls, 'When we dropped him off at home, Janet opened the door and said, "What am I supposed to do with him?"' She sought out professional help by taking John to Belgravia for a private psychiatric consultation. As Janet remembers, 'He had one quite long spell at the Priory in Roehampton which was just after the Banshees dumped him by letter. I think it must have been the Madrid gig that had got them all a bit worried. They were about to go on tour and on the eve of the tour John had a bit of a breakdown. So, we went to see a private doctor in London and he said, "I think you should go away for a bit, go to a nice little hospital," so he put him in the Priory. As they were just about to go on tour, I guess they saw it as John not being able to fulfil his part of the bargain any more, so they dumped him.'

Dave Woods and Severin went to visit John in hospital. Severin says, 'We discovered that John was in the Priory, which at that time was relatively unknown. It didn't yet have its reputation as a celebrity retreat. It was a mental health hospital and it's quite possible that John was referred there by the NHS or possibly Janet had him sectioned. It was decided that Dave and I would go down to see John the next day (Tuesday 2 November) as there was now real concern over our upcoming commitments. *A Kiss in the Dreamhouse* was out the following Friday (5th), we had an appearance on *The Old Grey Whistle Test* booked for the Monday (8th), a two-month long UK/European tour about to begin on the Saturday (13th) and dates in the US and Japan in our thoughts for the New Year.' Of John's condition and state of mind, he adds, 'We were told John was available in the evenings only, so Dave and I arrived at the Priory around 8 p.m. only to be told that he was down the local pub! He had left a weird scribbled note with a map so off we went. There was John surrounded by his new fast friends, sporting a still fresh tattoo and with his head shaved on the sides. He got up, came over to me, hugged and kissed me! All of this was extraordinary and really, really off. I recall thinking, "Are they preparing to lobotomise him?" Yet I don't have any memory at all of what was actually said. I think Dave did most of the talking; I was too stunned by it all. What was absolutely patently obvious was that John was never going to be ready for the *Whistle Test* or the tour and that we needed a back-up plan.'

According to Janet, John had heard by letter that he was out of the band. However, it's more than likely he was told face to face or over the telephone. Either way, at that point he was incapable of fully grasping the severity of the situation. He was where he ought to be in the short term, getting the professional help and support he had long been in need of.

Siouxsie reflects on the decision to remove John from the band and his reaction to it. 'If he'd fought to stay in the band, maybe it would have been different, but he rolled over pretty easily, so I think maybe part of him didn't want to continue.' There would have been regret, naturally, that such a highly creative and exciting musical collaboration ended as it did, and not just for John, but for all of them. It had been a frantic couple of years, but – equally amazing – the music they had made together and the live shows they had played had been so special and iconic. John didn't deserve to go out like that. The ideal scenario would have been for him to leave on his own terms, having felt he'd gone as far as he could with the group. Something that unique and special deserved a more fitting end, but real life seldom works out like that. The reality was that it was over and John was out – and needing to rethink his life and begin a period of recovery.

Of that time and the end of his journey with the Banshees, Janet says, 'John was very upset about it at the time, but he was in hospital and he was receiving treatment. A combination of drugs, alcohol, and I think he suffered with a little bit of depression. That's partly why he was doing the drugs and alcohol.' Siouxsie says, 'It took time for it to sink in. There were other issues, but I'm pissed off it was handled that way. At the time we thought we were doing the right thing and protecting the band's integrity.' Siouxsie also explains that John had been made aware of his dismissal from the band prior to receiving the letter. 'John wasn't sacked by letter. The letter was a necessary formality after Steve and Dave went to see him in order to speak with him.'

On whether the band could have done something to halt John's slide, Budgie looks back with regret. 'If something would fill me with grief and guilt, it would be that. It would be, why couldn't we together or individually take him to one side?' On the build-up to the events that led to him being removed: 'With *A Kiss in the Dreamhouse*, we'd expanded the line-up with the girls on stage with us – The Venomettes, as they became known. So, that was a distraction as well that made the party atmosphere push outwards. I wasn't aware of anything being wrong musically, really, until that gig, and not equipped to say anything about it either. That's what I mean. I think I was developing my own set of addictions or whatever they were, which certainly eventually messed me up. Is it that with John, once the ball started rolling, that it went much faster for him? It caught Severin later, I think. It took me a little while longer, because I kept stopping and trying to get a grip on another way of doing this. I did notice John always had red lips; I'd never seen that before. The joke of the Berocca in America, the vitamin

B and C and the Alka "plink-plink fizz", this was common. John was the first to have the Fernet-Branca the next day to settle the tummy. If I'd have had a Fernet-Branca, because I did eventually go to one of those morning drinks, that would be me for the rest of the day. I knew very early that I couldn't take a drink before I'd got the gig out of the way. Then I'd probably drink all night and have the rest of the next day to recover. I was noticing I wasn't seeing the band the day after the night before – sometimes I didn't see myself. It was the loneliest place, on the road. Yeah, I noticed it, but you don't notice. You don't notice because, who am I to point the finger?'

John's close friend Nicky Tesco feels that more should have been done, possibly starting with the industry. 'Musicians are a strange breed. There's no duty of care for them. You wouldn't notice with John, but there was something within him. He needed help, there was a battle going on inside him.'

Janet would spend time with John at the Priory while he recuperated and shares a particular memory. 'I remember visiting John one day at the Priory and he said to me, "The doctor has said it is OK for me to go and get my motorbike," and I said, "Really, are you sure?" bearing in mind he was quite spaced out. So anyway, I drove him back to Cricklewood and he got the bike and said he was going to head back to Roehampton, and I asked him if he wanted me to come back with him he said, "Nah," and he ended up riding the bike into the back of a parked car! I knew he was too spaced out. So, he ended up in the hospital next door to the Priory in Roehampton, St Mary's, being treated for minor injuries.'

John's recovery was slow and steady. It's sad that it took something as unpleasant as what happened in Madrid to start the healing process. To get the help he was in desperate need of, to begin a process of reckoning and recovery. To understand his limits, to realise he was not made of steel.

Janet recalls his hurt at being dismissed, but also his resilience. 'Creatively they [the Banshees] drew from each other. John was very upset when they dumped him, but eventually he came out of hospital three or four weeks later, [and] started working on other projects.'

John was nothing if not pragmatic, and somebody who would go on to play a significant role in his life a few years later – drum tech-cum-PiL tour promoter and friend Philip 'Trigger' Hamilton – has this to say of how John viewed his time as a Banshee. 'John never harped on about that period with the Banshees. He was very proud of what he'd done as a guitarist and about the albums they made. John didn't bad-mouth people – there might have been an odd occasion where I asked a question or we put a Banshees album on and I asked something, but there was never any malice. Never. No malice at all from John towards the Banshees.'

Severin agrees: 'I don't think John begrudged our actions, after all he wanted the tour to go ahead as we were all fronting it and stood to lose quite a lot of money in cancellation fees. I heard that he came to the first night of the tour in Birmingham and hung out with the crew. He says as much in his little segment on *Rock Family Trees*. In fact, the last time I saw him was at a lunchtime launch party for *Rock Family Trees*. We had a great time, had a few drinks and nearly, very nearly, went off in search of a gram to keep on going into the evening. Luckily, we thought better of it and so my final memory of John is a lovely one.'

Michael Jobson, who had got to know John back in his days with Magazine, remembers how McGeoch had made him feel a part of the Banshees fold and acknowledged the demons that they were all battling. 'John welcomed me into the Banshees world and all the crew were super nice to me. At that point I was sitting up on the side of the stage and being treated as one of the family. The Banshees were serious, serious users. They were into everything. I think John loved being in the Banshees. He loved the cool of it. They drank a lot back then – that's how it was. Was it the pressure for John of being in the Banshees? I really don't know.'

John Frusciante looks back on McGeoch's time as a Banshee and as a uniquely innovative guitarist. 'I have to say, though his playing is extremely creative in any setting from Visage, Magazine and the other things he did, there is something about that particular chemistry in the Banshees that really… I just don't think there's any guitar playing in history that stands above that. It's as good as chemistry can be and it's as creative as somebody can be, working within the limitations that have already been set – a band already has its theme, many of its boundary lines set and you figure out a way to not infringe on any of that and yet seem to be free, completely free.'

On how he operated within the band, Frusciante says, 'I would never want to downplay the roles that the other members of the group had. That's all part of being a guitar player. A guitar player can't exist in a bubble; the way people tend to compliment guitar players and put some on pedestals usually seems to have a lot to do with how they stand out or how they draw attention to themselves. I don't think that's right. Whether you're talking about flashy guitar players or whether you're talking about post-punk-type guitar players, the whole group really matters, and that's what John McGeoch seems to have understood. He understood how to make Budgie sound like a better drummer, how to make Severin sound like a better bass player – you look at some of those bass parts by themselves and, as creative as they are, when you add McGeoch to them, they seem very plain, you know? So, it has to be seen in that light. It's hard for me to really appreciate guitar players if I'm not learning the bass parts and taking a good assessment of where the accents of the drums are and what drums are being hit. I can't see a guitar part as being separate from that and I think that when I did, my thinking was very askew and I had a hard time being a musician in a band, because I felt that I had to isolate myself and that's wrong. You have to be thinking, "How do I make the rest of the band sound good?" – and he was a master of that.'

On the nature of serving the 'greater good' of the music and the band, Frusciante makes a key observation. 'It's a feminine quality that you have to have as a musician. It's that combination of having true artistic confidence and having a feminine side to your personality where you absorb what the other people are contributing. You're not intimidated by it; you're open to it and to where it can go, and you absorb it and contribute only what rounds it out and be as creative as you can within that. Some people will attempt to do that but they wind up just being a weak element in the picture. You can see that their whole intention is to round out the sound of the group, but they don't sound as vital as McGeoch's playing does. That is really where somebody just has a God-given connection with music that makes that possible. So, if you were to ask me, why is he important? It's because he was him, because he played exactly those notes at the exact time that he did in the way that he did. That's what it's all about, really, and I don't think I could explain it in any other way.'

So, why was John dismissed? John and Dave Woods had an uneasy relationship. John recommended bringing a lawyer into the fold after Nils went, and for a manager who could see dollar signs, having somebody like McGeoch asking questions would be undesirable. Woods had gained a promotion, arguably a once-in-a-lifetime opportunity. In his eyes everyone was expendable other than Siouxsie. She was the main draw, the leader, the prize asset. Without her there was no band. All that is true. A guitarist, however, well, they can be replaced... can't they? It seemed Severin had lost patience with McGeoch – his drinking had certainly pushed the two further apart. It's unlikely he felt that Robert Smith could become a permanent member, given that The Cure were still his main concern. But with encouragement from Woods, replacing McGeoch may have seemed easier to achieve. You simply get someone else in temporarily, and why couldn't that be Robert?

Severin explains the thinking at the time and the pressure the band were under to come up with a solution. 'The only person who could pick up the pieces at such short notice was Robert Smith. He'd come up to London from Crawley and stayed at my place several times during the *Dreamhouse* sessions, and had been coming with me into Playground, so he had heard the new songs and he had done this before in 1979. I don't think for a moment that we allowed ourselves time to speculate how all of this would unfold because we had a tour to do and John needed a prolonged period of rest and recovery.'

In my opinion the band were poorly advised. Rather than getting rid of John they should all have been protected from the heavy demands of endless recording sessions and tours. Rather than fuelling the fire of discontent and resentment towards McGeoch, they should have been encouraged to have a bit of space and then to work towards reconciliation before moving forward together. Musically this would have made perfect sense. The three albums were all different, all showcasing the band in exciting and different moods. This wasn't as much about musical direction and creativity as it was about profitability and a grudge, and for that I think it would be unfair to say the band were at fault. The pot had been stirred; egos would naturally be involved, but good management isn't just about filling the coffers. The band were flogged to death, both during and following McGeoch's stay. The Banshees were the band that didn't stop. They were viewed, as so many successful groups are, as a commodity.

Budgie recalls taking part in a documentary for TV some years later, which John was also involved in. 'What really choked me up much later, I was with Siouxsie living in London and [we were] being interviewed for a series [*Rock Family Trees*] and John was also interviewed. John talked about how much it meant to him being in the band, what a great time he had had and if he could just turn the clock back. It really got to me.'

Severin opens up on the guilt he felt following John's departure. 'I've beaten myself up over this for years wondering if we should have – could have – done things differently. I know Siouxsie has too. But I'm done with that now. For one thing, I only discovered years later that Dave had given John a Valium in Madrid to calm his nerves, which I think could have been a deliberate ploy on Dave's behalf. He'd never really got on with John; they had clashed over money and things had stalled a bit on the signing of a new Polydor deal. I think Dave considered John a threat and he certainly didn't advise us to postpone things – quite the opposite. We parted ways with Dave in 1988 and he simply vanished. I believe he manipulated John's latent stage fright in Madrid and subsequently played on Siouxsie and my fears that – just like in 1979 – we were being let down, being betrayed. For that alone, he deserves to be thrown under the bus.'

John Frusciante admires what McGeoch brought, not just to the Banshees, but also to his own understanding of the guitar. 'He was a good communicator; he knew musically how to communicate with the people he made music with and how to communicate with an audience. The best guitar players are the ones that put themselves out there more than other ones. I rate guitar players, personally, more on that, rather than any technical thing or any flash thing. It's really about, "Am I hearing the feelings the person playing feels inside?" And are you hearing their creativity at work? In somebody's style you can hear how they hear music, what they like about it and what they don't and what it means to them. It's usually all there inside their playing, and the more you study it the more you get a sense of how they broke music down and what their taste was. Who they were on a soul level, and so for me those are the guitar players who stand out because you get a real clear sense of who they are as a soul – because nobody is able to say what they said with the instrument. That's how it is with John McGeoch. I see him influencing people and I see the influence he's had on me, and that doesn't mean that anybody is going to say what he said with the guitar because what he said was really truly his and his alone.'

Siouxsie looks back on the McGeoch era with immense pride and, despite the way it ended, reflects, 'It was stunning work that we did together, and I just think it's such a shame that it couldn't have gone on a bit longer. We were all proud of the stuff we did with him, all of us.' Siouxsie goes on to reveal just how highly she regarded John and how unique he was. 'We kind of evolved and went a different path as opposed to keeping on a well-trodden one. For me, John was irreplaceable, as the original members were, and they were all different for different reasons. Of course, we didn't try to replace him, but you know, out of all the musicians I've worked with in the Banshees line-up, I could see myself working with McGeoch again, and that's not the case with anyone else I've worked with.'

A Kiss in the Dreamhouse was released on Polydor on 5 November 1982 and peaked at number 11 in the albums chart.

SIX

WAITING FOR THE FLOODS
After his dismissal from the Banshees, John travels to Sweden before forming the post-punk 'supergroup' The Armoury Show

---

Richard has been a friend for a long time and we'd always intended working together at some point. This was just the first chance we'd both had to put it together with the right people.

ZigZag (February 1984)

FOLLOWING HIS DISMISSAL from the Banshees and subsequent period of recovery at the Priory, John was ready to begin new projects. The past few months had been arduous; a lot of soul searching had been done but just as the Banshees sought to move forward John was determined to do the same. An unusual opportunity gave him the chance to escape familiar surroundings and use his experience of studio work in a brand-new way.

Lars Kronlund takes up the story of how John ended up working in Sweden in 1983. 'I can't remember how I met Michael Dee, but he was instrumental in connecting me with John McGeoch. Mike was a Swedish artist/journalist who lived in London. John had produced a single by Mike called "Hurra, Hurra, Vad Det Är Roligt i Moskva" on which Idde [Schultz] had done some backing vocals. I asked Mike if he thought

John would want to produce our album, and he made the connection. I spoke to John a few times over the phone before he came to Stockholm. We immediately got on very well. I obviously knew him as a musician as I was a big fan of Magazine, Visage and Siouxsie. From his guitar playing, I understood that he was really into getting original sounds and arrangements, which was what I was also into.' Lars had formed a group with sisters Idde and Irma Schultz, whom he had met while busking in Paris. Zzzang Tumb were signed to local Stockholm label Stranded Rekords, with the idea of pushing on with a new wave-inspired sound, which was yet to gain momentum in Sweden. As ever when it came to being creative, taking a risk and trying something new, John was happy to assist. As Idde recalls, John stayed close to the studio during the recording process. 'I think John spent three weeks in Stockholm. The album was recorded at Studio Decibel at Katarinavägen and John stayed at Sjöfartshotellet, a hotel very close to the studio.'

Lars remembers John's dedication and professionalism, although one thing in particular confused him. 'I remember being surprised that he really didn't want to play guitar. I mean, we were in a studio full of guitars and amps, and there was a lot of tweaking with knobs and boxes to get sounds, but he never once grabbed a guitar to strum it. It was as if he had made a deal with himself to stay away from guitars. We kept asking him to play some guitar or saxophone on the album, but he refused. He only appears on the recording with his voice shouting over the talkback mic. John was very easy-going in the studio. In fact, most of the time, he would just let us get on with recording tracks while he sat back and relaxed. And then, every so often, he would have an idea about some weird sound that we should try. I remember us recording the sound of smashing bits of glass in a bucket, which we would sample into the PPL sampler and use [as] a tambourine sound on the song "Molotov Cocktail Party". That must have taken the better part of an afternoon, and it's hardly noticeable in the end production. John cut his hand on the glass.' Irma has fond recollections of John and his time with the band in the studio. 'It was nice working with John. I remember him pretty much as a low-key person. We were very disciplined in the studio, focusing on getting the work done, so it was not so much chatting and hanging around. John was only engaged as the producer, so he never took part in the songwriting or as an additional musician.'

Both Idde and Lars recall that, despite the problems of the previous year, and particularly the last few months with the Banshees and his period of recovery, John was still struggling, as Lars explains. 'I remember John as a very sweet and likeable person. I always picture him smiling. It quickly became apparent to me that he was looking for a new experience and stretching his boundaries. He spoke about how he had found touring with the Banshees very stressful and how he eventually had to quit the band after he broke down at a gig in Spain. I also got the feeling that it had been difficult on a personal level between himself and Budgie. But it's also possible that Budgie was playing bad cop to Siouxsie's good cop. I think, generally, he was really proud of the music he had done with Siouxsie, but it was not a happy house (if you'll pardon the pun). I think that John had been dampening his depression on the road with alcohol, which was also the physical reason for his Spanish breakdown. He was still drinking a lot during the recording of the album. I remember him coming into the studio the first day with a case of white wine, which he would keep by the side of the mixing desk.' Idde adds, 'We normally started to work around noon and recorded until late in the evening. John had the same request every day: two bottles of white wine. I can't remember if he talked about Siouxsie and the Banshees with me and I guess I didn't ask either.' John was credited as producer on Zzzang Tumb's self-titled album which was released in 1983.

John returned to Janet and the UK without a band and without too much on the horizon. He was determined to get back into songwriting and, for all of his reluctance to play while on studio duty in Sweden, he was ready to pick up the guitar again. It was just a matter of waiting for the right opportunity.

John had previously worked with Richard Jobson and bassist Russell Webb on a Skids John Peel session in September 1980, just prior to making his live debut as a full-time Banshee. John was friends with both, in particular Russell, who aside from music shared a love of motorbikes. 'I initially met John at the first gig of Magazine's *Real Life* tour in 1978. John was very likeable to everyone who met him. I guess he felt like a kindred spirit with me because we became friends and stayed that way until time ran out.' The timing for working together couldn't have been better. John was in limbo post-Banshees; Jobson and Webb were both coming to terms with the break-up of Skids. Throw long-standing friendships into the mix and the idea of making music together seemed a no-brainer. And so The Armoury Show were born. A collective of talented, prominent punk and post-punk musicians with a heavy dose of Scottish determination and grit. As Jobson recalls, 'The name for the band came about from a poem I wrote called "From Brussels with Love" which was about the original Armory Show in New York, which brought new European art over. Essentially the name was about a big change – something new is coming. It was a cool name, everything felt right. Then there's the sound of John's guitar – a lot of the stuff he did with the Banshees is silvery cold. I worked with Stuart Adamson who was very inventive, and you can see that these guys have their own template that they work with, and how they impose that on the song.' As both Jobson and Webb knew, John's ability to come up with wholly original and inventive guitar parts offered them all the chance to make something truly new and exciting.

Russell recollects about how the group got together and John's initial misgivings: 'The Armoury Show was put together (minus the name, which came much later – in spite of what Jobson might say!) when Richard came looking for me at Eel Pie Studios in Soho to see if he could rekindle our writing relationship, which had soured after the Skids' *Joy* album. Not long after we started tentatively trying out some ideas, John lost his job with the Banshees. I got right behind John to do whatever I could to hold him in his desperate hour. I had been booked to go to Sweden to produce an album for an artist called Mike Dee. I thought that it might be a good opportunity for John to get back on track creatively, so I asked Mike and his manager if they would consider swapping me for John, which they agreed to. When John returned from Sweden I had done a bit more work with Richard and I suggested inviting John to join the project. Richard was up for it but John was very reluctant to work with Richard. I can't remember if John ever said why but it took a lot of persuasion before John got on board. There was never any real warmth between Richard and John.'

They underestimated how much of a hard sell the band were

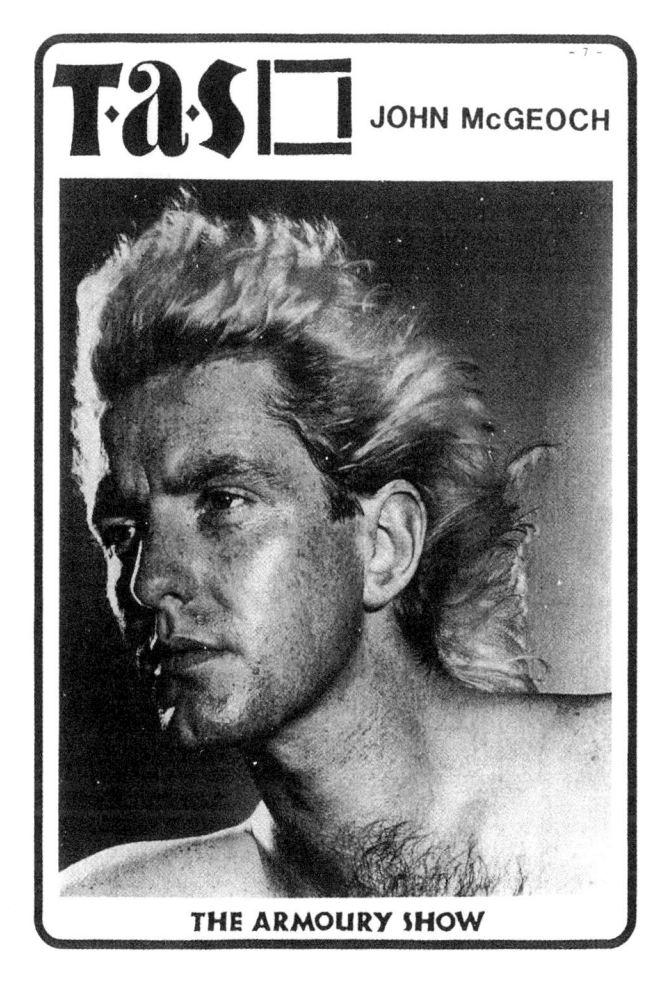

John in *The Armoury Show News* magazine, 1984.

going to be in securing a deal. Given the pedigrees of those involved, it's surprising that it would take a big mover from the US to get them signed. That would be for later. The immediate objective was to get a sound together, enjoy what they were doing and follow their creative noses and noises to put them all back to where they wanted to be. With the three friends on board, attention switched to finding a drummer. John Doyle takes up the story of how he came to be reunited with John. 'I bumped into Janet at a record company thing and she mentioned the band and that she would put my name forward. It all derived from that actually. I can't remember if they'd had a drummer prior to me or if they'd just been using drum machines.'

The move made sense, and John would have been more than happy to welcome his old Magazine colleague into the fold, not to mention that Doyle was a highly accomplished drummer in his own right. The band got into rehearsals, working on material while putting the feelers out for potential label interest. John Doyle remembers the take-up was slow and money tight. 'He supported the band for a while. We [John Doyle, Russell and Richard] were all pretty penniless at the time and it was John McGeoch that set up and paid into a fund that then paid us a wage. I can't remember how long for, but I'm pretty sure it was months rather than weeks. This was before anybody had any interest in us, which was small anyway. We had to force our way in, in a sense. We knew what we were doing, we were enjoying it and we'd got a few gigs through people we knew. As far as record company interest went, it was very limited. So, John supporting us like he did shows how into it he was.'

Richard Jobson had seen the drive and ambition that McGeoch had to be successful. The concept of The Armoury Show was very much a combination of the clever arrangements and songwriting of Magazine with the appeal of Skids. Jobson describes what he saw as one of the big contributing factors in John leaving Magazine and seeking out different musical experiences. 'One of the problems for John [with Magazine], because of being in London and associating with lots of different people and the high profile he was building – people were in awe of this new young Scottish guitar player who was super intelligent, a brilliant artist and very well read. I think John had a taste for the finer things in life – he was a bit different from everybody else. He coveted success, not just creatively but also in a much more materialistic way – he liked motorbikes and the nice things, he liked the things success could bring you. He was the first person I knew of that gang who owned his own property. By the time we worked together he owned a great car, he had motorbikes, every toy and trinket you could imagine. I think that paved his downfall in the end because he did believe in the myth. I loved the guy – obviously I worked with him and he was my friend and he was always the most kind, generous and respectful person. He loved to sit and talk about stuff – not just music, but books, painters, and he was an amazing cook. We used to go for Sunday lunch at his house and John was an absolute maestro in the kitchen. He had taste, he knew about fine wine, you know – we were still quite feral by comparison. I almost felt a bit out of my depth, other than cultural stuff where I felt I held my own.'

Richard's younger brother Michael was brought into the fold to work alongside John as his guitar tech and general fixer. Michael, who had already formed a bond with John back during his days with Magazine, recalls his role with The Armoury Show. 'I became that kid that looked after everything for the band when they were starting off, I was the backline guy. My relationship with John really flourished there. I knew about his drinking and all of that, and while he was cool and everything at the beginning of The Armoury Show, he really was drinking a lot. White wine in boxes – "Michael, go down the shop and get me two cans of this and a box of white wine." John was more rock'n'roll than the rest of them, really. He'd been on tour, he'd been to America, he'd been to Japan – he'd done all that stuff. These guys were provincial people, really, by comparison. Richard was the man about town, Webb had never done anything, really, and John Doyle had been with Magazine. John was the senior man in the rock'n'roll ranks. What you could never, ever do down with John was the parts he wrote.'

Richard remembers the early days of putting the group together and of his own living arrangements with one of McGeoch's recent collaborators. 'I was living with Steven Severin for three or four years and I was still living with him by the time John got fired from the band. It's kind of weird because there I am sharing a flat with Severin and beginning to work with McGeoch. Steven always said how much he adored John. Steven and John retained a friendship.' Which Janet affirms when she says, 'John was really close to Severin, they made friends again. There was a period of hurt and then a period of healing.'

Richard explains what happened after John had been axed by the Banshees and started getting the new project under way. 'He was supposed to go into rehab and sort himself out, but by the time he was working with us he was still drinking a lot by anybody's standards. Then there was the other stuff, the drugs, and they are a fatal combination. The drugs enable the people who drink a lot of booze to drink even more booze. There were some days he was not recognisable as the person that you regarded as a close, warm, compassionate and generous friend – he just seemed like this wreck, you know, with a vicious temper and then he was fine again. It's all the absolute signposts of addiction, I've seen it all before. I could have done more for John, but I didn't and that's something I'll have to live with.'

As Russell reflects, 'John didn't really talk to anyone about what happened to cause his departure from the Banshees. His work had taken them to a place where they would perhaps have never gotten to without him. It was a magical time for all of them, but drugs and alcohol (two things that somehow exposed John's terrible weakness) were definitely a major contributing factor in that time coming to an end.'

Whatever may have been going on, the reality is John wasn't coping well by this point. The 'stated' reasons for his dismissal from the Banshees were still an ongoing issue, but there was no shortcut or easy cure for what John was going through. A tendency towards depression and a dependency on alcohol in particular only made the situation more toxic. Here was a man who needed serious help, living in a world of excess and surrounded by men. As a rule, men tend not to support and check in with one another. Things are left unsaid or, if they are brought up, often it is not in any sensitive or constructive way. John needed support, but he wasn't going to get it here. That's not a reflection on the people involved in the Banshees, The Armoury Show or any other band for that matter. This is a problem that is deep-rooted in society, where we ignore uncomfortable issues and conversations, a typical reaction being, 'What's your fucking problem? You're successful, what have you got to be down about?' How many people fall through the cracks due to our ignorance and, more often than not, embarrassment?

The fledgling group struggled to attract interest from the industry, which, especially for John at that point, must have been frustrating. There was pedigree, there was a good concept, but there were no takers. As Webb recalls, 'It was almost impossible to secure a deal at the start, mostly I think because of the reputation of the two frontmen. Jobson could be difficult to manage. Raf Edmonds (Magazine's ex-manager) helped us out for the two Johns' sake at the beginning but had no intention of staying any longer than he had to.

John's reputation was – from a musician's point of view – unassailable; however the circumstances of his departure from the Banshees caused potentially interested managers, labels, etc. pause. It was a really long, hard slog until [Peter] Mensch came along.'

PETER MENSCH, ALONG with his partner Cliff Burnstein, ran a management company, Q Prime, based out of the USA. Mensch already had experience of successfully managing big names. Take for example AC/DC's most successful albums to date, *Highway to Hell* and *Back in Black*, as well as looking after Sheffield rockers Def Leppard and his most recent significant signing Metallica (eventually the biggest metal band on the planet).

Peter takes up the story of how he became involved. 'This is all Richard Jobson's fault! Richard put together, this... I don't know what you would call it – British alternative supergroup? Jobson and Webb had been in Skids, Doyle and McGeoch had been in Magazine. It wasn't my area of expertise – I never really listened to a Skids record although I knew who Stuart Adamson was because he had Big Country and he had hits. I mean he was the guitar player in Skids, he wasn't even the singer. Richard was married to Mariella Frostrup who was a press officer at Phonogram or Mercury UK and I was busy visiting Phonogram on a regular basis because I was waiting for Def Leppard to make an album – which took years. So, I had been trying to get other UK clients as I only had one in Def Leppard. We had started to manage Metallica but they were based in San Francisco. Mariella said, "Would you listen to my husband's band?" and I really can't lie and say I was like, "Oh, my God, this is Richard Jobson of Skids and John McGeoch!" I can't remember but they played demos which included "Castles in Spain" and I played them to my partner Cliff. Listen, when you managed Def Leppard in 1983 you weren't the hippest guy in the room by any means! I remember trying to manage The Tourists and they wouldn't even take a meeting with me. Everybody wanted to be managed by Paul McGuinness who managed U2 because that was the biggest European band that wasn't a heavy metal band; they were hip! I was thrilled to bits to be able to manage Richard's band. That's how I got to meet John McGeoch, who was a fairly unassuming guy, then I would listen to him play guitar and realise that he was great and, well, let me put it this way, more successful guitar players in more successful bands had nicked a lot of his playing style and I realised he was the unsung hero of the movement. I think that if you pushed the Edge hard you might get him to admit, not that he stole it, as that is not what I'm saying, but that he spent a lot of time listening to how McGeoch played – that's what it sounds like to me anyway. You know, I made the mistake once of saying to John, "You sound a lot like the Edge," and he didn't get really pissed but he did say, "No, I was playing guitar like that before he showed up!"'

Having somebody like Peter Mensch on board was a solid move – surely here was somebody who, despite being a hard rock and metal guy, could ensure the band got the exposure they sorely needed. The band continued to write and rehearse; material was created at a steady pace. What none of the band could have imagined was just how tough getting a deal would prove, as Mensch explains. 'The biggest issue was just trying to get people interested. The problem is, and I've had this all along in management, people will say, "That's a really good record." Well, you know the problem with really good? There's lots of really good. The difference is, it has to be great, and with a song like "Castles in Spain", to make a name for yourself you need a track that is a ninety-seven or better. "Castles in Spain" was a ninety-three, you know what I'm saying? There was a buzz but there wasn't a big enough buzz. We just couldn't get arrested. I couldn't get an English record deal; I signed a deal with EMI America. I signed an American record contract because nobody was interested and, believe me, I went round to everybody. Maybe it was Jobson? Maybe Skids had a bad reputation? I've no idea.'

Despite their new management, the band just couldn't break through. 'Castles in Spain' was meant to be the single that would set out their stall, that would let the world know that here was something new and worth paying attention to. Perhaps John was seeing a familiar pattern unfold. Magazine had suffered from being misunderstood or even rejected throughout almost his entire time with them, save for some moments of critical acclaim. He had only really experienced true and sustained success and recognition while with the Banshees. Stepping into something equally fulfilling creatively and commercially would be a slog. As you move upwards in your career, just how much of that do you want to do? Magazine had been a labour of love at times, brilliant though they were. The difference is that he was just at the point of establishing himself then. He took the shit he was dealt and put it down to experience.

With the Banshees John had endured pressures and 'failures' of a different kind, yet there had been success. The Banshees – thanks in no small way to McGeoch – had become a marketable group that wrote amazing songs and delivered consistent and seminal albums. That was always going to be a tough trick to repeat. Yet with McGeoch involved, the possibility was there for something genuinely innovative and brilliant from The Armoury Show.

Here we come to what, for me as a fan, is one of the saddest facts of John's career, as Mensch explains. 'I didn't even know who John was until I got the chance to hear him play guitar and realised that he was absolutely fucking brilliant. If you had to make a list of great lost guitar players who weren't super famous from Britain, McGeoch would be top five. You know, people know who Paul Kossoff is, people know who Richard Thompson is. McGeoch for his whole career was kind of under the radar. Maybe it was because when you're in the Banshees people are only looking at Siouxsie, I don't know. [...] A lot of those early English punk bands or whatever you want to call them didn't pride themselves on playing ability. McGeoch was a player. He could really play, his solos were great, he was a good rhythm player. He wasn't just up there flailing away with a guitar; he knew what he was doing. It is just that he was never in a band that broke to a point where his own cult of personality could develop. It's like we know every member of The Clash, but they wrote hit singles. Ask most people to name you a member of the Banshees and they'll say Siouxsie, or Magazine and they'll say Howard Devoto. John was pretty shy and retiring and his biggest problem was that he drank.'

Further to Peter Mensch's point about John's lack of recognition, Andrew Graham-Stewart – the man who had been in charge of Magazine at the beginning of John's professional music career – says, 'I don't think John was ever really a vocalist. Many of the guitarists who've got the glory, as it were, were also vocalists. They were also working with less overtly dominant characters than Howard, Siouxsie or John Lydon. He was working with people who either had a superb stage presence and charisma, such as Lydon, or in Howard's case

– who I don't think had much natural charisma – worked so hard on his performance.'

It's important to remember the musical landscape following the group's establishment in 1983. U2 were about to become huge; New Order were on to their second album and had released 'Blue Monday', which became a behemoth and the biggest selling 12-inch of all time; The Cure were fast becoming a massive draw; and The Smiths' self-titled debut was around the corner. The world was changing, tastes were changing and so whatever McGeoch chose to do musically had to be exceptional to stand out. His guitar playing on The Armoury Show's *Waiting for the Floods* was on point and criminally overlooked in his catalogue, but maybe the timing was just not right for the band.

What was so interesting about John and his approach to the guitar was that, as with any great artist, he was able to reinvent himself from group to group and to some extent from album to album. McGeoch was a different player in the Banshees than he had been in Magazine, and the same is true with The Armoury Show. Equally exciting, interesting and challenging, but very different. That is McGeoch's greatest strength, for me, as a player. Always being sympathetic to the music, always delivering exactly what is needed and never overstepping the mark. Of all the players I adore, I can't think of one where I haven't at some time or another thought, 'That's too much, what are they trying to do here?' With McGeoch he has that uncanny ability to make me want more, teasing almost, and getting it right time and time again. John had a serious musical brain, which meant he understood that to perform at his best he had to be tuned in to those he was playing with. He knew how to make everyone feel comfortable and sound great. To understand that is to understand true genius and what makes a musician like John so very distinctive. The tragedy of genius is that it is often misunderstood or too ahead of the game to be fully appreciated at the time. You could never deny the immediate appeal of songs like 'Shot by Both Sides', 'The Light Pours Out of Me', 'Christine', 'Happy House' or 'Spellbound'. It is when you delve deeper and appreciate the solo on 'Permafrost' or the sheer modernism and funky flexing of a number like 'Philadelphia' that you see the bigger picture. 'Into the Light' is a prime example of being cutting edge but also confident enough not to swamp the track and to use effects to perfection. John was combining styles in such an ingenious and often subtle way that it was easy to miss it.

With The Armoury Show you can hear the influences of other players, but given the McGeoch twist, as Richard Jobson explains: 'The beauty of John's playing, for example on "The Light Pours Out of Me", is that it is so simple, but to come up with something that simple in that kind of song you've got to have a brain that works in a particular way. Other people would be looking for a complicated sound, but John knew perfectly what the song required and it's amazing. "Castles in Spain" is another one, you know, that riff – it's almost like something Cream would have done. He applied that sound to my lyrics and it's great.'

Richard goes on to reflect about Peter Mensch's involvement and the direction of the band. 'Peter, for some reason, thought we were going to be the next U2 and we didn't want that. In our minds, perhaps subconsciously, we imagined we were going to have the commercial viability of Skids mixed with the artistic creativity of Magazine – and some of the amazing stuff John had done by reinventing the Banshees, because he did reinvent the Banshees, you know, there's no doubt about it. Those albums that he worked on with Siouxsie and the band would never have had the praise and the classic status they rightly hold without John's playing on them – especially *Juju*. These are amazing pieces of work which are both commercial and creative. So, that's what we thought it was going to be or at least could be. We wanted to have that "edge", which comes easy when you've got John McGeoch as your principal sound, because the sound was based on John, it wasn't based on anything else. John just gave us that instantaneously with a song like "Castles in Spain". I remember we did a TV show and we did two songs, "The Glory of Love" and "Castles in Spain", and the next day we got bombarded with offers from record companies, but we only had two or three songs at the time that were any good. It was only when we really started getting down to it that we started to sculpt some really good material together. I listen to John's work on "Higher Than the World" and "A Feeling" and it really is remarkable guitar playing. He had it all there, but he wasn't easy to work with because of the booze and the drugs, you know, it was really tough. I was the opposite and so it made it really hard for me to be working alongside people who thought getting wasted was part of the deal and it really isn't.'

Nick Launay was brought in to produce the album, an intelligent move given his reputation for working with great British bands and artists of the late seventies and early eighties. 'The first I heard about this record was from Peter Mensch and Cliff Burnstein. Now, I didn't know who they were even though Peter lived [near us] in London. Peter actually became a really good friend, because once the album was done I think there was a bit of a gap between recording and mixing. Peter was a really big American manager and I remember him being very easy-going and funny, but his reputation is of being really heavy. Some people said that the manager in *Spinal Tap* is based on Peter Mensch – the scene with him going in and threatening people with a baseball bat! I never saw that, but it would make sense because he wore a baseball cap and was no doubt into the sport.

'There was another guy called Steve Robowski who was the A&R guy, who at the time was at EMI/Capitol in America. Now, he was a major part of it and he called me and said that the reason that he and Peter wanted me to do the record was because I was known in that circle. I have a lot of respect for these guys, because I wasn't like a big rock producer in the way of selling a lot of records but I was credible in that I had made a lot of credible post-punk records. So, I think I was a good match for Skids or Magazine or Siouxsie and the Banshees, although I hadn't worked with any of those bands. That was pretty cool because they could have easily got a big American rock producer in, especially as they were signing them to be big in America. England had nothing to do with it and I don't think they were even signed to EMI in England until later on. So, that's how the whole thing started.

'Then I got to meet the band, we all got on really well and had some rehearsals. They were very passionate people. Richard Jobson is a very commanding presence when he's in the room and very charismatic. Russell had been in Skids, quite cocky and taking the piss all the time but equally very funny with it. John Doyle was definitely the quiet one, a sweet guy who was very mild-mannered compared to the other three. Richard Jobson was a very famous face and then there was John McGeoch who was this incredible guitar player who was just absolutely brilliant at everything he did. John's ideas and melodies were just incredible; he is one of the most talented guitar players of all time as far as I'm concerned.'

Launay adds that from the get-go there were unusual circumstances about the making of the album. 'The weirdest thing about this record was that it was a completely American-driven record. They were signed to EMI, which I believe may have been Capitol at the time in America. All the A&R – in other words, all the control and decision making from the record company, i.e. the budget and all that stuff – was all coming from America, which was very bizarre in England. All English artists I had worked with previously, their record company was English and it was in London. You know, you'd have people come down from the record company and listen now and again and a lot of them were idiots! You would want to avoid them as much as possible, because quite honestly, a lot of A&R people and record company representatives are either failed musicians or failed managers – they are a weird lot. They want to be cool and hang out with the band, but certainly in my area of music they were allowed down to the studio for a few hours and then pushed out of the door as quickly as possible. More often than not they didn't understand music but you had to keep them happy, you know?'

Michael Jobson spent a lot of time with the band and with John in particular. He could see that the difficulties John had during the latter part of his time with the Banshees still cast a shadow over his latest venture. 'I lived in West Hampstead and he lived in Cricklewood, so I was up there all the time. If we weren't at the studio I was at his house, building patios and probably drinking and doing as much blow as we could together. My naivety as a kid was I didn't get the gravity of John's problem. I thought we were just hanging out, doing a load of drinking and having a smoke – I was 18 or whatever at the time.' On the time spent at the studio, Michael admits, 'I started to notice how bad it was when we were together at The Manor [in Oxfordshire], because every second day I was getting handed the car keys and sent to London to buy more charlie, you know? The drinking up there was pretty intense in what was a residential studio. If you're not in the studio playing, you're by the fire drinking.'

There were tensions early on in the recording process between

Richard and John, both strong personalities and both coming at things in a different way. Richard wasn't a drinker and John was battling an addiction. The working relationship could be fraught, and again factions were appearing. John was very close to Russell, who had been around during his days with the Banshees, and Russell and Richard had a prickly relationship at the best of times. It may be that the last thing John needed to be involved in at this point was another group, which even though it was just starting was already showing cracks. John could have used time out, space to work through the issues he was struggling with. Time to take in just what a rollercoaster he had been on. But ever the grafter and creative dynamo, he didn't give himself that chance to breathe and possibly wasn't at a stage to fully grasp just how bad things were. Bad habits developed during his time with the Banshees perhaps, where the philosophy was that to be relevant and to attain success you had to push yourself to breaking point.

Nick Launay recalls the recording sessions at The Manor: 'There was a lot of drinking going on and he would get pretty angry. I'm a very passive person and I tend to use humour to get out of a difficult moment. I've worked with a lot of difficult people – Johnny Rotten, Nick Cave and Lou Reed, for example – and I tend to end up working with these people who reach out to me to work with them. There's always a meeting involved and they are able to see that I'm not a dominant person – I listen and then try and work out how to make the album. With John, doing the guitar overdubs was challenging because he was drinking quite a lot and so he would throw this anger about, like he'd be playing this part and getting visibly frustrated with himself so he'd blame the assistant engineer about recording this or that bit – when it was clear that he'd just had too much to drink. I remember trying to water down his drinks, because I didn't drink at all so I wouldn't have made a good drinking partner.

'With John his playing was so extraordinary and the sounds he had were so extraordinary that all I wanted to do was capture what he was playing. For the most part he played brilliantly on all the backing tracks when the band were playing together – we recorded everybody in the same room as a band and that was easy, they were great musicians. We recorded at The Manor up in Oxford and we all lived there for about a month. I remember it all being the normal juggling of personalities, but there were occasions where John's temper was out of control and I ended up just leaving the control room. "I'm going for a walk and I'll be back when you've calmed down." It was quite funny, really, and he would always be very apologetic. I was concerned about how much he was drinking.'

Launay also remembers the conflicts between the band that made things difficult, but equally very comical, and at times it must have felt like being part of some weird British sitcom about a dysfunctional family. 'John was funny and never physically threatening. He did pick on you a bit, but in a funny way, and he'd try and get you to bite and get into a verbal confrontation, which with me didn't really go anywhere. With Richard and Russell it did – it was really passionate, and that's what I would say more than anything. Russell was really into the making of the record, so he would be in the control [room] a lot, saying, "Why don't you do this or do that?" He would always be taking the piss but it's a very British thing, isn't it? Using humour to wind you up, and I think that me and John Doyle were the targets for that, as we were both pretty passive. I was a geeky young guy who didn't drink and I can only imagine they thought I was squeaky clean, but I've always been able to handle difficult people. With McGeoch he wanted a bit of confrontation, but I was never going to give it to him, whereas Richard would.

'It was very fiery – wild, really. There were three big characters in the band, and it's that Scottish thing as well, and this is true of whenever I've worked with Scottish people: they are passionate, they are like warriors and it goes deep, I think. They are loud too. There were arguments going on between the band that I couldn't decipher because of the accents; it was like a scene from a Viking movie. Then there were the wives and the arguments. It was fucking mental up there! Living up at The Manor, it was like one big shouting match. I found it more humorous than anything, mainly because of the shouty Scottish accents. I remember me and John Doyle looking at each other quite often and our eyebrows going up, like, "What the fuck?!" It was nuts, but totally hilarious. Richard and his wife Mariella really went at each other. Their relationship was fiery but they'd always make up. I remember John's wife, Janet, being really sweet and very nice and

McGeoch for the most part was calm, he wasn't super energetic. Richard was the energetic one.'

Russell adds, 'The dynamics in The Armoury Show were toxic rather than fiery. I guess I was the one who was most fiery, borne out of frustration at Richard's standoffishness and John McGeoch's unresolved alcoholism. John Doyle was the most stable member of the band, a sweetheart who got a lot more frustration and abuse thrown at him than he deserved.'

To add to the whole bizarreness of the situation, naturally Stephen the English bull terrier would have to play his part! Nick Launay says of this: 'The other thing I have very strong memories about was his dog, Stephen, which had a leather jacket which said "bones" on the back and had a skull and crossbones emblem. Stephen was grumpy, and to be fair they are angry-looking dogs anyway, I think. He'd just look at you like he was going to bite you! He looked like a little bruiser; he'd come in with his studded jacket and sit upright at the edge of the couch with his front leg stuck out like it was an arm. It was the most extraordinary thing, and when John was playing, we'd have it really loud, I'd look at the dog and see his right ear twitching up and down almost in time with the music. I said to John, "What is up with your dog? Its ear is nuts!" And he'd go, "Yeah, I know, watch this!" And so John would play a note, and I remember it was an F – whenever he played the F note on his guitar the dog's ear would go up, then when he went to another note it would go down! Then John did this thing on the guitar, de-do-de-do-de-do, and the dog's ear would be going up and down and up and down. Fucking hilarious! John loved that dog so much. It was like it was a critic – John would turn to it and say, "What do you think to that one? Should I do it again?"'

The band toured domestically and in Europe from their inception in 1983 and right through to after the release of their debut album, as John Doyle remembers. 'One of the first tours we did, we did in a white transit van. Just the band travelling together. This was when we toured Scandinavia and Germany. We'd use the sound engineers and lighting that was just available from gig to gig. I think we had maybe one tech with us.'

Of the live performances and general feeling within the band, Michael Jobson reflects, 'The gigs, living through a show with somebody

A signed Armoury Show setlist.

that you're that close to, the communication, you know, it's not even in words, it's eye contact. John never, ever gave me any shit when I was his guitar tech. He taught me how to be a good one, or as good as I could be. His patience with me, the smile when things were great, and the shows were awesome. We used to love doing the thing of the guitar change, you know, it was so fast – he'd break a string and I'd have it restrung and tuned and stretched and ready for him by the time he got to the next song, no problem. We used to laugh about those things and have such a great time with it all. Then there were some nights where he was pissed, and he was rubbish and it was stressful. My brother, for all his faults, he was an absolute perfectionist at work, he hated the drinking and the sloppiness. John hated the sloppiness – he'd be tanked up and fucked up and make a mess. Then the next day there would be a bad vibe around the room, but he'd created the bad vibe. It would be easy to blame Richard as the moody guy, but he was only moody because of what had happened. When things were great, they were awesome. When the four of them were riding around on their motorbikes, going from gig to gig, having a great time with no pressure, they were awesome.'

Richard admits that his own way of dealing with John's drinking was perhaps not as supportive as it could have been. 'As long as people are delivering the goods, you let the other stuff go. It's only when that stops happening, things going wrong at gigs, and you realise that it's not right. There were days where I did confront him with it, but not in a way that was helpful – aggressively, you know – and John didn't respond to aggression very well.'

It is often all too easy to overlook the human side of addiction, to paint a picture that is far from a fair reflection. John was in the grip of an illness. Far be it for me to say that he should be free of responsibility for his decisions, but what is it that makes someone need a crutch? Michael describes what made John not just a once in a generation talent, but a man with the biggest heart. 'John showed way more interest in me as a young lad making his way. As I say, he was more of a brother to me than my own brother was. I was getting paid £100 a week by The Armoury Show, my rent was £40 a week and I struggled to survive. Whenever I went round to John's there was always a tenner in my pocket when I left. That stuff meant an awful lot, that was groceries, and he knew that it was a struggle for me to deal with all that. I'll never forget him.'

It appears that there was something in his character that was all too ready to give someone a helping hand, to nurture and yet neglect his own needs, as Michael recalls. 'Inside of him, to me he was generous to a fault. He was a teacher to me, he brought me up, really, as a teenager. I became a man around John, he taught me how to conduct myself and without John's help I would never have become a tour manager. He was hard on me, he was really tough on me if I made mistakes, but he was also like a conciliatory brother to me. I always learned things from him and I never, ever had trouble with him as his tech. He allowed me to become a tech, which I wasn't, and he never judged me for my lack of knowledge at the beginning – he always praised me and was always there to thank me after shows. There were lots of complex things with John's playing, tunings and a lot of guitar changes and stuff. He made me a pro and then I stopped working with John, which I never wanted to happen, but I left because of [Russell] Webb.'

The band were lumbering, not achieving recognition and failing to find that one song that would set them up to succeed. Friendships aside, John may have been losing interest and focus on the venture by this point. He had staked a lot in the group, even turning down an approach right at the start by John Lydon to join him in Public Image Ltd, but his patience was wearing thin.

Prior to the release of the group's debut LP, John once again turned his talents to participating in some session work, as Paul Morley explains: 'I was doing ZTT at the time and working with a band called Propaganda. I got John in to play on a remix of a track called "p:Machinery". It was an incredible day and one of the reasons I'd done it was there was an internal battle in the making of the ZTT records. The producer of Propaganda was a guy called Stephen Lipson – an incredible producer who has since gone on to work with Hans Zimmer and Rihanna, but back then he was one of our house producers. He came from a prog rock background and he got Steve Howe to play on [*A Secret Wish* by] Propaganda, which absolutely mortified me. So, as a corrective to that world I thought, "Well, if they are going to get Steve Howe to play on ["p:Machinery" by] Propaganda – who I had signed and thought of as a more edgier/artier electronic group – I'm going to get John McGeoch in." I got John McGeoch in to play on this remix of "p:Machinery" and it was a brilliant day and he was fantastic.

'What I always remember is just how committed he was this day of coming in, playing on this track and getting it right. Different ways of playing and coming at it and I remember he got this session fee of something like £75 and I was always embarrassed by that – here he is, John McGeoch of Magazine and the Banshees, playing on this track and making it one of my favourite experiences of working at ZTT for a few years, and he gets paid about £75! He was so thorough and so gentle and so committed to this one riff, and then I asked him to play a solo and he did. It was a great moment just to witness that level of concentration. I guess that was just the world he was in, of playing the guitar and creating sounds. In the long run you think about the troubles he had and everything, but this was what he did that was so important to him, and kept him going and made him unique. It is sad to think about when other things can overtake that escape or finding yourself through playing the guitar. I had that one day of hiring John McGeoch and I've always been very pleased about that. He was my first thought, you know, when I was thinking to myself, "Well, what is my antidote to Steve Howe?" – obviously it would be John McGeoch. It was recorded at Sarm West, Basing Street – which then became Trevor Horn's studio where they did Band Aid. I remember John talking about going off on tour and being very matter of fact about it, as if it was just a part of his job and having to go to work. I think it was a bit of a grind for him. I got the feeling it didn't really suit him and he had to adjust to something which wasn't really for him. You could sense he was after something more. He wanted to find a way to express his soul. John was a very soulful player.'

The Armoury Show album, *Waiting for the Floods*, did receive some positive reviews upon its release but, given the competition and the lack of a killer single, it went largely under the radar, and lack of interest outside the group was mirrored somewhat inside. As a creative experiment it had been good, but from a personalities point of view this wasn't going to last. There were too many divisions, too many differences to overcome, and ultimately having failed to achieve an immediate success there was little incentive to carry on. Richard Jobson reflects on what may have prevented the album from being what he'd hoped it could be. 'I've got two feelings about the album. It was very difficult for Nick Launay because Russell Webb really thought he should be producing the album, so he gave Nick a tough time, I think. So, I felt Nick never fully relaxed into the album and what it should have been. For me, the album should have been totally concentrated on McGeoch's guitar playing and then everything else would fall into place, I would do my vocals whenever.'

Michael looks back with fondness on the project and thinks that given time it could have succeeded. 'I thought they were brilliant. I think they were well ahead of their time. The songwriting was brilliant

– streets ahead of what was going on at the time – but people just didn't get it.' Of the pressure put on the band to be a success from the off, he says, 'They had a huge deal with EMI America/Capitol. Mensch set the project up for success, and perhaps too much success, without letting it breathe.' Peter Mensch reflects on the experience: 'The Armoury Show didn't really work. You know, we made that one record and Richard did his best. I think it's probably a way better record than it gets credit for, but we couldn't get a British hit single and that's what we needed. I couldn't put a tour together; I don't think we even got a chance to make a second record – the whole thing just fell apart.'

Of the album's highlights and McGeoch's playing in particular, Michael remembers, 'John's playing on those very early songs such as "Tomas", he was using all these open tunings. There's a song called "Higher Than the World" which is the only one that survived in that D tuning, I think. It's amazing that he was able to play that way – I mean really incredible parts that he wrote for the songs.'

He recalls the set-up John had that gave that distinctive McGeoch tone and magic. 'He loved the sustain of the Yamaha. He was able to take a mid-range-sounding pickup and make it a puffy-sounding pickup with the push of a button. John had quite small hands, so the necks on the Yamaha suited him as they were flatter, it sat in his hand nicely. They weren't the greatest of guitars really, the SG-2000 was better as it was "neck through" and may have the best sustain of any guitar ever made. The problem with the SG-2000s is they were heavy, so heavy they didn't suit John. Those SG-1000s worked for him because they were just so light, and I love them just because they were his. He had a Gibson SG that was a Banshees guitar with three humbuckers on it, but I'm not sure what happened to it. Then he started using all those shit American metal guitars later on. I set John up with the Washburn [guitar] deal and I got him some stuff from Ibanez.'

Michael also remembers getting a pedal board made up for John and what gear he was using to keep it simple but exciting. John was never an effects nerd but he always found new sounds and ways of delivering interesting guitar parts. 'An MXR Flanger on a plate that screwed into a plate attached to a mic stand. We would always go first into a BOSS compressor, but he never used it as a compressor, he used it as a level booster, so it just made it louder as opposed to squashing things. A chorus and a DDL on the floor. Then we started using an Ibanez DDL. We had him a rack built and took all those pedals apart. I went up to Birmingham and somebody out of the same team as [audio engineer] Mick Hughes built his very first rack and it was basically taking the pedals apart and putting them into modules. A really nice pedal board was built for him which was always switchable, and that stayed with him through The Armoury Show days. John knew his sound, very simple. There was never one amp on, he always went stereo with the Marshall master volume combo giving the chug while the JC-120 was all the jangle that went on. The beauty of the flanger he used was that the regen knob had a spring in it, so he would play something and turn the regen up and it would bounce back so he didn't have to mess with it. That was why he had it fitted to the stand, so he could do it all by hand.'

Nick Launay acknowledges John's love of sound and search for the 'feel' he was looking for while recording. 'John had all these guitar pedals, a stereo pedal box running through the Roland Jazz Chorus that gave him his distinctive sound. He always played these Yamaha guitars, which I found to be really unusual – most people had Fenders or Gibson Les Pauls – but this Yamaha [SG-1000] was a Japanese Les Paul copy, effectively. That was his sound and he had two of those guitars. We'd get the sound together and he was very particular about it, "Bit more this, bit more that" – he really had an idea in his head of what it should sound like. He also had all these parts worked out and we'd record one part and then he'd say, "Give me another track," and I had ideas so would suggest, "Well, why don't you double track that part?" We definitely had, creatively, a good relationship and we worked very well together. I was really into sound – I'm an engineer-producer, I don't play anything myself, so I am all about the sound. John would play it and I would get the sound, he would like it and then we'd record it. We had a lot of fun with all that.'

Perhaps there is regret that the band never got their big break but, as Richard explains, 'I loved the concept of the band and what it could have become. We fucked it up. It wasn't the idea or anything else – it was the participants. In retrospect I don't think I tried hard enough to get John to focus and ultimately get him some help – he needed help. He left the Banshees and went to detox and got himself together to become that John McGeoch that we all knew and loved, because when John was a mess, he wasn't the John McGeoch that you knew or thought you knew – it was a real Jekyll and Hyde thing. I think maybe I was too in awe of him to sit him down and say, "John, you're fucking up, mate. You're ruining your life and you've got to do something about this or it's all going to end in tears." I just don't think I was brave enough or courageous enough to say that to him, because he was the main man.'

The end for the band was fast approaching and was instigated primarily by an offer that was just too good for John to turn down, especially as he had already given it a miss at the first time of asking. However, as John Doyle remembers, both he and McGeoch knew the writing was on the wall. 'Me and John pretty much left at the same time as we realised that that was it. We both just had the sense that it was time to move on. It may not be correct, but the story doing the rounds at the time was that the management team took us on as a bet. One of those involved thought they could make or rather manufacture another Big Country and it was a bet between them, where one of them said they couldn't and one of them said they could. That was one of the telling elements of "OK, thanks, goodbye." It was one of the stories and it could just be concocted.'

On any perceived rivalry with Big Country, Mensch says, 'There was never any idea of a rivalry with Big Country because they didn't write the same kind of songs. We'll never know how it would've developed because The Armoury Show only made one record, so it would be kind of unfair to compare the two. The theory would have been to progress, because the project came together very quickly. I'm assuming with Big Country Stuart had these songs written down for years before Big Country, or at least the ideas, when he was still in Skids. I don't remember a lot of reviewer comparisons: "Well, two ex-members of Skids have come up with two albums" – by that time Big Country were already big. I don't know when Skids made their last record and when Richard turned up in my kitchen, I don't know how many years it was. I wasn't a Skids fan, you know, I wasn't sat writing letters to Richard Jobson c/o the Skids fan club asking, "When are you making your first Richard Jobson solo record?" For me with The Armoury Show it was a case of it sounds like fun – I was living in England and so it made sense.

You know, in my forty years of management, I've never taken on a band whose first album with me has blown up, other than with *Highway to Hell*, which was purely by luck. Everything is a work in progress until we get there, so it takes a while and I would've liked to have got to a second album with the band but we never did, so that was that.'

Of John as a guitar player, Nick Launay says: 'John's playing was very melodic. He wasn't all in on the riffs – he could do that; it's the memorable melodies, and the thing about McGeoch is that it wasn't a macho thing. A lot of rock is all about being at the front of the stage, "Look at me, I'm a man and I'm making all this noise." He's not that. John's at the back of the stage making these absolutely beautiful melodies, which are also very odd and dark. There's a darkness there, his choice of notes is dark. It's not typical pop melodies, it's this other thing. The stuff he came up with in Siouxsie and the Banshees is just extraordinary to me. To me that is his most memorable work.'

Looking back at *Waiting for the Floods* and its lack of exposure, Launay admits, 'It's very of its time, that album. There are things I listen to now and think, "Why the fuck is that so loud?" I know where my head was at the time – big drums were in. Most of it is good, "The Glory of Love" is a great track. You know, I'd never been involved in the politics of record companies until this album. I'd just make the record with a band and then it would come out and that was it. This was quite different. First of all I got contacted by the label and management and then the band, so that was unusual. I remember Peter Mensch and Steve Robowski in particular were ever present and deeply involved, and then all of a sudden they weren't. Steve Robowski basically disappeared off the face of the earth. I think he might have got fired by Capitol/EMI and it was a big deal – I remember it was on the front page of *Billboard*, so it must have been a massive clash of power. We hadn't even mixed the record at that point. I got a call from Capitol asking, "Are you working with this band? Because we are getting bills from the studio and we don't know who they are, what kind of music are they?" At that point I knew that this record wasn't going to be heard.'

Then, and probably not unexpectedly, at least from John's perspective, the call came from old pal John Lydon. Lydon had made an initial move for McGeoch around 1984, shortly after The Armoury

Show got together. The two had met for the first time a few years earlier. Lydon was now more determined. He was a bit of a hero to McGeoch, somebody he acknowledged as a renegade and a talented songwriter. John was also a massive fan of PiL and in particular the guitar parts Keith Levene had laid down on the first two albums. PiL had released *Album* in 1986, the year after *Waiting for the Floods*. It had been very much an album made up of Lydon playing with assorted, and highly regarded, names, but there was no intention of getting that line-up to go out on tour. One thing you could say for Lydon was that he recognised interesting and capable musicians. It had always been the same with PiL, and it wasn't going to be any different this time around.

Russell understands what caused John to bail. 'John's biggest frustration was that The Armoury Show didn't get to tour America. We were making progress slowly in the UK and in Scandinavia but in spite of having one of the biggest US-based management teams in our corner, America was always out of reach, which frustrated us all. I think John always wanted to break America and the frustration of not achieving it in The Armoury Show was probably quite a big factor in his decision to go to PiL as they were a fairly big draw in all the other big territories worldwide – Japan, Europe, America, etc.'

Michael Jobson looks back on the time he spent working closely with John. 'I always stayed in contact with John after I left. John was sad that I'd left. I wasn't just his tech but I'd learned about guitars and, really, I learned how to play from John, just from watching him. That was the sadness for me – leaving him. I wasn't sad to leave my brother – I was sad to leave John.'

As Launay says, 'John McGeoch was a lovely guy who had a bit of a drink problem and that's all. Not for a moment did I think he was an arsehole. He always smiled – he had a cheeky smile about him and that's how I remember him. An extraordinary man. We are all very grateful that he did what he did and that he played what he did.'

SEVEN

BRAVE NEW WORLD
John joins John Lydon in Public Image Ltd

That first Public Image single in 1978 really had the greatest impact on me. I thought it was a stupendous piece of work.

Guitarist magazine (April 1991)

THE TWO JOHNS had met back in 1981 when McGeoch was in New York on tour with the Banshees. Ken Lockie takes up the story: 'When John came to New York we met up and I, at John Lydon's request, introduced them.' The two got on and, according to McGeoch, Lydon invited him back to his apartment and cooked a turkey.

Given Lydon could choose to work with diverse and challenging artists, the idea of bringing McGeoch into the fold would seem a no-brainer. With John having only recently joined the Banshees and with Lydon still working with Keith Levene, it would be put on ice, but not for long. Shortly after The Armoury Show came together, Lydon and Levene parted ways and McGeoch received an approach. Possibly with a pang of regret, John turned the offer down, but he must have harboured hopes that his dream of joining PiL would one day be realised.

John didn't have to wait too long; Lydon, looking for musicians to tour *Album*, made his move after its release. John wasn't going to pass up the chance again and threw his lot in with Lydon. At the same time as McGeoch joined Lydon's reinvigorated line-up, an American bassist was recruited to tour and ultimately record with the British post-punk trailblazers. Enter Allan Dias. 'When Lydon was putting that line-up together, these guys were all heavy hitters. I got a call saying, "John Lydon wants you to play bass for PiL." This was right after "Rise" had come out – *Top of the Pops* '86. This was a big thing – PiL's return, so to speak. So, Lydon had got the guys from Big Audio Dynamite to back him up and did *Top of the Pops.* Shortly thereafter I get the call saying that Lydon had heard about me through [PiL drummer] Bruce Smith who I used to jam with. I'd been doing promos and TV stuff with Bryan Ferry at the time – basically just a clothes horse holding a bass! So, I was like, PiL, what?! There was no audition, I met Lydon in a pub, we drank a few beers and he asked if I was interested and I was like, "Yeah, OK." So, I walk into rehearsal and I don't know if I knew who was going to be there, other than Bruce and Lydon. I met McGeoch. Given his background he was one of the movers and shakers, you know, he was one of the architects of new wave or post-punk, whatever you want to call it. So, I had John Lydon, John McGeoch of the Banshees, Magazine, Armoury Show, Bruce Smith of The Slits and Pop Group, Lu Edmonds of The Damned and me – an unknown guy! All these guys were like ten years younger than me, it's another generation.

'Getting back to McGeoch, you know, there were no airs about him. Salt of the earth, man, he had that sense of humour and that sharpness. We became friends pretty much instantly. He wasn't like, "Who is this guy? Blah blah" – there was none of that, he just took me for what I could bring artistically and that was that. Great sense of humour, down to earth, but he was a tough guy – he was hard man, you know. He didn't take any shit.'

Richard Jobson recalls how he felt when John told him he was teaming up with Lydon. 'The Armoury Show was as much John's band as it was my band or Russell Webb's band or John Doyle's band. I was absolutely furious when he decided to chuck it in and become a member of PiL. I remember the day he called me up to say, "You've got to understand, this is like Mick Jagger calling me up," regarding

John Lydon, and I said, "But why do you want to work with him?" It was to do with success. The Armoury Show were not successful. In fact, I'd go as far as to say The Armoury Show were a failure. I don't think it was a failure creatively – the album was good and John's guitar playing is exceptional – but we weren't a commercial success. I think that was a disaster for him because he had staked a lot on that. After being with the Banshees he was used to playing big stadium gigs, big festival gigs, going on tour and everything was done for you and they were "punk rock stars" in a sense. The Armoury Show had all the noise of being a big band, but we weren't a big band. We had to start all over again and I think he always found that very difficult. He was already in a very elevated position both culturally and financially. For me at the time, it didn't really matter, it was a new journey, and I knew it was going to take that bit longer. I always felt that if we got to that second album then the band would take off. The biggest difficulty was keeping John focused. With the Banshees, there was the drinking and the excesses and, unfortunately, he brought that with him to The Armoury Show. It was very sad to watch – this dignified, super-intelligent guy really falling to bits because of believing in the myth of booze, drugs and the "lifestyle". It was borderline idiotic for such an intelligent human being. It was his Achilles heel and biggest vulnerability.'

Russell Webb confides that John had not made him aware of Lydon's offer. 'John didn't say anything to me about the approach from Lydon, but he took the opportunity to leave The Armoury Show within days of me ending up unconscious in hospital following a collision between me on my motorbike and a careless taxi in Paddington. I don't think John and I had any contact with each other for about five years after that.'

Peter Mensch recognises that for reasons out of his and the band's control, the future for The Armoury Show was always going to be tough going with or without John. 'It fell apart really because John got the chance to join PiL and I remember him telling me, because I was bummed, I didn't really have anything else to do and I was waiting for *Hysteria* [Def Leppard] to be done, which took four years, "Imagine if one of the guys in Def Leppard had the chance to join Led Zeppelin, because that's me getting a chance to join PiL," and I said, "Really?!"

He actually asked us to manage PiL and I think we met up with John Lydon but it was weird because one of the band members lived in Manchester and Lydon lived in Venice [California] on a houseboat with his rich wife. So, the band were writing songs and ferrying them over back and forth, which was not a situation conducive to management success. Half your band is living in England and your leader is living in southern California, so for all his "Johnny Rotten" stuff, by that point John Lydon was leading quite an upper middle-class life.'

From those early rehearsals Lydon not only felt validated in his pursuit of McGeoch but realised that there was an opportunity to take PiL in a new direction, with the same edge but musically very different from its foundations. Keith Levene, whom McGeoch particularly admired as a guitarist, can see why McGeoch was the right man at the right time for Public Image. 'I can totally get my head around John [McGeoch] recognising the potential space that I left in PiL. The work he did with Magazine and the Banshees, it's amazing, and I can see him seeing this little [opening] and I can see him totally getting what Keith Levene did on guitar and thinking, "I'll have some of that," and the thing is, he didn't have to play like me to be able to do it. I sort of automatically gave him the blessing of being able to do that stuff, but there again he always sort of played like that anyway. I know I like Magazine's guitarist and it has to be him, right.'

Johnny Marr echoes these sentiments. 'When John McGeoch replaced Keith Levene in Public Image, albeit with a few years' gap between them, it was just such an obvious fit. The guitar playing by Levene on the song "Public Image" is not only really original and out of the box and quite brilliant – the only other guitar player who could have come up with it at that time was John McGeoch. It does sound like something McGeoch was doing. Both McGeoch and Keith Levene were the opposite of heads-down, drink a load of beer and just thrash it out… let's put it that way.'

The band started its 1986 touring schedule at the Victoria Hall in Stoke-on-Trent. After a pretty packed set of UK dates, the band took in Germany, Holland and France before crossing the Atlantic. The North American leg was fast and furious. Mark Arm recalls PiL coming to Seattle where his then group were the support act. 'Green River opened for PiL. The problem was PiL's gear and with us being a five piece. The guitar players had half-stacks and there was just not enough room to set up the drums. We asked politely if they could pull some of the keyboards back and they were like, "No, no," and we just tried to explain that we were a pretty energetic, wild band and that if they didn't pull some of this stuff back then we couldn't guarantee what kind of condition it would be in by the time they came to play. Anyway, they did move it back, which was nice, but we were young, dumb and a little bit cocky; our friends came upstairs when the band went back to their hotel and Andrew from Malfunkshun, who later went on to be the singer in Mother Love Bone, got into John Lydon's wine! I had a very brief interaction with McGeoch at the gig, again just telling him how much I loved his playing, but the whole thing was just clouded by Mr Lydon's attitude and our response to it.'

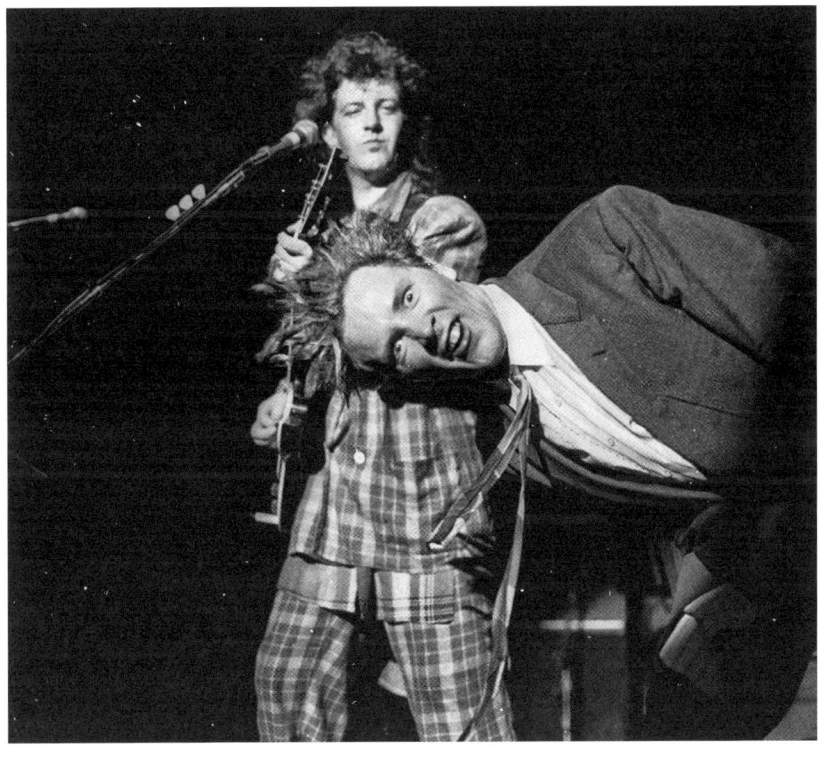

John in Public Image Limited, on stage with John Lydon, Washington DC, 1986.
Chester Simpson

By chance John was reunited with an old friend when Michael Jobson was asked to step in and help out with the tour. This followed some down time from his more recent commitments with Echo and the Bunnymen, as he explains. 'I got a phone call in '86 – the Bunnymen were on a break – asking me if I'd go on the road with Public Image, and I just assumed it would be to look after John but it wasn't, as John already had somebody taking care of him – it was for Lu Edmonds, and what a beautiful human being he is. Still, it gave me the chance from late spring through the summer of '86 to spend time with John and we had a great time. But as always with Lydon there was trouble. Their tour manager, a guy called John Martin, never made it – I'm not sure why exactly, something to do with a visa maybe. Anyway, I had to step up and become tour manager for that period of time. So, I was back in that same place with John that I had left with The Armoury Show and he was quite ruthless with me. I had gone up to quite a different level in my career by that point, but he was quite hard on me but in a good way, in a professional way. Outside of the boozing and that weakness that was in him, he was a super pro and he loved the whole thing about being a pro.'

PiL had always had frequent line-up changes, and what that gave Lydon, creatively, was a new vehicle – often from album to album and tour to tour. People came and went, and some stayed longer than others. McGeoch had been brought in with Edmonds, Smith and Dias to take the new (and older) material out on the road in support of *Album*. It was after returning from the American leg of the tour that one of the most significant events happened that was to have deep and long-lasting ramifications for John, not just musically but also in his personal life.

Allan Dias takes up the story of what took place on 12 September 1986 at the Donauinsel Festival in Vienna. 'There was a lack of security, and basically while we were on stage people went into our dressing room, drank our wine and ate our food. Somebody goaded some kid to get into the audience and throw a wine bottle, which hit John. So, John's been hit, and we are midway through a tune. Dude, the bottle caught him in the face. That shit would have knocked me out. He's up there and his knees didn't even buckle. He's still playing, and he turns around and I'm just like, "What the fuck?" with blood everywhere, all down his shirt and guitar, and he just says, "I guess the gig's over, huh?" Hard as nails. He was still playing.'

Lu Edmonds adds his own memories of that night and how it escalated. 'In Austria John got bottled and needed forty stitches in his face. Who was it that found the fucking bottle on the stage? That was me. I pulled it off stage and I looked at it and thought, hang on a minute, that looks like the bottle we had backstage. What had happened was someone had gone in while we were playing, nicked this 1.5 litre bottle of Austrian wine, necked it and threw it at John. They knew who it was, and the security, who were all Hells Angels or some dodgy Austrian motorcycle gang, did nothing. Then there was this weird process of about a year with a lawyer; they were trying to get compensation. In the end I think Lydon turned round and said, "Look, this should really be for John," and I don't know if there ever was any compensation.

'Honestly, it was this total nightmare for McGeoch. It changed him and it changed everything. It was just such a shocking moment. There was blood all over the stage. It was terrible and I'll never forget it. I was the only person with half a brain; I was sorting stuff out: "Keep the bottle, get this, do that, keep the evidence." I did it all. Everyone was all over the place, but I kept my head. What had sparked it was there was some spitting coming at us from the audience and McGeoch, being the senior guitarist, went to the front of the stage and started having a go at the audience and next thing he had a bottle in his face. He turned round to me and I'll never forget it – he made the sign waving his two arms to say that's it, the gig's done, and I looked at his face and there was just blood pouring. His clothes were soaked in it – he must have lost a pint of blood before he even got backstage. I didn't see that bit, because the medics took him away and then that was it, the tour was cancelled. Lydon, to his credit, just said, "That's it, we are going home."'

Just over a month later the band were back on the road to finish some dates in Europe. Allan Dias explains just how confrontational and disgusting those early gigs could be. 'We had to take some abuse with PiL, and those guys, because of their experience with the punk scene, they knew how to deal with it. I wasn't prepared for it. We are talking 1986 here when we did our first gigs as a band and kids are gobbing at us. You go to reach for a note and there's a big lump of phlegm on the fretboard. I remember being in Sheffield and a cue ball got thrown at the stage. McGeoch and Lydon could just play through it. You know, Lydon used to wear this big yellow raincoat with his back to the audience because of the spitting. Pretty gross! I was in for a shock, man. It was sort of exciting too, because it was a charged atmosphere at gigs. After the first tour that stuff went away.'

Lu Edmonds saw a change in McGeoch following the events in Austria, which he feels had a lasting effect on him. 'He did recover, but something was different. I remember asking, "What's happened to him?" and being told, "Oh, he'll be all right." Imagine going through that. He totally changed at that point. Up until that moment we'd had a fairly creative interplay and I used to do a lot of improvised feedback and noises. Whereas he was the mainstay of the guitar, I'd play a bit of keyboards and weird shit on top, for example using the Greek bouzouki.'

In the immediate aftermath of the incident, John went on holiday to Nerja in Spain with some mutual friends. It was there that he got to know and go on to fall in love with Denise Dakin, somebody he had known in passing since The Armoury Show days. She recalls the extent of his injury. 'John needed laser surgery and he had to have forty-four stitches in his face. It was awful, to be honest. The doctors who performed the surgery, which was basic plastic surgery, advised John that, "The best thing you can do is go somewhere warm where there is sea and you can get in the water and it will help your wounds heal quicker." I was due to go on holiday. There were four of us going together. One had to drop out due to work commitments and my friend Su told me that Janet had said John needed to go somewhere hot and would I object to him coming? I was just like, well, whatever. I knew John so it wasn't as if he was a stranger and it would have been a shame to have had to cancel the holiday.

'So, that is what happened. John came along to heal his wounds and the rest is history – it was just like two magnets. We went on holiday vaguely knowing each other and came back joined at the hip. It was really hard for us because for the first few weeks after getting back we really did try not to see each other but it was just too difficult. It sounds soppy, but we couldn't stop looking at each other. We came back on the plane holding hands across the aisle! We had to get to San Sebastián and we were at the airport, we missed the flight because we were just sat there and we couldn't stop googling at each other. It really was like people say about finding your soulmate and falling head over heels. So, that was the start of me and John and that was in September '86.'

John had found his love match. Not that it was going to be plain sailing. He was still a married man at this point, and despite the fact that the marriage had been going through some turbulence, breaking up was a big decision. Likewise, for Denise, she would be returning to Def Leppard frontman Joe Elliott and having to make the break in order to be with John.

By 1987, having experience of touring and working together as a unit, PiL were ready to head into the studio to begin putting material together for the first album of the newly established line-up. Putting the horror of the previous tour to one side, McGeoch was able to work with a familiar face when he drafted in Banshees tech Murray 'Muzz' Mitchell. 'I had no idea he'd joined PiL. I hadn't seen him for some time since he'd left the Banshees and then I bumped into him at a gig somewhere in London and he suggested I come down to the studio because he was making an album with Public Image. I was like, "Nah, you're all right," because I'd never liked Rotten, and John said, "Come on, come down and keep me company." It was only just out of town. So, we went out there and I spent a couple of weeks there with John saying, "Help me get some guitar sounds," and so that's how I ended up working with PiL and had a couple of glorious years with that version of the band. That really was great stuff. He seemed to have found himself again, you know?'

The album – *Happy?* – was recorded at Great Linford Studios, Milton Keynes. The band, or Lydon, had opted to use Gary Langan, better known for his work with Art of Noise, to produce. Not a decision, in hindsight, that all the band are happy about. The process itself was generally a good one and something which McGeoch threw himself into wholeheartedly. For all the concerns about the quality of the production, there were some highly original and innovative McGeoch guitar parts on display. Following the disappointment of *Waiting for the Floods*, John was back. Here was someone who'd suffered a very challenging few years – ever since being fired by the Banshees – sounding like John McGeoch again and giving fans the prospect of PiL returning to what they had once been. Had the production been brighter – it does sound squashed – this could have been an exceptional album.

For all its the faults, however, John's playing does sound surprisingly vibrant and cuts through the cloudiness enough to ensure that all is not lost. There was definitely a change in his approach. Yet again he was embarking on a period of reinvention, as Lu Edmonds recognises. 'He split up with his wife and got with Denise. I went to see him once – I think it was out towards Guildford or somewhere like that. Denise had this amazing bungalow with massive grounds, and she had these dogs called Hunter and Ronson, two lovely boxers who were fabulous dogs. Musically, his whole thing changed. He really got into rock in a big way. He became really fascinated by rock, rather than the whole innovative Banshee-type thing – the arty side. I don't know how that happened, although it didn't really manifest itself in his playing that much, it was kind of an attitude thing. It was odd.'

John was clearly on point again as he had been at the start of the fallout from punk. Stadium rock was the order of the day and he dipped his toe in without cheapening his talent. This was a bigger, cockier-sounding McGeoch. You can imagine him strutting around the studio like a peacock, a new-found confidence or indeed 'fuck it'-type attitude, no doubt in part due to Vienna. The dynamics were also different. John would have been eaten alive by Lydon had he been anything less than bombastic and self-assured. He'd been in the game long enough and worked with incredibly talented, powerful and forthright front people in Howard, Siouxsie and Jobson to be more than up for dealing with Lydon.

Keith Levene sees the sense in the trajectory of John joining Public Image. 'It really fits that John ended up in PiL; he was perfect for them [after the] journey he'd been on from Magazine and then the Banshees. Magazine were one of my favourite bands – when Devoto left Buzzcocks I found that really interesting. Devoto was in that interesting, weirdy-punk mystical/militant area. He was intelligent and had skin in the game. Looking back on that period, we were of our time in our time. He was perfect for PiL and it would seem that at that point he was putting himself back together again.'

Happy? was released on 14 September 1987 by Virgin and got to 34 in the UK albums chart. The group also put out two singles: 'Seattle' on 10 August, peaking at number 47, and 'The Body' on 31 October, which got no higher than 100 in the UK charts.

John, left, with PiL, 1987.
Adrian Boot

IT WAS AT this point, with the band hitting the road to support the album, that Philip Hamilton, known to his friends as Trigger, came into the fold, initially as drum tech for Bruce Smith. Trigger was invited into the PiL camp on the recommendation of Paul 'Suspect' O'Reilly, who was half of the Heavenly Management team. 'I met John [McGeoch] in 1987. John Lydon had got the group together to tour, he'd done a couple of studio albums and he'd wanted to put a band together that could take his studio stuff out on the road. It was Paul O'Reilly who brought me into PiL for a tour, quite a big tour on the back of the *Happy?* album. My first introduction to John was, "Wow, this is the famous John McGeoch." You know, the mad Scotsman. I'm not a guitar player or somebody that would be able to wax lyrical about his abilities as a guitarist but obviously it went without saying that he was great.

'So, the musical side of it I left alone. John did what John did and I did what I did, but we just got on well. We got on like a house on fire. He was about two years older than me. Big character, mad Scotsman, been there and done it all. I was relatively new to touring, I'd done a bit but the thing about it was at that time Public Image Ltd were massive in America – everything was coming out of America. That was one place I'd not done a lot of touring and John [McGeoch] loved that, because for him it was like, "Great, I can show you how this works," and he sort of educated me, well he did it for all of us really – Murray [Mitchell], there was a big crowd of us. John would always have the answer if you were going to a certain city or venue – you know, John had been there. He sort of took me under his wing – I was a little bit green around the ears and he liked that. So, throughout the period I worked with him and PiL, within about a year, well it would have been about 1989, through a gradual progression I took over the stage management, I took over the production management and then, mainly because for one reason or another tour managers ended up falling by the wayside, I found myself tour managing – which went on to 1992. Because in those days the band had American management, they needed somebody in the UK who would primarily look after John [McGeoch]. John Lydon had places in America and he had places in the UK, so he would be flying between America and the UK and wherever, so they basically needed a UK base. There was a UK label and there was a bit of UK interest, but the money was in America.

'So, I ended up in this position where I was put on a retainer, paid a salary by the band, so that if they were on tour I was the tour manager and if they weren't on tour I was readily available if anybody needed anything. Nine times out of ten it would be McGeoch – quite demanding, I'll give him his due! Sadly there was also a little bit of a tussle between him and Lydon – they got on but there was a little bit of artistic stuff between them and John [McGeoch] used to like to get his share. He would occupy my time; John did a lot of session work so I would do that for him and in and amongst all that we just became incredibly good friends. In and amongst being demanding and being a pain in the arse and just being John – he was a sweetheart. There was nothing that he wouldn't do for you and I was always learning from John. He was someone I could go to and if there was anything I wasn't sure about, certainly business related, John was the man. So, we had close contact for a good five years.'

Although McGeoch and Lydon were friends, the frictions had arisen early on due to musical differences, differences in approach and a clash of personalities. Lydon had carved out a fearsome reputation – as confrontational as he was witty, intelligent but at times lethargic. Never dull. McGeoch was more than a match intellectually, but his musical talents were what really set him apart. He had quickly found himself to be the driving force from a writing perspective and Lydon needed McGeoch to be at his creative best in order to produce the goods. As gifted a lyricist and frontman as Lydon was, he couldn't match the musicality of McGeoch.

Allan Dias makes no bones about just how influential McGeoch was on the sound of the band: 'Regardless of what anyone says, Bruce and Lu both know and sadly McGeoch is no longer here but the other guys know. McGeoch was *the* major contributor of the songs. As the guitar player, he brought more ideas to the table than any of us. Lydon brought mostly lyrics. We would have to gang up on Lydon – not physically, but verbally and artistically beat the shit out of him so that he would get pissed off and he would come back and write these fantastic lyrics and hooks.

'Those two [Lydon and McGeoch] were the two alphas, and me, Bruce and Lu [at that time], we pitched in where we could. It was a group effort in that we shared all the publishing, the five of us, until Lu left, then the four of us, and then when Bruce left it was just me and the two Johns. If I wrote the whole song it didn't matter, we shared everything 33 per cent. McGeoch was pretty prolific, he had a lot of ideas. Great textures. The mindset we had as bandmembers was that we could offer Lydon something different. Something that without our input he might not have thought of himself. We were there on merit and McGeoch, in particular, was very instrumental in supporting Lydon to find and explore new characters and parts of his palette, which drove the group forward.

'McGeoch had a wide range. For a bass player it was awesome and for a songwriter, which I eventually became, it was incredible. I used to take his guitar parts off multitracks to sample it, in the early days of samplers. We were using floppy disks and stuff, you know, eight megabytes of sampling and that was dope. Fifteen megabytes was unheard of! So, I'd be using the early Steinberg software and use McGeoch's sounds and when I presented the demos he knew exactly what was going on. John's playing in demos, for instance on a song like "Disappointed", the bass line was just suggested by the way he did his chords. He was a consummate guitar player. He could have had a big head about it because a lot of movers and shakers in the post-punk/new wave arena like Edge from U2 and Johnny Marr, they all speak so highly of him.'

By the time of the tour to support *Happy?* John had changed his gear. The Yamaha, so long the McGeoch mainstay, was shelved in favour of Washburns, Charvels and Carvins and he was establishing his own position as *the* PiL guitarist, as explained by Lu Edmonds. 'He stopped playing the Yamaha for some reason. He had this amazing guitar rack that he was very proud of, that somebody had made for him. He had impeccable taste in pedals and in speakers and all that stuff; he was incredibly knowledgeable. He had very good techs, having been with the Banshees and working at a very high level and therefore worked with excellent techs who had helped him out. I'd been in the doldrums really, doing a lot of world music. I'd done my share of touring, but nowhere near his level. He never really discussed his preferences with me. He was quite cagey with me, in a way, about his position and he was very much the senior guitarist.'

The relationship between John and Lu, while perfectly fine personally, hadn't gelled musically, at least from McGeoch's perspective, as Edmonds recalls. 'I don't think he'd ever worked with another guitarist before. Some people will have different opinions, but I'm not entirely crap on the guitar. I really wanted it to work with John and myself. I'll adapt to anything and, you know, now that I'm the only guitarist in PiL it's fine and I think I hold my own. Even though I was the second guitarist with The Damned and then again when McGeoch was in PiL. I'm adaptable, I like playing. McGeoch wasn't very good playing with me, and by that what I mean is, I don't think he felt comfortable. He liked me playing keyboards and I had to programme the Prophet 2000 – that was an absolute nightmare as it was one of the early sampling keyboards. He liked it when I programmed a sample of some crickets and I gave him that. I can't honestly say, however, that we ever really clicked. He was an amazing bloke and, remember, everyone has an ego – everyone. To get up on a stage – to do all the stuff he did, especially with Magazine and the Banshees but also with PiL – and to be sure about what you're doing is really difficult. He always had it, he never lost it. I'm not saying we didn't get on personally – I got on really well with him and he was an amazing guy. He was prone to fisticuffs and he could hold his own, but we never fell out. What I mean when I say we never clicked is that I don't think he ever got his head round working with another guitarist. I wanted it, but he didn't. He would have been happier had I just played keyboards.'

Edmonds left the group shortly afterwards during the recording of the follow-up to *Happy?*, on which he didn't play but did help write, leaving McGeoch as the main man and recognised second in command to Lydon as the face of PiL.

By 1987 John and Janet had gone their separate ways and Denise moved in with John at the house in Cricklewood. 'I was still living in the house I shared with Joe, and John was still in the house at Cricklewood, so we had to sort all that out. I sold the house in Surrey first and moved into John's house just for a month; I bought Janet out of that house. We then moved up to Blyth near Worksop [in Nottinghamshire] as we'd decided we wanted a family but we didn't want to do that in London. We were looking in the Derbyshire country-side, but we couldn't find anywhere as it was boom time and everything was going rapidly. We ended up buying somewhere in Blyth.'

One of the biggest sacrifices John had had to make when moving in with Denise involved his faithful, biker jacket-wearing canine amigo, as Denise explains: 'When John and I got together he had a bull terrier

[Stephen], and he loved Stephen and Stephen loved him, but one of my dogs, Ronson, was a fighter and we just couldn't put them together, so he had to give Stephen up. That must have been really hard for him, but he did it because he wanted to be with me. He used to play games with Ronson; my other dog had died when he was only six so Ronson was left on his own. John was so concerned that Ronson would be grieving, so he'd play games with him to keep him occupied. He actually increased Ronson's mental capacity – he would lock Ronson in a room while he'd hide a ball, but he'd make a point of running all over the house so Ronson wouldn't know what room he'd gone in. He used to hide it in the most ridiculous places, like behind the top of the radiator, and then he would come back downstairs and say, "OK, go get it Ronson!" Ronson would then run round the whole house trying to find the ball and they'd happily do that all day! He would be the homebody – cooking, foraging, playing with the dogs, and that's what he loved.'

John the homebody, 1989.
McGeoch family archive

Things were changing rapidly for John. By 1987 he was divorced and in a new relationship. By 1988 he and Denise were married. He'd left London not long after and by 1989 he was about to become a father. In many ways, he was exactly where he wanted to be. Professionally and personally everything had come full circle. He'd been through the fire, but he was proof that out of hardship the best things can be realised. He was the happiest and most secure he'd been. He'd also made a big commitment to Denise by leaving London. London, for all its pitfalls and distractions, was always the place to be as a musician. John would need to do a fair amount of commuting to keep everything ticking along, but by this point Lydon was mainly based in the US anyway. He was absolutely delighted at the prospect of becoming a dad. For all the excitement of creating music, for all the highs of being a sonic pioneer – it wasn't the be-all and end-all. He was ready for big changes, for the stability that domesticity and fatherhood offer. In many ways, this was the single most pivotal point where his thinking changed. Where he was forced to take stock and decide what he really wanted from life. He was in control of something, unlike being in a band where you can get swept along – John could navigate a path for himself.

The band began putting ideas together for their second LP – what would become *9*. Producers were sounded out, including Bill Laswell, who had produced the album prior to McGeoch's arrival, and the musicians flew out to New York. Laswell proved to be a non-starter as he wasn't keen on the band as it was and disliked the direction it was moving in. The trip left a bitter taste in the mouth, to the point where Lydon and Laswell fell out. Instead, the album was produced by Stephen Hague and Eric Thorngren, with additional input from the band themselves. McGeoch was hands-on, having had plenty of experience when it came to producing and engineering. The band headed to both Comforts Place Studios and The Manor (where McGeoch had previously recorded with The Armoury Show) in the UK.

The album contains some of John's most memorable playing with the band, but upon its release he had misgivings. Though largely pleased with it, he had a nagging feeling that given the strength of the material it could have been better. Again, it is perhaps let down by the production, a recurring issue during McGeoch's time in the band.

Ed O'Brien feels it really was the production of those albums that ultimately hampered their success. 'I liked it on the whole… because he was such a great player and "riffmeister" but I didn't like all the eighties production… I don't think it complemented his sound, but I had 9 and enjoyed it at the time.'

On the production of the albums, especially 9, Dias has this to say: 'I just wish we'd had a little more say in the production. I mean, McGeoch could bully and boss the producers around a bit, Lydon I don't think was that into that side of making a record at that point. I think he let McGeoch have more control over that. For me, I mean, I was happy with Stephen Hague, I just thought that my bass sounded a little thin and lightweight – not enough bottom. When we got to *That What Is Not* there is more bottom to that.'

The album was released on 30 May 1989 and reached number 36 in the UK albums chart. The band chose 'Disappointed' and 'Warrior' to be the single releases from the album. 'Disappointed' came out in April of '89 and 'Warrior' in the July, peaking at 38 and 89 in the singles chart respectively. The album wasn't the most significant development in John's life at this time, however, as in February of the same year, he and Denise had welcomed their first child into the world. Emily Jean McGeoch was born on 23 February in Hendon, west London. Denise takes up the story: 'I had Emily in Hendon, at a private natural childbirth hospital. I didn't want to go in the NHS as I'd heard horrible stories about women giving birth unnaturally. We rented a flat for a week, went to the hospital to have Emily and then drove back to Blyth. We stayed in that house until Emily was three. My family lived in Sheffield and the roads weren't very good to Blyth and with Emily being little I wanted us to be nearer my family. So, we moved back to Dronfield, which is where I was born.'

The band went out on a comprehensive tour starting on 9 June 1989 in Vancouver and concluding at the back end of November at the Lisner Auditorium in Washington DC. The band were not getting the level of appreciation or bookings in Europe, and specifically the UK, as they were in North America. Everything was geared up for success Stateside, a move that would have suited expat Lydon, but which weighed heavily on McGeoch. Being away from his little family was proving more and more difficult, as Denise explains. 'He just wanted to be with us, he didn't want to be off on tour – he really hated it. I remember when Emily was smaller and we bought a video camera so I could film her every day while he was away on tour so that he wouldn't miss anything. He could see it all when he got back off tour. At that point we were having the house in Blyth made bigger: we'd gone into the loft, we were having it extended from a two-bedroom bungalow to a five-bedroom house. So, me and Emily had to live with my dad in Dronfield while the work was being done. I said to my dad, "Look, I'll pay the phone bill because I'm going to be using it a lot to speak to John." For a quarter it was £1,300 and that's because John used to call me and reverse the charges. He would be so upset on the phone that I would have to talk to him for so long to make him feel OK because he was off on tour and he didn't want to be there. It would make him anxious thinking about having to go out on tour, it just made him anxious.'

The band supported New Order at this time for some festival dates, along with the Icelandic outfit Sugarcubes, which featured a young singer who would soon go on to receive wide acclaim as a solo artist, Björk. McGeoch would go on to collaborate with Sugarcubes on their 1992 album *Stick Around for Joy.* Of those gigs, New Order co-founder and bassist Peter Hook recalls, 'I remember the tour we did with PiL was pretty whacky, because supposedly they'd had to tell Johnny Rotten that PiL were actually the headline band but that they were going on before New Order. Of course, when Rotten got there, he was full-on Johnny Rotten. You'd be sat there with him and it would just be me and him and he'd be "Fucking this, fucking that, fucking cunt," and I'd be like, "John, will you give it a fucking rest, mate. It's just me and you!" He never fucking switched off and he was off his rocker. It was very difficult, so after being sober now I can empathise and sympathise, with somebody [McGeoch] trying to keep a handle on their drinking within that. It must have been fucking horrendous.

'I remember that we were quite ebullient, shall we say, especially our English road crew. PiL were wearing those ridiculous outfits, all that neon stuff which was a bit weird. We were the antithesis of it, we never dressed up and nobody knew who we were and nobody cared – they just loved the music. With them they were going through a difficult musical period, I'd say. The dress-up bit didn't quite feel right and I think McGeoch knew it. I think it rankled with him and I think he knew it was a bit stupid and he didn't like it. What that band must have gone through on that tour must have been really difficult.'

One incident in particular sticks out and caused a bit of tension between McGeoch and New Order at the time, as Hook relates: 'I remember one night which I felt really bad about. John was a strutter on the stage with PiL, always running around – you know, he really gave it his all. We got a load of banana skins and put the banana skins on his foot pedals as a joke and, fuck me, he went fucking berserk! He just did not appreciate it at all – you know when you do something as a gag and you think, "Oh, my God, I've caught him at a really bad time." Fuck me, did it backfire! It was my idea as well, you know, I thought they'd laugh. We'd definitely caught him at a bad time, and I felt really bad and regretted it immensely, I must admit. So, we sort of fell out for a while.'

Allan Dias recognises why success was perhaps easier to find in America than in the UK. 'PiL did well in America because we brought the right music. We brought a music that the kids would love. Still to this day I meet people who are like, "Man, I saw PiL down in Florida when I was 13 years old!" Moving forward it was about trying to gain exposure in America. We opened for INXS in '88, they were the big draw around that time. Michael Hutchence was a big fan of PiL and Lydon, so they invited us to do the tour. We went from doing theatres on our first couple of tours and then on to arenas, albeit opening for INXS. MTV was putting us on alternative rotation and an alternative night thing. That was back when MTV used to play music videos in the eighties, it was a big deal. We got big exposure. It was my first foray into being in a band playing these big venues. It was nice working with guys who'd been through that before and McGeoch really was a professional. He had that shit together. Basically, I just mirrored what he did! Stuff like how to move around on stage and entertain. I was used to playing small clubs and bars. Places like the Odeon and bigger venues, McGeoch had been there and done that, as had Lydon. I just learned a lot, it was a good time.'

Muzz remembers tensions that arose over the set list now that the band had put out *Happy?* and *9*. 'There was always a bit of a struggle because the band wanted to play the songs that they'd helped write. There were a whole two albums' worth of songs and they wanted to play more of those and less of the older songs that they weren't party to. McGeoch used to pastiche it up a bit on the Steve Vai songs, because Steve Vai is a big metal kind of player, really, and McGeoch would take the piss a bit. I think John played some fabulous guitar on those two records.'

As had been the case with the Banshees and, to some extent, Magazine, tensions within the group were brought to the fore much more on the road. Naturally, the bandmates were in each other's company a great deal more than would otherwise be the case and PiL were by now very much a heavy touring band in the true sense of the word. This was a very different animal from the band that the likes of Levene and Jah Wobble had helped get off the ground – unrecognisable, in fact. Lydon was at the peak of his carefully crafted stage persona. McGeoch had had to develop his own presence on stage, which was not something that came naturally to him, as Denise remembers. 'I remember Peter Mensch saying, "You've gotta throw shapes, you've gotta throw shapes!" because John would just stand there and play his guitar whereas the rock guys would be leaping about all over the place – "You've gotta throw shapes, man!" He wasn't a showman and he wasn't a businessman either, which is why he got ripped off a lot.'

Perhaps by this point John had taken his eye off the ball somewhat from a business perspective and was less bothered by it. He had never been full-blown greedy, but artistically at least, when he was at the height of his powers, he had spread himself pretty thin and taken on a lot of work outside the bands he was involved with at the time. He had enjoyed the trappings of success, but by now his priorities were quite different. His primary focus was elsewhere – back in Blyth with Denise and Emily. He loved recording, he loved to be creative and he was never shy in pushing for the music to go in the direction he felt was best for the band and the best showcase for his abilities. That being what it was, he was getting older (although still relatively young in terms of being a successful working musician) and most of his habits had changed. Drinking was still haunting him, though at home it was generally manageable and didn't impede on his family responsibilities.

It was on the road that his old demons of hard drinking and bouts of aggression tended to reappear. Out of frustration, out of dependency. The road was a lonely place for the John McGeoch of the late eighties and early nineties. As had been the case with the Banshees, John wasn't alone in his addictions. Both Lydon and Dias were prone to excess, and in Allan's case this was heading towards something akin to what had done for McGeoch all those years ago in Madrid.

Dias looks back on the effect the drinking had, but also on the power of those performances when it all came together. 'It got a little crazy at times, for all of us. Drinking on stage, being sloppy, missing cues. Bruce didn't like that. Listen, when you work with John Lydon you never know when he's going to come in. It's not like verse, chorus, verse, chorus. We used to have to play, with me looking at McGeoch, with Bruce looking at both of us, and listening to Lydon wondering and waiting for him to come in with the verse or the chorus or just space out and not fully knowing what he's going to do. So, Bruce would come in with the downbeat and then Lydon would hit the lyric and McGeoch and me would come in. Literally, you had to be that quick. We got to be great listeners. When you're in a band you get familiar with what people are going to do. This is especially true when you are playing gigs night after night and you can anticipate. Lydon would be dancing about and spinning round and that meant we never really played the songs the same way twice. McGeoch and I, at first we would just look at each other and I would be stage left and he'd be stage right and we're both at the front with Lydon in the middle and we're looking to see if he's going to come in with the change. It's funny, but that's how good a musician McGeoch was, and I mean he wasn't a jazz player or anything but he could anticipate and you couldn't throw him off. He knew when to hold back or come in. We developed that feel as a band and got good at what we did and we had some amazing gigs. I mean, imagine playing "Holidays in the Sun" in Berlin in a circus tent that was just a stone's throw from the wall just before it came down! Dude, it was spiritual. Kids were crying in the audience, it was magic. Now you're talking about the power of music.'

The heavy schedule was one thing, but decisions surrounding the making of McGeoch's third album with the band would bring tensions to the surface. These would culminate in the complete collapse of PiL.

Trigger picks up the story: 'There was one period, which was in 1991 when John's daughter, Emily, would have been about 2 years old. Basically, the band were due to record an album. Now historically, and this was certainly the case for all the time I'd been around, they'd always recorded in the UK for various different reasons, be it costs, producers or whatever. Suddenly, in 1991, John Lydon decided he wanted to make a record in America and what that meant was basically a minimum four, five or six months away from home because in those days it was old school, it was pre-digital and it was residential. John [McGeoch] was living at home and he was flying out there and the band was flying out. Just before John was due to go he lost his licence – he got done for drink-driving. So, there was a major "Shit, what are we going to do?" situation. So, I was then asked if I could fly out to America and basically live out there for six months with John.

'In LA if you haven't got a car you can't make a record, basically. So, we did. John's daughter was 2 and my wife was pregnant, as luck would have it. So, the pair of us went out there. Neither of us wanted to be there – John wanted to be home desperately, he was missing his daughter and Denise, and I didn't want to be there because my wife was pregnant. We shared an apartment in Santa Monica on the beach for six months and we just recognised that we had to get through it and that it wasn't going to be easy. We'd be in the studio a good four or five days a week, and then every now and again John Lydon would decide he didn't want to work for a week, which was adding to the pressure, given we didn't want to be over there anyway. We joined Gold's Gym, which was McGeoch's idea – the Schwarzenegger gym – and went bodybuilding three times a week. John bought two mountain bikes, so we had a bike each and used to go up the highway on the Pacific coast. We looked after each other – we were like the odd couple! Finally, we got the job done and flew home, but yeah, it was a big period for both of us and sadly it was when it all started to fall apart thereafter, really.'

There was a simmering resentment from McGeoch towards Lydon. Both were formidable characters with strong opinions and at times the tensions could bubble over into rows. Perhaps McGeoch felt that he was being stifled, perhaps Lydon felt McGeoch was becoming too vocal. Allan Dias explores this further: 'There was an artistic battle going on in the band, definitely. Things could get tense. If McGeoch felt he wasn't being heard he might turn on Lydon, but it was out of frustration more than anything else. There were lots of ideas floating around for songs and naturally if you think it is for the benefit of the album then you want it to be heard. McGeoch could tell John Lydon to "Fuck off and go write some real lyrics – you're a man of a million words." McGeoch would be the only one who could say that to his face because it would be a case of, "What you going to do about it?" I couldn't say that! I mean I could infer that or I could support McGeoch, but I don't think I was ever able to get to Lydon like that. For the most part I would always support McGeoch with his ideas because it was for the greater good. You see, McGeoch knew how to push Lydon's buttons and he had the strength of character to be convincing about it and not take any shit.

'We all knew that without John Lydon there was no PiL but at the same time we were equal partners and had to be up to the task. It was a great dynamic and it shows in the music. Whether it be something like "Warrior", or with Bruce and Lu, we had this EPC drum machine when it came out and Bruce figured out this beat and then McGeoch had these chords and it became like this tribal thing. The bass was easy because McGeoch just had these abrasive chords that were like fire and intense and we were just like, "What!" You know it became a big hit and then it was in the Billboard dance chart with a remix by Dave Dorrell. McGeoch had that kind of versatility, ear and emotional connection to be able to express himself like that. Big chords, dreamy and airy kind of lush stuff without sounding like he was trying to imitate something.'

There were frustrations among the band, but it's hard to lay the blame for what was unfolding solely on Lydon. He had come from the shadows, a part of London that wasn't on the tourist itinerary. He'd had a tough, solidly working-class upbringing, overcome meningitis and the loss of his memory as a child and been propelled to fame and notoriety at a young age with the Pistols. One can assume he had built a shield for himself, in many ways through necessity. His turbulent time with the Pistols and the fallout with record labels and management had fuelled the Rotten 'caricature'. Lydon has never been an easy character to properly get a handle on, certainly from an outsider's perspective. I'm sure he wouldn't have it any other way.

For all their differences it is clear McGeoch respected Lydon's talent as a lyricist and performer – he loved PiL and always had. From the very start of PiL it had always been about Lydon. The press wanted their piece, the videos were focused on him and the band were considered by many as nothing more than Johnny Rotten's backing group. Few had any understanding of the dynamics that went into creating those records or of how crucial all the members of the band were. McGeoch in particular was the musical heart of the group.

As Dias sees it, 'Lydon, Bruce, Lu, they all brought [something] to PiL and everyone accepted me for what I brought to the table, but I'm telling you, without John McGeoch that version of PiL would never have sounded the same. I like what they're doing now with Lu and Bruce but John McGeoch pushed PiL forwards musically and commercially and he understood stadium rock, that concept which you could say is bullshit or sell-out. No, dude, to move big crowds – that's not easy.'

McGeoch still admired Lydon, still wanted to make music with him but without the drama. He wanted to go in, get the job done and spend as much time as he could with those he cared about most. For all his success, he was happiest in his pack, be that family or his network of close friends. For John there was a very definite line: there was family and there was music, and unless he was working in his home studio he rarely, if ever, just picked up his guitars. Time was too precious for that and he was keen to get the work–life balance right. He also recognised that music or the pressures associated with it brought out a side of him that he was wary of, the lifestyle of being on the road or in a studio setting tending to lead to excessive drinking.

That What Is Not was released by Virgin on 24 February 1992 and climbed to number 46 in the charts. The album had been produced by Dave Jerden and co-produced by the band themselves. The only single to come out of it was 'Cruel', which features some of John's best playing with the band, as described by Lu Edmonds. 'McGeoch loved being in PiL and he was flipping amazing. The sound he got and the way he played and the parts he came up with. You know, we recently did a version of "Cruel" and I'd listened to it about eight years ago and thought, "Nah, I can't do that" – it just seemed too difficult. Then I listened more carefully and I thought, "Ah, I see how he's done it," and it's really clever. He was a really intelligent player and he was good at playing by himself using delay pedals and effects.'

Trigger has particular memories of the time they spent sharing an apartment while working on *That What Is Not*, not least disputes over the choice of radio station! 'There were certain peculiarities about John. Anybody you speak to will say that he was *the* post-punk guitarist. He had his influences and he loved rock music, he loved big guitars. I was a punk rocker, that was my thing, but John loved the rock guitar sound. When we were in America he'd always have KROQ on the radio blasting out and I'd be like, "For fuck's sake, John," and he'd say, "Shut up and listen, you might learn something." He adored the big guitar solos, the big arena rock sound which I hated. If it was metal, whatever, he loved the guitar and the largesse of it. He loved Steve Jones, who was basically a heavy metal guitarist, which I didn't know at the time. He used to force me to listen to this stuff. He used to say, "Look, I pay your wages. You're driving, put KROQ on!" And it was so funny because we used to have these arguments and trade-offs.'

This love of the big show and the arena rock shtick carried on back in the UK as Trigger remembers of one particular occasion. 'He rang me up one day and said, "I need you to come up at the weekend, I've got some work for you." This would have been in the early nineties, and so I asked what it was and it was a ruse, basically. What it was, Def Leppard were playing the Sheffield Arena and his wife Denise was the childhood sweetheart of Joe Elliott. So, there was a big connection from the advent of Def Leppard – she'd sold the T-shirts and she'd run the fan club. They were still massive friends and John loved all that because Def Leppard were the biggest band, possibly, on the planet. To me it was hell! Def Leppard? I'd rather die! So, I went up and brought some of his guitars and amps and a bit of nonsense. When I went up I would stay the night and he said, "Oh, really good timing. Guess what? Just by pure chance Def Leppard are playing." I said, "John, I'm not going to that," and he said, "Oh, but I've got you tickets." I said, "John, I am *not* going to that!" and he said, "Who pays your wages?" So, I'm like, "OK, we'll go." So, he basically forced me to go, but in fairness we had a really good night, we had backstage passes and hung out with [tour manager] Ivan Kushlick and got all the treatment and met the band. See, John loved all that arena stuff, he was just so happy to be there. Where I was like, "John, *please* for the love of God!" and he's just saying, "No, come on. You've got to learn!" We had that all the time I knew him. John adored guitars and that's how he learned.'

PiL took to the road again in what would prove to be McGeoch's swansong with the group. It would also see Allan Dias drop out due to the stress of touring and mounting addictions. The tour kicked off in Tampa, Florida on 13 March 1992 and finished in Buffalo, New York State on 18 September of the same year. The band took in some large festival dates, not least Reading, the same year as Nirvana performed their now legendary set. A couple of the UK dates were cancelled or simply not booked, despite having been scheduled.

Muzz remembers his last time on the road with the band, and how McGeoch was feeling about the set-up at the time. 'The last gig I did with PiL would have been Alton Towers that James headlined and PiL were the support. It had all started to fall apart a bit by then as Bruce Smith had left and Mike Joyce had joined. I think by that point McGeoch was feeling a bit deflated with it and thought that it had all gone a bit crap. They'd made another album that none of them had liked.'

By now, however, his anxieties about touring were all-consuming. For weeks leading up to the start of a tour these feelings would torment him and the separation anxiety while away from home would fuel his drinking. It was his escape from the reality of being thousands of miles from home, of being stuck with a lead singer who he was finding increasingly difficult and irksome. There was also a sense of frustration that he hadn't found the spark that he'd had with the Banshees, and the fact that times had moved on. The music scene had been forever changed by the advent of rave culture, and the guitar music of the day was the sound of Seattle. McGeoch and PiL just weren't on the cutting edge any more. John was all in for creativity, for being enthusiastic about what you're doing, but the truth is the band were coming to the end of the road. It was more about sticking with it out of a sense of duty and keeping a steady income coming in; given the less than spectacular record sales, the bulk would be earned through touring.

Nobody wanted PiL by 1992. How cruelly that would be demonstrated, as Trigger explains: 'I remember the last PiL gig in America in 1992 and we flew back to the UK. None of us could have guessed what was going to happen and that it was all over, and I'd say it took a good year before it all came crashing down. I'm not in the business of contradicting anybody else and I've not read what Lydon has said, because my relationship with John Lydon was very different to my relationship with John McGeoch. I don't have a problem with John Lydon and I don't believe John Lydon has a problem with me, I hope not. Lydon is very good at rewriting history because he's John Lydon. Because John Lydon says something, people believe it and that was part of the problem between him and John McGeoch. John McGeoch was a genius guitarist and a beautiful man and, in his own right, a legend. John Lydon always had to be in charge because of who he was, which is fair enough and I get that, but it was difficult for McGeoch because Lydon didn't see it the other way round, where McGeoch just wanted to be himself and get on with his life, and he used to get a bit beaten up by it. I have on occasion read the odd thing that Lydon has said, and they are very much as John Lydon saw it.

'Now, what happened with PiL is very simple. In the period I worked for Public Image there were three different management teams involved. When I first started there was a London-based management called Heavenly Management. Very early on, probably as early as 1988, they were fired and Lydon took on American management and brought in a guy called Danny Heaps. Danny managed the band for a couple of years and that was why I got the job in London to take care of UK stuff. Danny Heaps got fired and somebody by the name of Bill Diggins came in. I won't say too much about Bill, but it didn't work out. So, in 1992, the last album that McGeoch was on, the one we'd made in America, was called *That What Is Not*. We came back from America in the summer of 1991, toured throughout that summer and toured throughout '92. Then Virgin Records, who Lydon was signed to, decided to sell in 1992 to EMI. Suddenly it was all looking pretty rocky. We'd toured the full cycle of the previous album and what needed to happen was to make a new album and sadly there was no label.

'Obviously McGeoch and myself were in contact the whole time. John was doing his session work, but the other thing that was happening at the time, and this was very sad for John, was people didn't want guitarists any more. The early nineties was the advent of dance music. The world changed, people discovered ecstasy and the world changed. What was happening in Britain in the nineties meant there wasn't the requirement for John McGeoch to do sessions. Suddenly, as a band member, McGeoch didn't have a label and also nobody wanted him as a session player, so he was in a really bad place. Eventually, probably late '92, I'd had to take other work as the American management had said we can't keep on paying you if we don't have a deal. So, my job was surplus and I just got a phone call one day saying, "Really sorry, Phil, but we can't employ you any more."

'I got this phone call from John McGeoch one day and he was heartbroken, he was absolutely fucking heartbroken, because somebody, and I can't remember who, had offered John Lydon a deal and it didn't involve PiL. So, Bill Diggins had rung McGeoch up and said that he was going to come over to the UK to talk to him about what was going to be happening for the future. This guy flew over from America, got the train from King's Cross to Sheffield and John's wife drove them out to this little country pub in the middle of nowhere. This guy is from LA and doesn't know his arse from his elbow. So, they went to this country pub 20-odd miles from Dronfield and John's thinking, "Great, we're going to sit down and discuss the new deal." Obviously there would be an advance involved, so financially John is in trouble because they are waiting for the advance on the new record, but there is no advance. So, Bill Diggins tells him in this pub, "Really sorry, John, there is nothing out there for PiL at the moment and therefore John Lydon has had to sign a solo deal. Give it a couple of years and I'm sure we'll be able to sort something out for PiL."

'I remember John telling me, John being a martial arts expert, that "Two things crossed my mind. One: I could take him out in the car park and kill him. I'm just going to take him outside and end it. Then I thought that was probably not the best idea as there would be consequences." So, he just told the guy that he needed to use the toilet and he just left him sat there. Denise came and got him and they drove off leaving Bill Diggins sat at a table in a pub in the middle of farmland. That is what happened, and that conversation was the end of John McGeoch's career as a professional musician. You may hear other stories, but hand on heart that is what happened.'

Trigger expands on how John was crucial to creating a new sound for PiL: 'The thing with John is, if you gave him a guitar there was nothing he couldn't play. If you got him to listen to a song and said to him just play it, he would be note perfect on first listen. I'm not sure how common that is. I possibly underestimated that side of it. John wrote lots of the PiL stuff on piano. John was instrumental in the musicianship of the records. Lydon wrote and sang the lyrics but the music was coming through McGeoch. John would spend weeks after Lydon had done his bit and gone home, working with the producer and tweaking stuff. John McGeoch was the engine room and he never got the recognition for those PiL albums that he should have done. People always go on about his guitar work with the Banshees, but he never gets the same compliment for his work with Public Image.'

Paul Morley looks back on McGeoch's career post-Magazine and Banshees. 'The sad thing is that it became hard for John to find a place in the end. His sound and way of playing was so wrapped up in the moment of being in Magazine and then with Siouxsie. By the mid-eighties pop and rock is in a very different place, and even in PiL he's in a group who by that point aren't at the centre of attention that, in a way, Magazine or the Banshees would have been in his time with those bands. So, he's already drifting in a way by that point. It can get to the stage where it almost becomes that dreadful thing of being "the guitarist for hire", which must be soul destroying for someone like John. You don't want to take over or be the focal point, but also you don't want to feel you're just being used as a sort of convenience.

'It must have been very difficult for John that he couldn't really find a place into the eighties and nineties. Thinking about the way he played guitar – yes, he played guitar, but he played in such a way as to almost not make it sound like a guitar. He was trying to find detail, which is why I think he worked so well with Siouxsie, coming off her voice. It was abstract, it's not pedantic or colourless – it's incredibly mysterious and moving. If you don't have good collaborators, then it becomes very difficult to know where that works.

'You had this great period of time where so much changed and so much music happened and so many characters emerged. The fact that he worked with both Devoto and Siouxsie was incredibly apt – because before '75 and then after about '85 there would be no one around like that for John to attach to. Even Johnny Marr, to an extent, since leaving The Smiths has had difficulty finding a place and has had to go on a similar journey to John to try and find the right place, the right collaborators and moments to stop yourself from being that person that just plays the guitar – which is not necessarily what you thought you were doing, as strange as that sounds. Whilst they might not have been as obviously influential as The Smiths, in their own way they were – both Magazine and Siouxsie and the Banshees were giant groups in their way. Distinctive, unusual, epic and influential to groups like Radiohead and other groups of that era. It all comes from that world.

'After it, what happens to John? Howard becomes very reclusive. Siouxsie becomes a kind of icon. John becomes invisible in a way and he can't lift himself up again as he could in the seventies and eighties to be part of something, which I suppose is what you lose. You lose being a part of something. With Magazine and then with Siouxsie for a short while he was a part of something that seemed important. It was written about in a way that made it seem important. The artwork made it seem important. Siouxsie was a fantastic pop star. Devoto was a great enigma. It must have been amazing to be associated with all that. Then when that goes you definitely lose something. John was on a fabulous adventure when he was working with the best people that he worked with. They loved him because Howard, Siouxsie and Steven missed what he could bring and create when he was no longer there.'

So, with that, John's career with PiL was at an end. All the promise and all the hopes were dashed and John found himself with a family to support and without the security of a regular income or prospect of a new record to record and promote. It is unclear what was said between McGeoch and Lydon and if they ever spoke again; I can only assume they did and that it wasn't pleasant. It's likely that John felt let down by the whole experience. For all the dilemmas surrounding his personal problems when touring, for all his dependency issues and the frequent tensions between the two Johns, he had breathed new life into PiL, he had galvanised the band and Lydon especially. This was PiL as much in McGeoch's image as it was Lydon's, and now it was over. One of them had a deal and an immediate future and one of them didn't.

EIGHT

DIAMOND

John as the family man, and starting up his own group, Pacific

---

I paint, I write songs, I play guitar, but I can't sing. Oh, I can hold a note, but that doesn't make you a singer. There's a strong possibility I'll do a writing and producing project soon, but we'll see. I do write stuff that couldn't possibly be done by PiL, but so does Allan for that matter, and so does John! I really think of myself as a songwriter and not just the guitarist in the band – a noble profession though it is.

Guitarist magazine (April 1991)

THE PREVIOUS TEN years or so had seen John join and leave three bands, tour the world several times and even dabble with producing other artists. Marry and divorce, remarry and become a father – it had been quite the journey by any standard. Having recently found himself without a band in Public Image Ltd, it was back to the drawing board.

As Trigger explains, the messy end with the group and in particular its management had left a bitter taste, but John wasn't one to sit around feeling sorry for himself. 'John McGeoch was quite pragmatic about things, which is something he taught me. Sometimes you have to accept life on life's terms, there's no point carrying baggage with you. John was a great believer in facing facts. What is the situation today and what can I do to make the best of it? McGeoch was very stoic and didn't feel sorry for himself. He got on with the hand he was dealt, because he had to. Why did Public Image stop? [...] Its demise couldn't be landed at John McGeoch's door, sitting up in Dronfield minding his own business, waiting to make the next record while this useless American manager and Lydon tried to play politics with record companies. Which is why McGeoch was so incredulous at the time when Lydon took the band off the roster due to the EMI deal.

'I remember McGeoch saying, "What on earth is he doing?" Because he understood the industry, he knew how it worked and could see that the band weren't in a position to start dictating terms. He was mortified by it all at the time. Thing was, you had American management managing PiL but only ever listening to John Lydon. Both the American managers that I worked with, all they were ever interested in was John Lydon and getting him on TV. They didn't have the foggiest idea what they were dealing with in John McGeoch. They didn't have the history and, to be honest, John McGeoch was probably a bit of a hindrance to them because what they really wanted was John Lydon and *his* band and they got Lydon and McGeoch. They never knew how to handle him, they couldn't figure him out, and to them it was a case of why doesn't he just shut up, why is he speaking up, who's this guitarist with an opinion? Did the Banshees sell records in America, had Magazine been successful there? What I mean is, to any American manager you can see them looking at John Lydon and seeing the dollar signs chinking up. It was always constant attempts to get him on TV, to get him in films and that was their dream, but it never really happened. It's all very sad because, come 1992, the dominoes started to fall for John McGeoch.'

At the beginning of his time with PiL John had been moving on to new pastures in his personal life. Having met Denise, he knew, as did she, that this was the connection they'd both been waiting for. The great music John made, the amazing albums and the calibre of artists he worked with all paled into insignificance for him once he met Denise. It was as though all the previous hardship had led to that point over in Nerja, Spain. The couple had got married, in secret, on Denise's birthday – not a move that went down especially well with the families when it was announced after the fact, but they all got the chance to celebrate with the couple and wish them well.

Of all the many achievements and blessings in John's life, it was the birth of his daughter that brought him most satisfaction and completeness. Given his background of touring, excess and adulation it is almost hard to believe that McGeoch was a natural father – but he was. He took to fatherhood like a duck to water and revelled in the role, as Emily explains: 'I found a list he'd made of my first words and how I pronounced them all. He would send me things all the time, even when I was a baby and couldn't read, he'd send a postcard saying, "Here's a big hug from daddy," and I found a note the other day where he'd written, "Hi pumpkin, found this funny 50p in my change hope you like it?" and it was like a foreign coin, but he saw it and thought, "I'm going to post that to Em." We spoke every day on the phone, we spoke about everything.' After PiL John threw himself headlong into

John and Emily on holiday, 1992.
McGeoch family archive

domesticity, as Denise recalls: 'I remember once when it was Halloween, I'd gone to collect Emily from school, he'd completely transformed the living room into some kind of Halloween den! He'd made it all out of household items – he'd not been out and bought decorations. I remember a black rubber glove was part of it, like a spooky hand. Emily's jaw just dropped because it was so fantastic, but that was just him.'

The family had by this point moved from Blyth and were living in Denise's home town of Dronfield. He would return to London from time to time, meeting up with old friends and looking out for potential opportunities to get back into the saddle, musically. He had a clear idea of how he wanted to proceed, mainly as a studio artist playing one-off shows rather than full-blown tours.

Clive Farrington takes up the story of how he came to know John and eventually work with him: 'Andrew of our band, When in Rome, had been out, I think it was a Saturday night, and he came back to the studio with John Lydon and John McGeoch. So, I'm in awe of course, thinking, "Wow, here we are in my studio recording the album for When in Rome and these two superstars show up!" One of my favourite songs of all time is "Shot by Both Sides" – I wore the 7-inch out – and so meeting John was just a magical moment. Of course, they'd been out for the night and were therefore a little worse for wear, which meant we didn't really get talking about anything at that point. When in Rome went our separate ways in 1991; we'd lost the record deal, but Virgin had arranged a few dates for us over in Brazil in '92. So, when I got back I was looking for people to work with and then one day out of the blue McGeoch called me and said, "Would you like to put something together?" So, I started travelling to Dronfield, to the little studio he had in the house up there. We got to working together and things really sped up from there – this would have been around '94. I'd met this guy called Keith Lowndes down in London. I lived in Camden Town and there was this antique shop opposite me where Keith worked. He was very different, looked a bit quirky, and you could see that he was into music so we got working together and went up to Dronfield to make some tunes.'

By chance, on one of John's trips to the capital, he met up with an old acquaintance – Glenn Gregory of Heaven 17 fame. Glenn takes up the story: 'I hadn't seen him for ages and ages, and I just happened to go in a pub called the Lansdowne in Primrose Hill and he was sat there with a couple of guys I didn't know. One of the guys, Simon, lived just across the road from me but I had no idea what he did and it transpired he was kind of managing John, Clive Farrington and Keith Lowndes and we just drank and laughed and had a really good catch-up. Then a couple of weeks later I got a call saying, "John wants to meet you to talk about a few things," so we had a meeting and he said, "Look, we've got this thing going on, a new band, and we'd love you to come along and sing with us." So, that's how that started. Eighteen months of misadventure and excitement!'

Glenn had initially got to know McGeoch back in the early eighties at the start of the New Romantic period, as he explains: 'It was in the really early days of Heaven 17. I'd always been aware of his playing with Magazine and all of those things he did that came out of punk. So, I was always aware of John, his playing, and absolutely loved it. When Human League split and Martyn Ware and Ian Marsh formed B.E.F. and Heaven 17, one of the first things we did when they made the B.E.F. album *Music of Quality and Distinction*, which was all about working with the people you wanted to work with, John was one of the first people we thought of and it was a case of, "Let's get McGeoch in," and he did, which was just fantastic. That must have been in '81. Also, Human League had toured with the Banshees prior to that. We retained a loose connection after that. You know, we didn't see each other often but you'd bump into him at bars or parties and he was always an absolute pleasure, a total fucking giggle whenever you did hook up with him. He was such a funny guy, great sense of humour. He was really sharp and quite caustic as well, and not afraid to speak his mind to anyone.'

John had been doing bits and bobs since PiL, the odd bit of session work, but nowhere near the volume of his busy schedule of the eighties. Effectively, he had become something of a house husband for the past couple of years, devoted to spending as much time with Emily as possible. He'd also been incredibly supportive of Denise as she sought to further her own career. 'He had an aptitude to be extremely intuitive and caring. When we were together, I did a diploma in clinical hypnosis and he was incredibly supportive of me doing that.

I would have to go to Manchester every weekend to do the studying and he would just stay at home with Emily. I would be gone long days; Emily would be more or less in bed by the time I got home and that went on for nearly two years. Once I'd actually got my diploma I then started working for the college where I had studied and that then involved me having to go away on the weekends as well and he was very supportive.'

John certainly was intuitive and recognised that for Denise, as with Janet before, there are big sacrifices that have to be made in being the partner of a successful musician. This was the time he could give back, while fulfilling a role at home which suited him down to the ground. Denise believes that nurturing side of him was a trait inherited from his father: 'John was an exceptionally giving person. He was that way with everybody, unless someone had done him wrong or been unkind, but generally he was very generous with his time, emotions, an ear. I think he is a credit to his parents. His father passed away thirty years ago and that actually happened in our house – it was pretty traumatic. Emily was nearly 2 at the time, his parents had come to stay and his father suffered a heart attack in the night in his sleep. That was traumatic for John, who had tried to do CPR on him, but the heart attack was just too massive. His father had had a heart problem, either a double or triple bypass in his late thirties, and he couldn't work after that. So, the roles were reversed where his dad stayed at home and John's mum went out to work. John's dad was a very, very caring person. Very quiet, very giving of his time and his energies and I think that's where John got it from. I believe John observed his father being very doting and attentive to his mother and he thought that was good and right, and it is how John was with me and no doubt with Janet as well.'

John's upbringing had been so crucial in his development as a child and into adolescence and adulthood. His parents had always been encouraging of both their sons' pursuits and offered them the best opportunities in life that they could. John's youth wasn't a story of neglect or feeling alienated. He'd always had a strong bond with his parents and was, in many ways, a reflection of them. He had the caring side of his father and the high intellect of his mother, Annie, as Denise explains: 'John got a lot of his intelligence from his mother, who was in MENSA and is exceptionally bright. He was softly spoken, he was intelligent and he had the advantage of having words and being able to use those words effectively. He learned that from his mother. His mother is everybody's friend, but she will take no shit and she will tell somebody if they are out of line. She won't tell somebody nastily or aggressively; she'll tell them so everybody can hear and then they know: you don't mess about with Granny Annie.'

John, Clive and Glenn pressed on with their new project, entitled Pacific, and were joined by John Keeble and Keith Lowndes, who had been introduced to John by Clive. Glenn has his own memories of working with McGeoch up in Dronfield: 'He was living in Dronfield with Emily and his missus and their big fucking boxer dog called Ronson. They had a house that backed on to the woods, a really nice, steep hill, then there was a studio in the basement. It was one of those houses that from the outside looked like it was all one floor, but at the back it was like three or four floors – it went down and that's where he had a 24-track studio. That's where we used to do our work and I'd come up from London and pick Keith up from Camden, drive up and we'd stay for a week. Most of the time I'd stay at my mum's over in Sheffield, which was only a twenty-five-minute drive from John's place, but occasionally if we worked really late I'd just sleep on the sofa. That bloody dog Ronson would lay on you and try and sleep with you and he had the smelliest breath and the stinkiest farts! I would be like, "Oh Ronson, will you fuck off!" and McGeoch loved it. I'd wake up in the morning and he'd be sat in the chair laughing, with this dog sprawled all over me.'

John was still going through his battles with drink and this would lead to him becoming frustrated, in the main, with himself. He knew what he was capable of producing but the alcohol hindered that, as Glenn recalls: 'The songs were good actually, but nothing ever came out. It was a weird time really because, sadly, John was drinking heavily at that point and it was a bit of a tightrope working there, but interesting and I loved it. He was very serious about his work and it had to be right. So, I think that was what annoyed him when he'd be drunk because he just couldn't play the way he wanted to play. John liked to work late through the night and sometimes he'd just be laid down flat spending a couple of hours trying to get this guitar part right, and it probably was right 70 per cent of the time, but not right enough for him, if you know what I mean.'

John ran the project, and the house, almost like a musical B & B – when they weren't busy working on material or crashing out with dogs etc., he would be rustling up some delight in the kitchen – conventional or otherwise, as Denise explains: 'He was a morning person where I am a night owl; he would leave me and Emily to do what we would do in the morning. He would be up with the larks, out picking mushrooms – he had a whole book on mushrooms and how to pick spores from them, which he taught me. He would love to go out foraging to see what he could find and cook with it. The worst thing he ever put on the table was when we had the guys who were using the studio [Pacific] round and he'd cooked chicken's feet! We all just looked at them and said, "Well, that's great and you're sterling for doing it but there's nothing to eat there… it's just a foot!"' Glenn remembers being presented with the feet: 'He was quite the chef! I never did eat those chicken feet he cooked. He was desperately trying to make me eat them and I was like, "John, I don't want to eat fucking chicken's feet! Stop it!" and he was sat there sucking away on them and saying, "Oh, they're really good. Just try one!" Yeah, he was a good cook and it was really strange because for the eighteen months or however long it was we were doing that, it kind of got into the routine of being in the studio and working away then he'd go upstairs to spend time with Emily and Denise and he'd make a lovely meal. We'd all go and sit upstairs and have dinner together, but the strangest thing was he'd never eat the dinner. He'd always leave and go back into the studio and start working on something.'

The arduous nature of recording and coming up with material was broken up by the antics and humour that John was renowned for, as Glenn recalls: 'We had such fun and such a laugh. One of the funniest sights and memories I have of anybody ever was when Keith and I were in the studio working and the blinds were closed. It was winter and there was deep snow on the ground. At a lull in the music I heard this cracking noise and thought, "What the fuck's that?" split the blind to have a look and John was naked in the garden with a bull whip, whipping the snow from the top of a bird-feeding station! Hilarious, and I still laugh about it now. He was such fun, he really was.'

Emily recalls just how much her dad loved the winter, and snow especially: 'He loved the weather. Looking at the snow reminds me of him, because he was completely obsessed by it. He'd be like, "Right, it's snowed, let's go out in our pyjamas and roll about in it!" That's the kind of person I remember, that taught me to read, taught me to ride a bike and roll about in the snow in his pyjamas with me!' Here was a man equally, if not more so, enthralled by the natural world and all its wild beauty and idiosyncrasies as he was by making music. Nothing was quite as awe inspiring to him as the intricate beauty of flowers, as Denise remembers: 'He was always taking pictures of flowers. He just thought nature, and flowers in particular, were just so perfect. That house we had in Blyth, the garden was about a quarter of an acre and it really was a garden-garden. It had been properly planted and he'd just go round all day taking pictures. Emily would say as she got older, "Oh, here's another picture of flowers that my dad took!"'

Nature was a major inspiration, not just for his photography but for his painting. He'd never lost his passion for creating art and, if anything, in the time since he'd been largely at home, he'd been able to devote far more time to it again. One of the most striking discoveries I've made in the course of writing this book is that music may not have been John's truest passion. It certainly wasn't his healthiest pursuit. Yet it was his calling, and the art form in which he created the pieces for which we admire and respect him so.

As Denise reflects: 'I could probably go as far as to say he fell into the music business, even though he was very good at it. He was young so he liked the lifestyle at that particular time, [but] it wasn't him as a person and it didn't suit him. I think that is where the monkey on his back came in with alcohol, because that was his way of dealing with feeling uncomfortable in that environment.' A sentiment shared by Emily when she looks back on who her dad was away from the stage. 'My dad was never about the fame and would have rather not had to deal with that side of it. If he could have been a creative musician and spread his art and his music worldwide without anyone knowing who he was, I think he would have probably preferred that. At first, I'm sure, he was into the attention but later on I think he would have preferred a quieter life. He did suffer with nerves and anxiety about performing and especially touring. He was always tinkering about in the studio, which may be why he did the session work, although I wouldn't want to speak for him. I definitely feel he would rather have not had to be out on the road and therefore he wasn't pushy with it. He would go on TV shows and find that he would be the one talking, because he was eloquent and had a lot to say.'

The question of what an artist has to give up, or give of themselves, on the path to success is an interesting one. Will it wear you down? How many low points will there be? McGeoch had his fair share of the latter. The path had probably been its healthiest for him within Magazine. By the time of Visage and then through the Banshees and finally with PiL, the success had turned to pressure, the pressure to addiction and a fragility that was only ever masked by the use of substances that don't really help, and so the cycle continued. McGeoch was a misunderstood man, contradictory and complex in many ways. His success paved the way for his own downfall. On the road, McGeoch was fun, confident, brilliant, confrontational and larger than life. Away from that environment he was kind, funny, highly intelligent, loving, sometimes a little gruff, but gripped by insecurities. Insecurity and creativity seem to go hand in hand – at that level of extraordinary and unique achievement there will always be those nagging doubts.

Denise expands on this when she says, 'John hasn't been credited for loads of work that he did. He was such a giving person that he would do work for people and not be credited for it. He didn't know how, or rather he didn't have that in him to go, "Well I did that, so I'm going to get something for that." He would just say, "Oh well, whatever. If that's so important to them." He wouldn't push himself forward and in a lot of ways if you were looking at John as an individual from a therapy point of view, you could say, "He's got low self-esteem, that guy." I know that he may have appeared like that in some areas and to some people, but when I was doing that hypnotherapy course he and I did a little psychological test, which I can't remember exactly, but it involved going into your mind and thinking about the contents of three different boxes. It was roughly along the lines of what's the picture on the first box you see, which represented what you portray to the outside world and what you want people to see. The second box was a bit smaller and was all about your defences, and then the small box in the very centre was how you feel about yourself, actually, and I remember his little box in the centre – what he really, really thought of himself – was a diamond. So, he knew what he was.'

Pacific struggled to get any traction but they did play one gig down in Soho at Madame Jojo's, as Clive relates. 'McGeoch and John Keeble were so loud! It was funny because when Keeble was in Spandau Ballet he was very subdued and restrained, but when he was playing with us in Pacific, he was using these sticks that were like batons, the kind of thing you'd run with! He'd play loud and John McGeoch would have to play even louder to be heard over him and so for a singer that was just impossible, so I think the Madame Jojo's gig was a John Keeble–John McGeoch battle for who was the loudest. Not that I complained; I was just delighted to be on stage with them. One of the reasons I wasn't too disappointed to not carry on, certainly from a gigging perspective, was John Keeble's drum kit was so heavy. We had to cart it all up the stairs and of course we didn't have or couldn't afford roadies, so I'd had enough of it by the first gig. It was like carrying half a car! Then it took about three hours to set up and soundcheck. I think it was worthwhile, even if it was just [to say] Pacific at least did that one gig. I ended up with a sore throat at the end of it.'

Glenn Gregory adds, 'I've blanked the gig out! It was quite a frustrating time because the guy who was managing us, there was all that promise and there were going to be deals and big gigs. It just never came off. John got very angry with me when I said I wasn't going to do it any more. It was the only time we fell out, really, when I told him over the phone. I just said to him, "Look, I'm really sorry, John, but I feel as though we've given it as much as we can, really, and it's just not going anywhere," and he was pissed off, but it had to end, you know, it just wasn't conducive. I think John recognised that deep down and he did call me back and say, "Look, you're probably right," although after calling me back and saying all that he did say, "Are you sure you don't want to try a bit longer?" and I said, "John, you've phoned to say you agree with me and now you're telling me you want to start again!" God, he was a really talented guitarist and a talented guy, writer and, you know, a lovely man. I would have loved it to work, I really would, because to have been part of something with John was a pleasure and an honour, but it would have been even better had we been able to get it off the ground.'

Clive admits that for a variety of reasons the project ran its course. 'I think we all just got pissed off with each other, to be honest! We'd all spent so much time together by then. It was a shame it never came to anything. I think we were a bit of a gamble for record companies, not that we didn't try – we did approach people but maybe by the mid-nineties it was a little bit past its sell-by date.'

Despite Pacific not working out, Clive and Glenn have cherished memories of that time. Far from it being about a failure to form a successful group or John's own battles with his demons, it is the sense of fun that they remember most. Glenn says, 'This is just so typical John McGeoch. We used to go clay-pigeon shooting – it was something John really liked to do. So, he had a couple of shotguns and we'd go shooting just outside Dronfield and we'd be driving back and he'd say, "Anybody fancy a pint?" So, we'd be like, "Yeah, go on then," and if you're carrying guns with you you're supposed to have it all locked up and you're not supposed to just leave them lying about. John used to leave them on the back seat of the car! Then we'd go and get completely pissed in the pub. He was just so funny, honestly. I'd say to him, "John, you can't just leave your guns there," and he'd be all, "Ah, it'll be all right! Everybody knows me around here, come on!" A real character.'

Denise recalls a particular incident that left John, with all his experience on the road, feeling shocked and disgusted. 'We once went to Twickenham to see a relative of mine playing rugby. After the game we went back to the players' lounge where the families gather, but John was absolutely horrified that the men had to go and eat in one room and the women were in another room. He couldn't abide not being with me, so for him it was absolutely abhorrent that the women and the men were separated. When he came out of that meal, he just said, "I've seen some things in my time, but I've not seen anything or experienced anything like that." He told me that the wine bottles were on the table and when the bottle was empty one of the players would urinate in it and put it on the table. He thought he'd seen it all but obviously not – rugby players far exceed rock bands in antics! He found all that kind of behaviour absolutely disgusting.'

John wasn't the typical 'bloke' in that sense – sport didn't interest him at all, although jokingly Michael Jobson does say that, put under pressure and with a few jars inside him, he had a slight allegiance to the blue half of Glasgow. 'John was a Rangers fan. He's from Greenock, so really that's Morton [FC]. He would say, "Nah, I'm not interested in all that shite." All that sectarian rubbish he wasn't into it, you know, but if you got down to it, with a few drinks it all comes out. You can always find the Hun in a Hun!'

Throughout the years, John had always gelled best with the people on the fringes of the industry. His friendships with Trigger and Muzz were not the exception, as Emily confirms. 'Dad preferred those people [road crew]. You know, when it comes to the industry, he wasn't best mates with the lead singers. It was the people in the background that Dad was closest to and whose company he enjoyed. So, when crew talk fondly about him and their relationship with him, I can say it was mutual. That's how he was.'

No doubt the failure of Pacific to progress would have hurt John who, inwardly at least, harboured hopes that PiL might soon resume. As Trigger remembers, it was the paucity of John's other projects that cut deepest. 'The real tragedy was that the session work dried up, because from his days with Magazine right through to PiL he'd always featured on lots of records. He had his own publishing deal with Chrysalis. Quite often he'd ring me up and we'd go off somewhere and do a session and he'd hand me an envelope with cash in – he looked after me like that. It all ended, which was so sad for John.'

John returned to something he had dabbled in prior to studying in Manchester, all those years ago in Goodmayes. He began working in care and trained to become a qualified nurse, supporting and caring for the elderly and in particular those affected by Alzheimer's. Sadly, by now John and Denise were starting to drift apart. John's frustration with the end of PiL, the failure to get Pacific off the ground and the general pressures of everyday life had all placed too much of a burden on the couple. Denise would have loved it to have been different, but by then it really was beyond salvaging. Naturally her first priority was to do what would be best for Emily in the long run. John struggled to accept that the relationship was over and did what he could to prolong the inevitable, as Denise explains: 'We sold the house in Dronfield in

'96 and I moved with Emily to Sheffield. John began doing nursing in Sheffield around that time because he didn't want the break-up, so he stayed in Sheffield, I think, in the hope that we would get back together. He got a job in a care home and I think that is where the nursing side of it started. John was such a caring person that that kind of profession actually suited him better.' She elaborates on how the work at the home impacted on John emotionally: 'He was a hit with the ladies in the care home. I think they loved him because he was gentle and he was softly spoken as well – there was nothing abrasive about him. He had a gentle touch, a gentle voice, just gentle everything. So, they all loved him and I remember him once saying, "It's a bit tricky because some of them are going on about being showered in cold water and it not being nice and they like me showering them because I don't do that." He would cry at things like that, it would really upset him.'

John didn't stay in Sheffield long and, before the year was out, he called on an old friend to come and bring him back down to London, as Trigger recalls: 'He rang me one day and he was in trouble and said could I drive up north because he was leaving Denise. So, I picked up a Luton transit van and drove up the motorway and brought him back to London. I put all of his gold discs and everything he owned, really, in some really obscure, poxy garage in Hammersmith.' Denise remembers the final words he said to her before leaving: 'He was a very loving husband and a very loving father. He was devastated when we split up and his parting words were, "You'll never find someone who loves you as much as I do."'

NINE

HEAVENS INSIDE
John's later years and untimely death

I've been playing the guitar for twenty years, and now it's really down to 99% perspiration and 1% inspiration; you pick up the guitar and it's very hard to come up with something you've never heard before.

Guitarist magazine (April 1991)

JOHN MCGEOCH WAS back in London, under very different circumstances and without a clear direction. His life had spiralled down, and he was having to start all over again at the age of 41. All the accolades, all the former glories weren't going to help him. His first priority was to organise some accommodation, as Clive Farrington recalls. 'He ended up moving down to Hammersmith in London. I actually shared a houseboat with him, living on a barge opposite the Blue Anchor pub. I forget where we'd got the connection to rent this barge, but we were living on there, opposite the Blue Anchor, which of course is where the film *Withnail and I* was set, just by Hammersmith Bridge. That was when I'd met him again after the whole Pacific thing. I was going through a break-up with a girlfriend and he'd moved away from Dronfield and Denise, so we were both going through a split and kept each other company.'

Around this time he connected with an old friend, Sophie Skinner, who had known John ever since he first moved down to London with Janet, shortly after Magazine had taken off. Denise reflects on what she knew of John's time in London and his relationship with Sophie. 'I didn't see him as John the guitarist in whatever band, I saw him as John my husband and Emily's father. I didn't look at him as a musician, really, whereas I think Sophie did. I think John and Sophie had got history going before me – she'd been around a long time. She absolutely idolised him and loved him and she was always there. I didn't really know that until later on. They had stayed in contact, sending birthday and Christmas cards. Then when John and I drifted apart I know now that they were in touch and he would be on the phone to her a lot, so it didn't surprise me that they got together when he moved to London.'

Once John had established himself in his new surroundings, which he did quickly – resourceful as ever – Emily remembers the regular visits down south and the work her dad took on. 'He'd trained to be a nurse, and when him and my mum had separated, he did some nursing work in Sheffield. Then when he moved to Hammersmith in London he did some nursing work there, but he also worked for the London hospitals delivering blood. He did that both on a bike and in his car for quite a while. He did some more nursing work while still doing bits of session work and writing [music] for TV. He did a lot of stuff for televised rugby, which may have been the World Cup. When he worked at the nursing home, he used to take me in with him when they did craft days and they all loved him. He was a very sensitive soul and as he would make friends with the people in the home that he was caring for, when they would die it was really hard for him – which I think is the main reason he left nursing, because he couldn't really cope with it. Sophie and my dad had a houseboat on the Thames, which as you can imagine was pretty small. Sophie also had a one-bed flat in Hammersmith, so that's where they lived. They just did what they did, without a big fuss.'

For John now, as ever, his primary focus was Emily and ensuring that despite not living close by, their relationship suffered as little as possible. Denise made every effort to bring Emily down to London, so that she got to spend that important time with her father. 'I used to take Emily down to London once a month and I would stay with my friend Su. Emily would spend the weekend with her dad and Sophie and then I would drive back with her. That went on until about 2000 when I had my son, and at that point it just wasn't feasible to be going up and down the motorway.'

Emily remembers the time spent with her dad in London. 'In Hammersmith I mainly slept at the flat, but I also loved sleepovers on Dad's houseboat, it was like a mini adventure. When the tide was in we would do "fishing" from the front of the boat. Obviously in the Thames you would collect all sorts of stuff, there would be different bottle tops, ropes, feathers, crab claws, and once we fished out two live crabs, so we went and got a tank for them and they lived on the balcony of his flat! Now when the tide was out, that was metal detector time. Dad got me this cool little metal detector and we would walk for ages finding old pottery, coins, keys and, weirdly, a lot of shoes. One time we even found a dead octopus! Looking back, it was probably discarded from a seafood restaurant, but at the time Dad made it into a mythical sea creature that had made an incredible journey to visit us on this houseboat. He was always telling the silliest stories and making everything seem so exciting.'

John's career in music was now effectively at an end, the session work was over and, in his own way, he'd accepted that and moved on. He wanted to take early retirement, as it were. There was no bitterness – he was immensely proud of the career he'd had, but he wasn't prepared to languish in the past. To that extent, he was at peace with where he found himself. McGeoch wanted to enjoy life, to travel a bit with Sophie and make the most of what he had earned. Sophie was working herself at the time, as Emily remembers. 'Sophie had worked for a law firm, or it might have been a law bookshop, and they had enough money to get by and to be able to do what they felt like doing, which is what they were about more than making money and working long hours. For both of them it was more important to be able to have a good time.'

The couple enjoyed trips to France and meeting up with friends. Being back in London, John was able to reconnect with old mates such as Joe Barry, and of course he was close to his mother Annie and brother Bill. Emily remembers spending time with the family down

John and Emily during one of her visits to London, 1997.
McGeoch family archive

south. 'Every year I would spend New Year with Dad, Sophie, Granny Annie and Uncle Bill in London. We always had Chinese takeaway and I was always allowed to stay up until midnight, when we would sing the traditional "Auld Lang Syne" in a circle in my granny's living room. One year my uncle even set off fireworks in the garden. Dad loved all that – he was really into making a big deal of it all.'

Of her dad's time living in London, Emily looks back with fondness on one friendship in particular that John had formed, which showed her just how in tune with the emotions of others he was. 'Dad had a friend called Reg, he was a fascinating man and a great friend to Dad. We spent many days out with him on wildlife walks or visiting places of history. He was a designer or something on the original Concorde windscreen, so we went with him to watch the last Concorde flyover. He became overwhelmed with emotion and I remember the way Dad embraced and comforted him – it was so lovely. Reg also worked for Disney Animation Studios and once snuck us into his office with him, and we got to see all the original artwork on the walls and he gave me a bunch of Disney goodies. Now, looking back on Reg, I think he was a really positive influence on Dad. They were very close and spoke about everything. He was possibly one of his best friends at the time.'

It is easy for fathers, following separation from their children, to overcompensate. This wasn't so for John; he had been the same from the moment of Emily's birth. Hands-on, keen to nurture her interests and spark her imagination, and always up for a laugh. Emily looks back on the dynamic between them. 'Every time I visited, the first meal Dad would serve was M&S chicken and vegetable pie. He loved to cook from scratch but knew that was my favourite, so we always had it on the first day. Dad used to love making up words for theme tunes – he would sing any words that vaguely described the show and just make them go along with the tune. It always made me laugh so much, even though it was never very clever. The best, or maybe worst, one I remember was just humming along to *The Bill* and at the very end just shouting "THE BILL" on the last two notes. I still do it now!'

Unfortunately, John still hadn't managed to kick his dependency on alcohol, and it was taking its toll on his health. As the century drew to a close, his decline proved too distressing for those who'd known him at his best and most full of life. As Michael Jobson remembers, 'I bumped into John in the street in Hammersmith and we went over to the Hammersmith Odeon to see Trigger, to see the Primal Scream gig. He had long grey hair and a big grey beard and I hardly recognised him. So, as John's old tour manager and mate, Trigger, was at the Odeon with Primal Scream I said to him, "Go home, get yourself ready and I'll meet you in the pub here and we'll go to the show together." We had a right good night out – but I could see he was very ill, and there was something very wrong there. I put two and two together – it's the booze – but despite that it was such a smashing night and

I'm forever grateful that we got that time together. We sort of put to rights all that was ever wrong, whether between us or any other stuff, we got that wonderful night together.'

Of that time, Denise recalls how he was seeing less of Emily, but equally how Sophie was able to get John's affairs in order so that Emily would be taken care of should the worst happen. 'Things started dropping off a bit because it would be down to John and Sophie to make the transport arrangements. John would come up to collect her, and Sophie, bless her, would do the same. She would come up for her on the train every few months and take her back. What Sophie did, because she was so besotted by him and his talents, it was down to

John and his final partner, Sophie.
McGeoch family archive

her that she made him go through his back catalogue and go with an umbrella company. I don't know whether it was John or Sophie that knew Paul Lambden, but she made him go through his back catalogue and register it with the company that Paul was working for at the time. That's why there is an estate for Emily now, and really if it hadn't been for Sophie making John do that, then there would be no estate.'

Paul takes up the story of how he became involved with John. 'I was running the music publishing company Rykomusic at the time, and was always on the lookout for back catalogues to add to our roster. I was a massive Banshees fan and spotted that John's share of the songs he wrote with them were unpublished according to PRS. Somehow, I got his address and wrote him a letter saying that my company would love to look after his songs for him. A while later he rang me, and we met up in The Dove in Hammersmith and got on swimmingly. Sophie had some music business experience and helped us sort out a deal. It turned out that Sophie's aunt lived on my road, so we met up a few times when they visited her. We always had fun!'

Trigger, who had been a close friend of John's since the early days in PiL, reflects on his friend's decline and his last meeting with him – the night at the Odeon with Michael Jobson. 'When I first met him, I remember he was moving to Dronfield. He'd got married to Denise, and Emily came along. He was sitting pretty. He was an internationally acclaimed guitarist with the world at his feet, really, over a short space of time. And I think a big part of it was the Public Image thing, but the biggest part was leaving Denise and Emily, who he loved dearly. Another aspect in his demise was the world changing with regards to music tastes and the dance explosion. Ultimately, all those things happened and the last time I saw John, which was quite tragic really, I was working for Primal Scream and they were playing Hammersmith Odeon, which would have been at the back end of the nineties, maybe '98 or '99. He came along to the gig and he was in a terrible state. He was scruffy – bear in mind John was always smart and he always looked after himself, he was a well-dressed man and he had a pride about him. His hair was long and he kept nodding off. It was so sad, but what do you do when somebody is in that predicament?'

John was going to have to dig deep inside himself; nobody could fight this battle for him. Sophie loved John dearly, but she was also in the grip of alcohol dependency. On the horizon was an opportunity that offered the chance of redemption and a clean slate. A chance to put to bed once and for all the demons that had tormented John for too long. John had the biggest heart and would do anything for anyone, but as Denise reflects, 'I think because I have that background of therapy, I also know that people that care also need to be cared for. People who go into nursing possibly need nursing themselves. You've got to have been there to truly help somebody who's there – it goes hand in hand.' Whatever John had done, he'd thrown himself into it fully. Whether being a creative force within a band, as a father and husband or as a caregiver. Now, more than ever, John's lifestyle was catching up with him. The substance abuse had naturally scarred him internally, but John was also dealing with the mental burnout that had taken hold back in '82 and had been provoked and stoked by the ensuing years as a touring musician.

John collapsed while out and about shopping in London. He was rushed to hospital, unconscious, having suffered a severe head trauma from the fall. Waking to find himself in a ward bed at Hammersmith Hospital, John asked for his wife to be contacted, meaning Denise. Denise recalls the conversation: 'He started fitting. As we later found out, he'd developed epilepsy. He suffered a fit in Hammersmith while in Marks and Spencer's and caught his head on a metal clothes rack. They called me and said, "We've got your husband in hospital," to which I said, "Do you mean John McGeoch?" and she said, "Yes, this is Denise McGeoch, isn't it?" and I said, "Yes, it is, but we are no longer together and I live in Sheffield." She was apologetic and passed on that John had said that I was his wife. I don't know whether it was due to the fit and injury to his head that his unconscious mind had taken him back to the time we were living together, I really don't know. I phoned Sophie straight away and she went down to the hospital.'

Shortly after his accident, John and Sophie made the decision to leave London for good and head to Cornwall, where Sophie's elderly father lived. The move was made primarily to care for Sophie's father, rather than have him going into a care home, and with John's experience of providing care the role would be a familiar one. It would also afford John the opportunity to recover and begin the slow rebuilding process of taking care of his own health. They moved into the house in Launceston and Emily recalls not only the change of environment, but the positive impact it was having on her father. 'When Sophie's father Michael died, Sophie inherited the house, and they chose to stay there. They lived the simple life. They lived next door to a farm so we would go and collect eggs in the morning – not very rock'n'roll! They used to go over to France all the time and stay in the south of France, and that was just what they did. They'd kind of retired early and did what they wanted really. They lived a very free life.'

John had found his spark again; the health scare had forced him to confront his own mortality. It had been a rude awakening, but now, more than ever before, he knew he had to turn it around. He began to evaluate his drinking habits and started to sensibly reduce his intake. He was back to being the well-dressed man that he had been and there was a sense of optimism and hope for the future. He was painting again, enjoying the local beauty spots, and wasn't averse to picking up the acoustic from time to time. He was finding contentment, with Sophie by his side and with Emily regularly coming to stay. He had all that he needed.

John's old friend Trigger remembers hearing from John again after he'd relocated from London with Sophie. 'A few years after the Primal Scream gig, I spoke with him again. I'd lost contact with him, but what happened was a mate of mine called Dan Mullaly met him. Dan was living on a houseboat and he'd met him in a pub in Hammersmith. He said, "Oh I bumped into a mate of yours, John McGeoch," so I said, "Did you get his number?" I got the number and called him up. So, I said, "What's going on?" and he said to me, "Great news: I've got this place with Sophie in Cornwall." We had a catch-up and he told me about his plans for the future. That was the last conversation I ever had with John.'

As Emily recalls, the house needed a bit of modernising, all of which John and Sophie were focusing on doing. 'I remember being at the house in Cornwall, probably around 13 or 14 years old. It was an old cottage and pretty much what you'd expect an old cottage to be, in that it had a farmhouse kitchen and an open fireplace and old people's carpet. I would go in the summer and spend a couple of weeks there. Dad and Sophie were slowly doing it up and I would help out with odd jobs. There was a beautiful big pond in the garden with an island in the middle. It was overgrown and needed dredging, so Dad and I spent a whole day pulling mud and weeds out of the pond and we started to discover all this wildlife living in there. So, we got lots of containers and buckets and started to rescue things, one by one. I think there were over a hundred newts as well as various frogs, toads, tadpoles and other swimming things. At the time I wanted to be a marine biologist, so it was absolutely fascinating to me! That was the last summer I spent there.'

John and Sophie became faces within the community and made friends with some locals there. Nothing to do with his career in music – this was just John and Sophie who'd come down from London. By the end of 2003 John had been sober for a good couple of months. Having initially cut back, he had now ceased drinking altogether and was in a place where he could see that his partner needed that helping hand to break free of her own dependency, as related by Denise. 'John had stopped drinking and he had told his brother, "Now we just need to get Sophie sorted out. I've nailed it, now I just want to help Sophie."'

Sadly for John, his ability to support Sophie was to be dealt a blow, as his epilepsy started to become far worse. The seizures were becoming more frequent and they were impinging on his ability to lead a normal life. Denise recalls speaking with Sophie about John's health: 'I remember Sophie talking to me about John's seizures and telling me that there was a pattern with them. Changes [to routine] could bring about these episodes and they were getting worse and more profound. I knew something was very wrong, as John missed Emily's birthday, and he never missed her birthday.'

Denise explains the events that unfolded on 4 March 2004, in part related to her by Sophie. 'He went to bed, having had an epileptic episode earlier in the evening. The episode he'd had is what you would call an absence, which means the person just blanks out, but they don't suffer a fall. He'd had this absence while watching *The Simpsons*. Afterwards he'd started complaining to Sophie that he'd missed *The Simpsons*, when in actual fact he'd been sat in the chair watching it, but he hadn't seen it due to the absence seizure he'd had. She'd tried in the past to get him to go to the doctors about his seizures, which had been getting worse, but he wouldn't. They went to bed that night and while he was asleep, he suffered a seizure which effectively switched off his brain mechanism and stopped his breathing.'

Sophie raised the alarm upon waking, but it was too late. John Alexander McGeoch died on 5 March 2004 as a result of SUDEP (sudden unexpected death in epilepsy). He was 48.

Michael Jobson reflects upon hearing the news that his friend had died. 'It stopped me in my tracks, you know what I mean? I kept thinking, could I have been there more for him? Could I have helped him?' The next time Trigger heard from Michael, it was to break the sad news to him, as he remembers, 'Michael Jobson told me and nobody knew, it was completely out of the blue and it wasn't public knowledge. He said to me that I might want to ring a few people to let them know.' The sense of loss and shock was felt by all who knew him and, naturally, his friends took the time to reflect on their memories of the man. For Dave Formula, 'There was a vulnerability to John. Despite the ambitious exterior, you could see underneath it all he was vulnerable. If you've got that artistry about you, you're inherently vulnerable. People would take advantage of John at times because of his sensitivity.'

This insight into John's nature tells us so much about the pressures he had to deal with in his life. His sense of betrayal at the demise of PiL is something that Budgie was made aware of in a phone call shortly after John's death. As he explains, 'After John died, and I don't know how this happened, I ended up in a phone conversation with the lady he was living with. I don't even remember her name, but somebody must have given me her number. I phoned her and we spoke and all she said – she was immensely sad and very angry at the time – she just had nothing nice to say about John's time in PiL, and that it had taken a lot out of him both physically and emotionally. She said that the bottle incident on stage, which had badly injured John, was a huge turning point for him.'

It was Trigger who decided to reach out to Lydon to inform him of John's passing. No amount of touring or working with him could have prepared him for the singer's response. 'When John McGeoch died, I tracked John Lydon down. I felt it would be better to hear the news from somebody he knew. I told him and all he said was that he already knew. Over the years I'd kept in touch with him. If I was in America doing a tour, say in LA, then he'd come and see me. Maybe I expected more of a response, I don't know. I felt sad that he didn't say more really; it felt cold. I haven't spoken to him since.'

John's funeral was held back in London and was attended by family, friends and people John had worked with. The eulogy was read by John's close friend and former bandmate Russell Webb, something which must have required great strength to do in front of John's grieving family and young daughter. Michael Jobson also spoke and read the words that Malcolm Garrett had sent to be heard by those in attendance. As Michael explains, 'I kind of tried to take a bit more interest in what was going on, arranging things, to try and support his brother and his mum. I got a little itinerary together and sent it round to everybody, made sure that everybody that came stayed together and were looked after.' Joe Barry recalls, 'Russell did the eulogy, as I remember. John's family were great people and I am especially fond of his mum. They may have felt that the music was what had ultimately taken John from them and you couldn't blame them for thinking that.'

Emily recalls her emotion and sense of disbelief at the turnout. 'The church was packed. There were people stood up at the back, all there to pay their respects and say goodbye to Dad. I kept saying to my mum, "Look at all these people." It was very moving. Maybe I hadn't quite realised until that point just how much he had meant to people. To the world he was the guitarist in Magazine, Siouxsie and the Banshees and Public Image, but to me he was my dad.'

Joe Barry recalls how his friends came together to remember and celebrate John's life. 'There was no wake as such. Understandably, I think, his mum chose not to have people back to the house because of the circumstances and with the prospect of boozing. It wouldn't have been appropriate.' Naturally, John's friends wanted to gather to remember the man, and made their own arrangements. As Joe explains, 'A group of us who were friends or had known John went to the local pub and we couldn't get in, as they'd locked it up. There was kind of a strange mix of strange-looking people, all old kind of rock and pop people. Somebody was on crutches and we looked like a raggle-taggle bunch. We went to another pub and eventually found our way to one that was open called The Joker over in Seven Kings [Ilford], which was an Irish pub that I knew. I went on my own to the door because I got in front of everybody else, and they said, "Ah, well, if it's just you... we'll let you in, because all the publicans are ringing up saying there's a group of gypsies and we didn't want to let them in," and I said, "No, no, I've got some mates with me but I can assure you we're not gypsies!" Prejudice still reigns in Seven Kings!' The friends shared their memories of the man who had so sadly left them behind.

Michael Jobson sums up John's impact on his life. 'John's imprinted in my heart really. I got back in touch with him a bit when he moved up near Sheffield. I was doing well in my career; he was always really gracious and he loved the fact I was doing well. Look, without John, I didn't have anything. Without John and my brother I was going to be a coal miner, and I have massive respect for the man who worked down the coal mine all his life like my father, but I was given the opportunity to not do that, and I was given that opportunity by my brother and by John McGeoch. John gave me so much love in my life. At his house eating fish finger sandwiches with ketchup and walks with Stephen, his dog.'

Nicky Tesco was also present at John's funeral. 'If John was around now, he would be encouraging young bands. He'd be seen as a mentor, as a teacher because that is what he was. I've seen how he was around people.' Nicky adds, 'I have a lot of respect and admiration for those bands that are still around today, like Radiohead, who can establish themselves, make albums, and then go off and do very constructive and healthy individual projects. In my mind that's what John could and should have been, where he could have had another outlet for his talent, creativity and imagination. You talk to anyone about guitarists, they'll go through the usual suspects and then you mention John McGeoch and they'll go, "Oh, my God, of course," because actually he laid the tracks for all those people to ride along.'

Perhaps it is a reflection of what the industry does, and more importantly doesn't do, for artists that is highlighted here. From back when John was establishing himself through to his final album with PiL, the commercial demands were such that the emotional and psychological needs of John and musicians like him would have been an afterthought at best. It wouldn't be right to lay the blame for McGeoch's untimely death solely on the music business, but it does beg the question, did the companies and bigwigs allow too much to slide in pursuit of financial gain? If so, how much has changed? As Richard Jobson says of being in The Armoury Show with McGeoch, 'I have to say the experience left a terrible taste in my mouth, and I left the music industry and I've only recently returned. I've been doing some gigs in some clubs with two young guitarists, doing Armoury Show stuff, really brilliant guitarists, but I need two of them to be able to do what John did. One guitarist is not able to do what he could do live, and as I say they are genius guitar players, technically brilliant, but I need two of them, so that tells you plenty.'

Denise takes up the story of how John's headstone inscription came about on the way home after the service. 'I wrote the words for his headstone and I think it was when we were in the car on the way back. It just came to me and I just felt that I had to write it and it was in reference to what John had thought of himself deep inside, all those years before – that the diamond part is included. I was thinking about it on the whole journey back to Sheffield. I don't usually write and I'm not saying it's fantastic, but what I am saying is that I don't usually do things like that. It was one of those times in life where you feel compelled to do something, and you've got to do it until you've seen it through. I ran it by the family, and they agreed, so that's what's on his headstone. When John died the family received a card from Siouxsie and she signed it off with the words, "Sleep well, big man." That was really appropriate, because John did suffer a bit from "little man syndrome" – he wasn't particularly tall, and he always liked wearing shoes with a big sole to try and make himself appear that bit bigger than he was. What I take from that was that Siouxsie acknowledged that, but was saying that you were a big man, and you don't have to be tall to be a big man. So, I took that from her card and put it on his headstone because it felt right.'

Sophie returned to Cornwall alone, devastated by the loss of her partner and best friend. The sense of hopelessness was too profound for her to bear. Without John there was an empty space in her life that was too overwhelming. Sadly, Sophie passed away four months after John's funeral on 17 July. She deserves to be remembered as the woman John spent his final few years with and with whom he enjoyed many happy and special times. Sophie was also always keen for John to maintain his close relationship with Emily. She was the one who pushed John into sorting his business affairs out so that neither he nor Emily would be deprived of his record royalties. Denise remembers the sadness that overshadowed Sophie's final few months. 'Sophie couldn't live without John, she was heartbroken. She didn't want to go on without him. She told me that she would walk around the house talking to him – she missed him terribly. Sophie loved him so much.' There is a genuine feeling of warmth when Sophie is mentioned by both Denise and Emily. She was valued.

Despite the sadness towards the end of John's life, culminating in his tragic death, it is important we remember the things that make him so special, not just to those who knew him, but to those of us who have loved his music and for the generations to come that will discover his work and derive just as much pleasure from it as those who heard "Shot by Both Sides", "Happy House", "Spellbound" or "Cruel" back in the day. John had finally turned the corner with his drinking before his death, and as Denise says, 'John was totally and completely alcohol- and drug-free and had been for several months. John was trying so hard to get his life on track and I really believe he'd nailed it.'

It is easy to see what the world lost in John. A guitar virtuoso, a visionary and a criminally overlooked figure in rock history. That's how I saw it initially. While all of that is true, what I now see and feel most poignantly is that a daughter lost her father and a mother her son. John was many things to many people, but it was those closest to him who felt his loss most acutely, and this was tragically true for his partner Sophie. Those who knew him best and loved him not as a musician, but as a man. The memories his mother has of taking him to the television studios as a toddler, or his artistic achievements with the Cubs, watching for the children who were left out of other children's games. The friends he made down in London and making a racket on the guitar. Janet trying to avoid his initial approaches, before succumbing to the natural charm, kindness and the famous McGeoch smile. John and his dear friend Russell riding around on their motorbikes in their leather jackets. Denise and John, true soulmates falling in love in Spain and making a family of their own. The jewel in his crown,

Emily, playing in the snow with her dad, both in their pyjamas, and making arty pieces together. How he loved them all and how they loved him. That's what this man and his life says to me. Love.

The following quote from his daughter, Emily, speaks volumes about the relationship they had and about the man he was. 'I remember when I got my first period. I called Dad as usual – we spoke every day on the phone – and I told him and he was so pleased for me, he even sent me a card in the post! Then the next time I went to stay with him, he had made this shoebox full of supplies for me and he sat me down and said, "This is for you and if you need anything else, just ask. I might be a man, but I'm not embarrassed, I'll walk right into any shop and ask for whatever you need." He was always so supportive and I could talk to him about anything.'

Death may or may not be the final destination, but this was never about John's death. It was always about the journey. It was about an amazing life. Full of drama, emotion, creativity, self-expression, kindness, warmth, highs, lows. To die at 48 is tragic; all the things John and his family should have been able to experience together have been denied them, but John McGeoch lived life on his own terms, a full life in which he gave so much to so many. History has not given John his due; this is our small way of saying thank you.

Before embarking on this book, when I'd put an album on that featured John, I knew I was going to enjoy it, no matter how many times I'd heard it previously, because his playing means something. It makes me feel. Now, having had the opportunity to speak with those who have contributed massively to this project, I just have to hear the name John McGeoch and the internal response is the same. Not solely for the music, but because I know he is somebody I would have been proud to know personally. There's a slightly twee but nonetheless relevant saying that could and should be applied to John McGeoch. It doesn't absolve him of the failings and flaws he may have had, but it does encapsulate the sense of goodness I have felt when hearing first-hand accounts of what he was like as a person. The saying is: 'It is nice to be important, but it is more important to be nice.' The image of John in my head as I write this final sentence is of a father with his daughter after an evening at the movies, as Emily remembers: 'When I was 14 he snuck me in to see the Kevin & Perry movie because I really wanted to see it but it was a 15! It's full of sex and some scenes are fairly graphic. I remember feeling so awkward, and then on the way out him saying, "Well, that was a bit awkward… I can see why it's a 15." We were laughing all the way home!'

    Rest easy, John.

───────────────────────────

TEN

THE ANTI-HERO

Tributes to John McGeoch from friends, family, contemporaries and admirers

---

Guitar playing isn't escapism for me, it isn't leisure, it's a responsibility.

International Musician and Recording World (April 1981)

Dave Formula (Magazine)

THE LAST TIME I saw John was in the mid-nineties in Sheffield. I was in the studio doing some session work on keyboards. While I was there, I had a room booked and I had been given a number for John and, as I knew he lived nearby, Dronfield, I phoned him and asked if he fancied meeting up. We'd not spoken for at least ten years prior to me phoning him. He was very receptive and said that there was a pub in town, called The Howard. So, we met there, had a few drinks catching up and then went for a meal and he said, 'What are you doing now?' to which I said, 'I've got a hotel booked,' and he said, 'Why not come back to mine?', which I did. We just spent the evening reminiscing and drinking, and it was really lovely. He had a daughter by this time, Emily, and he was just so delighted to be a father. John spoke about his time in PiL, as that had been more recent and it had clearly upset him in how it had ended. I think he felt hurt by John Lydon, who had gone off to LA after being offered a solo deal, which had left John and the other guys in the band in limbo. You could see it had left a scar on John, as he had considered Lydon a good friend. I left in the morning with a hangover, but it was well worth it for having had the chance to see John again. We had made tentative plans to meet up again. Sadly, it wasn't to be.

Barry Adamson (Magazine)

I WAS GUTTED when I heard John had died. I had a strange experience about thirty years ago; I'd got clean and I stopped drinking and some years after there is an idea that you go through your past and apologise to anybody you'd treated less than favourably during your addiction. One of those people I wanted to reach out to was John, and I just wanted to say, you know I love you and you're my friend. So, I was speaking to a mentor of mine about this and I said, 'Do you think it's a bit too soon to do this?' and he said, 'No, it's probably a bit too late!' So, I said, 'I've got to catch a flight to Los Angeles,' and he said, 'Write the names of those people you want to contact on a piece of paper and they will appear,' and I'm thinking, who are you – Gandalf?! So, I did and the third person on the list was John McGeoch. I'm on the flight, I touch down in LA and I'm going to collect my luggage and who's there but John McGeoch!

It was six or seven in the morning and John's there waiting for somebody, chaotic as fuck and falling over suitcases. He was quite drunk and stinking of booze and I talked to him for a little bit, and while I was in LA I got a call from somebody else who was on this list that I had lived with previously. They were in LA and they told me that they'd seen John and he had told them that I was in town. That was the last time I saw John and then I did an interview several years later for the Manchester International Festival, and I was talking about John and found myself getting very emotional because I started to remember the things he gave to me when we first met. He gave me so much validation and support, he even taught me how to tune the bass, where he said, 'Use these things called harmonics and I'll show you how to play any chord across the piano with three fingers.'

He was a great teacher, a great friend and he was very kind to me, and as much as he could be moody and quite a blustery character at times, he had a lot of respect for me. So, seeing him that last time and because of where I was in my life, I was able to tell that he wasn't very well. When he died it seemed unbelievable in a way, and I don't know why, but you just think people, especially people you made music with, are going to go on forever. Even now it doesn't seem right even though I've accepted it, but in retrospect maybe I can appreciate far more the moves he made in his career, and perhaps there was an urgency to get things done.

Siouxsie Sioux

I DO REMEMBER bumping into him in Covent Garden in the late nineties and it was just like, 'Hey John!' and 'Hey Siouxsie!' I thought there might be some bad feeling from back then, but he was just like, 'Nooo! Nice to see you,' and we hugged each other. I was out shopping, looking for a jacket or something, and I literally just bumped into him. It was lovely to see him but that was the last time. You know, I do regret how things ended with the band.

Steven Severin (Siouxsie and the Banshees)

THINGS WERE NEVER the same once we had lost John. For one thing – and it's a big thing – the whole dynamic was irrevocably changed as from then on it became the three of us plus the new guy(s). Of course, there were many more highlights as the years passed but hindsight shows us that we were at our peak between 1980–82. The intense pursuit of excellence, that drive and commitment, the hours and hours take their toll. It was all too much. P.S. Don't think I mentioned? BEST. GUITARIST. EVER.

Budgie (Siouxsie and the Banshees)

HE'S NEVER FAR from my thoughts because I feel I've been blessed with a second, third and even fourth chance sometimes. Now I have a little family, I'm busier than I've ever been, I've got a new project on the go and I think – John doesn't get that, you know.

Richard Jobson (Skids and The Armoury Show)

I REFUSE TO just remember the crap stuff. I remember John cooking lunch for all of us at his house in Cricklewood, doing his incredible dishes – roasting a chicken with sixty-four garlic bulbs in it, stuffed with fennel. We'd just sit and talk about movies, books and art and laugh our heads off and then get the guitars out.

Russell Webb (The Zones, Skids and The Armoury Show)

FROM THE DAY I met John at Redcar on the first date of the *Real Life* tour and saw him play guitar, I wanted to be in a band with him. We hit it off on a different level to the musical one that brought us to the same place at the same time. Although the connection burned fairly dimly for the first two or three years, occasional meetings at social gatherings after the *Real Life* gig, it turned into something a bit deeper than just an acquaintanceship. John began to invite me to the various studios where Magazine would be recording (*Secondhand Daylight* and *The Correct Use of Soap*). In fact that became a kind of thing with John; he invited me along to some of the sessions he did with the Banshees, too.

John was a loyal friend and was almost always there for me when I needed him. He invited me to come over to America to join the Banshees entourage on the West Coast for a few days. I had just finished producing the *Joy* album (Skids) and took a cassette of the pressing. John gave me the best feedback I could have asked for. He took the cassette and went into the rear 'listening' lounge on the Banshees tour bus. An hour later he emerged sobbing. He handed me the cassette without a word, but his eyes said it all: 'It was shit'… only kidding!

When John had his nervous breakdown and ended up in the Priory, I was one of the few people who regularly visited. Our friendship was cemented before then, but I think John felt that I would be there for him too. We would occasionally go for motorbike rides round London, fishing on the Thames or the lakes near Cricklewood. I was due to see John at Sophie's house in the South West but never got to keep that date.

I will always be wordlessly proud that I got to play and record two guitar duets with John, 'Avalanche' and 'Waiting for the Floods', both on The Armoury Show album. Two of the greatest achievements of my musical career.

Nicky Tesco (The Members)

I CAN GENUINELY say with my hand on my heart that he was one of the finest people I've ever been friends with. I really loved him. You're always left with that little bit of guilt when you've not seen someone for so long and then you find out that they died of alcoholism. You think, 'Why didn't I help?' and then you realise [it's] because life takes you in different directions. When you look at the body of work that he left behind, OK on paper it doesn't look massively broad and it was concentrated in a relatively short period, but he was the seed for everything that happened afterwards. You still hear it today – sometimes I'm listening to records and I could almost hear John playing that, because someone somewhere has listened to 'Monitor', or 'Arabian Knights', or 'Spellbound', or 'Night Shift'. I keep coming back to "Monitor" because of the sound that I heard when he played me that rough mix at about two in the morning in Notting Hill with our feet on the table smoking a doob. Suddenly there's that cut in the song with that controlled feedback, and it complements the sound and it's just one of the most powerful moments in rock music. It still gives me that feeling when I hear it to this day. I remember John as a modest and brilliant man who didn't realise his own genius or understand the regard that those who knew him held him in. I wish he was still around today.

Allan Dias (Public Image Ltd)

JOHN'S DEATH WAS a real shock. I had heard John had cleaned up his act, he'd been doing nursing and then – boom. It was a horrible shock and so sad. That guy had a lot to give, he was a genius pure and simple. John was salt of the earth.

Michael Jobson (friend and guitar tech)

HIS TALENT AS a guitar player, well, he was head and shoulders above everybody else. There's been some great guitar players that have come out of the UK – is there anybody as unique as John McGeoch? I don't think so. Johnny Marr might get close, in a different kind of way. Jez from Doves might get close, in a different kind of way. Is there anybody as accomplished as John McGeoch as a guitar player? Not a chance. The rock guys could play blues-based guitar all they want to, but could they play like he played? John could play all that rock stuff with his eyes closed and round the wrong way if he wanted to.

Peter Hook (Joy Division and New Order)

I DID ADMIRE him. I admired him as a man, I admired him as a player. He's done some fantastic work and he's left a wonderful legacy, hasn't he? The groups that he worked with, fucking hell, they're legends, aren't they?

Malcolm Garrett (friend)

GUITARISTS KNOW ABOUT him, and fans who follow the bands know about him, but he's not Mick Jones, he's not as well known. He was never a guitar hero, he was just bloody *good*, and he loved working with other great front people: Howard Devoto, Siouxsie Sioux, John Lydon. He was never someone who sought the limelight and was never a good self-publicist. He was *the* guitarist of his generation.

Phil 'Trigger' Hamilton (friend and PiL tour manager)

JOHN WAS UNIQUE, and I'd never met anyone quite like him before or since, really. Very unique character, very charming character is the word I would use. A big sadness because of what happened when it did. If John was around today, he'd probably be very busy, and had he survived, I dare say he'd still be in demand.

Murray 'Muzz' Mitchell (guitar tech)

FROM MY EXPERIENCE of working with brilliant musicians over the years, John was very unusual. You often find that, as good as they are at what they do, they are lacking in other departments. John really had the lot. Everything you could wish for. He had the whole package, which is pretty unique, I think. He was very human.

Steve Albini (guitarist and engineer/producer)

I ADMIRED AND sometimes emulated John McGeoch, though I don't think I ever had any direct interaction with him. In particular I liked the way his guitar played abstractions of the music rather than the structure of the music, even in a three-piece band setting, like with Siouxsie and the Banshees. I liked that he could play away from the song and let the listener figure out how it fit in.

Mille Petrozza (Kreator)

I'VE ALWAYS LOOKED up to the sound McGeoch got from his guitar. It had something that was lacking in metal, which was all about the big solos, the big chords. McGeoch brought a dark, chilling atmosphere – almost like it was set in ice. It was very expressive and creates images in your mind and I think it is especially true of his work with Siouxsie. McGeoch in that period took you on a journey. It was so influential to me.

John Frusciante (Red Hot Chili Peppers)

I DON'T KNOW much about McGeoch as a person, but I can say from the perspective of a musician that it really requires a genuine artistic confidence to not overstep those bounds [musically]. When I was 18 or 19 and starting my band, I had no ability to stay within that and it wasn't until I was about 20 that I started seeing how you could get more out of trying to stand out less. It's something that he seems to have understood from the very beginning of his recorded output, and understanding how to adapt to the people that you're playing with. How to do something, like I say, extremely colourful and creative within those boundaries that if you step outside of them you're going to be stepping on the other people in the group, and they're not going to sound as good as they can sound. He does a lot of fancy things, on *Juju* especially, there are so many sixteenth note-based guitar parts on there where he's very comfortable playing at that speed, and where open strings fit into it as well. I tend to think when somebody is playing that comfortably that they are actually capable of going even further than that, but they are staying within what's comfortable and that has a certain sound as well. I don't want to hear somebody where it's like they are doing the absolute top limit of what they are capable of doing; you want to have the sense that somebody could be doing more but they're not – they are restraining themselves in order to be more expressive, and that's a paradox. I think a lot of guitar players go their whole lives and never get that through their heads. Hearing somebody who understands it so well from the start of their career really shows what I believe to be true artistic confidence, and you can't get that by trying to make people see how confident you are – you have to just be that way inside yourself, and really appreciate the colour and the feeling that music produces.

It's incredible how much you can learn about somebody from studying their playing and trying to do exactly what they did and seeing the relationship to the other instruments. I'm always surprised when I hear about musicians that they learn how to play only from playing with other people – I wouldn't have ever gotten anywhere if I did that. It's only from studying what people have recorded – that's where my whole style comes from, that's where my conception of music comes from, that's where my songs come from. It's like getting to know somebody as a person even though they're not there. That's what it feels like – it feels like they are there and like their heart is there, their soul is there. It all just needs to be decoded and you just try to get better and better at decoding. It's an incredible thing what recording has brought to the possibilities of musicianship. I don't know if I would have ever been a musician if recording didn't exist.

Joe Barry (friend)

IN HIS LAST year at Manchester Poly art department he was getting plaudits for his artwork, as well as Magazine taking off and [doing] a lot of rehearsing. He was the first person in my world who looked like a success! I asked him one day how it had all come about. He said to me, in a particularly emphasised Greenock accent, 'I work hard.' It stayed with me. In a way it became my watchword. Genius as he was, there was as much perspiration as inspiration. He played hard too!

Liddy Papageorgiou (friend)

IF I HAD to describe John, first of all I would say he really was a genius. He was creative, so inventive and so funny, terribly funny. We shared a lot of space together and I remember in the house with Malcolm, John and I had this massive room. He would sit on the sofa and he'd play very well known songs like 'Out Home on the Range' or something, completely out of tune, but it made sense because it was so out of tune, and it was hilarious. On the last note he would look at me as if to say, 'Get ready for this,' and he'd just pluck this outrageous, stupid note and we'd start laughing. I'm sure he worked really hard at everything, but he was such a genius, it was in him, and talking to John was fab because you could talk to him for hours about anything – he was interested in everything. We went to Greece together and we had a very intense time as friends, and he was best man at my wedding. We were very, very close. I have nothing but huge love for him.

Sakis Tolis (Rotting Christ)

FOR ME WHAT made John McGeoch's approach so special was his simplicity, in conjunction with meaning. He plays for the good of the team and not for himself. He's not trying to prove anything or overplay, which is in contrast with the majority of other guitar players. Most important of all... he has talent in composing. All of the above makes an artist unique, for me. Maybe he didn't receive the level of recognition his talent deserved because he didn't try to achieve that recognition. There are so many silent warriors out there that do not achieve the recognition immediately, but I believe they will have their day because nothing is hidden behind the sun.

Johnny Marr (The Smiths et al.)

WITH ALL GREAT groups there's a collective vision that comes from all the members, really. You can't ignore that the name of the band and the titles of the songs like 'Permafrost' or 'Motorcade' go so perfectly with the music, and vice versa. Those words for me are synonymous with what John's sound is. You know, 'Permafrost' is a great word to describe his guitar sound and then maybe, later, when it gets to the Banshees, you could call it glacial. Not that it was soulless, but it was a long way from the down-home bluesy vibe which is the easy way out. It's a real sad thing that John McGeoch's not around to get all the appreciation from musicians and music fans. That's a really sad thing.

Ed O'Brien (Radiohead)

HIS PLAYING AND contribution to Magazine was so good, but I really think he hit his stride with the Banshees, and *Juju* for me was the epicentre of his playing... so, so good.

Ray Stevenson (photographer)

WHEN JOHN MCKAY left the Banshees I thought he was irreplaceable. Robert Smith seemed to demonstrate that, though admittedly he had no rehearsal time. McGeoch's versatility quickly had the band sounding like themselves pre-split, and then sounding even better. (No, I haven't forgotten about Budgie, but this is a McGeoch book!)

John was a 'gentleman' in that old-school sense. I never saw him lose his temper, sulk or throw a strop, though hangovers made him quite reclusive. And he always had time to answer my inane guitar questions.

Which reminds me... He had a Squire that over time he'd set up to his liking. Once he started to make some money with the Banshees, he bought a real Stratocaster and sold the Squire to Pete Petrol. A month later Pete got a call from John... 'Can I buy my guitar back?'

John really enjoyed food (he took me to my first teppanyaki restaurant). If he was around today I'm sure he would be on those celebrity cooking shows. His party piece could be Kobe beef, while playing 'Shot by Both Sides'!

Miss you, John.

Roddy Frame (Aztec Camera)

I FIRST SAW John playing with Magazine in 1978 in the Satellite City club in Glasgow.

I was already a huge fan. He played all the phased arpeggios and tricky chords with a stylish swagger. Magazine came alive in that sweaty club and were actually quite a visceral, rough-edged band. John brought muscle as well as intricacy and invention.

His guitar parts were like a signpost to beyond punk for any guitarists wishing to progress. Never naff or self-indulgent. Never improvised. It's something he brought with him to the Banshees and PiL. A style that wasn't rooted in the blues. It was edgy and audacious and playful. All grounded in a broad musicality.

Even his choice of guitar, a Yamaha SG, seemed to signify that he wasn't interested in rock'n'roll orthodoxy. Bill Nelson – another Northern innovator – was the only other person I'd seen play that model.

He was a one-off.

Mark Arm (Mudhoney)

HE WAS SOMEONE that I latched on to immediately with his playing in Magazine, and then with Siouxsie. There are things you could try to say about the music and how it makes you feel, but I just don't think that would be fully accurate. It can be easy to reduce it all to a game of comparisons and that doesn't do the music justice. He's got a very unique style, you know. It's not a style I've emulated – I'm not that good! He's a very original thinker and not an 'overplayer' – the little bits where he does a solo are really innovative and super cool. Whatever scale he was using on 'Permafrost', it's brilliant. Space is key, a secret ingredient for musicians which shouldn't be a secret. Knowing when to step back – John had that ability.

Noko (Luxuria and Magazine)

I FIRST PICKED up a guitar in 1977 at the age of 15 – at the time it seemed like I was coming to the table very late, which now seems a bit daft! The whole punk thing was in full swing and it felt like anyone could have a go, but I always felt ill at ease with the simplistic thugginess of the Steve Jones school of playing – that simply wasn't new. The bands that followed in the next wave (... post-punk, anyone?) blew the bloody doors off – the sound of rule books being comprehensively ripped up and thrown on the fire; in my opinion, the most creatively charged period of progressive musical reinvention ever. Guitarists like Andy Gill, Keith Levene, Tom Verlaine and, most importantly, John McGeoch, self-consciously rejected the hegemony of pentatonic blues tonality that had held sway for decades and explored the power of dissonance, finding unique ways to say the new things that needed to be said. My first introduction to John's playing was the jaw-dropping swagger of the rising Hungarian minor scale-inflected 'Shot by Both Sides' riff (actually originally Pete Shelley's, I believe, finally landing as 'Lipstick'). The intensity and urgency he brought to the notes as it corkscrews upwards are a thing of magnificence, setting the stage for Howard's incendiary words to drop.

In that instant, Magazine became my favourite band. I grew up in Liverpool – 'Shot...' was also used as the intro music to Tony Wilson's

What's On Granada TV arts round-up show, so ears always pricked up when that came on TV! There's an epic thematic aspect to John's riffs throughout his career (some of his heroic riffs from The Armoury Show deserve to be re-evaluated, by the way) and a fastidious crusade to avoid the obvious and explore dissonance, often in a quite minimalistic way. You only have to listen to the masterclass of flanged harmonics that is 'Happy House' by the Banshees to appreciate that aspect of his genius. The closest parallel for me is the way Robert Fripp wrenched out more brute power in *Larks' Tongues*...-era King Crimson, with a couple of well-chosen 'dark' notes, than a whole orchestra of Metallica's – John seemed to be driven by that spirit of invention, but also imbued it with a romantic lyricism as well. My favourite Magazine album is *Secondhand Daylight* and I later discovered, from Howard, that 'The Thin Air' was essentially John's work, even though the guitar playing on it is almost nonexistent. I really cannot overstate the importance of this man's influence on my musical aesthetic. *The* most important post-punk guitar player. I'd worked with Howard in Luxuria in the late eighties, making two albums for Beggars Banquet. Howard still had John's first Yamaha tobacco sunburst SG-1000 that they bought from (I think) A1 music on Oxford Road in Manchester with the first Magazine advance. I used that guitar on a few Luxuria songs and I always liked the idea that I was channelling a bit of the man!

For all of the above reasons, it was obviously an honour to play the Magazine reunion gigs in 2009 and I approached it very much from the point of view of the fan in the front row: what would I want the guitarist to be doing? This music was being played for the first time in decades and the last thing the fan in me would have wanted was for some guitar player to have the arrogance to make it all about them and their 'style'.

In fact, one of the first things Dave [Formula] said to me when he told me I'd got the gig was, 'I see you're playing [Gretsch] White Falcons these days – we can't have any of that, this is a Yamaha SG gig!' I went about it quite forensically, and got myself the exact signal-chain of gear that was the magical conduit to the classic Magazine sound: a '77 Yam SG-1000, a pair of late-seventies Marshall JMP 2x12-inch combos, an MXR Dyna Comp and of course the legendary 'flanger on a stick'. A few years earlier, Howard had given me the actual battered MXR Flanger, rescued from his damp basement, that Robin Simon had used on the 1980 tours that were documented so imperiously on the *Play* live album. Job's a good 'un.

Roger Cleghorn (friend)

HE WAS EXTREMELY talented. I was always jealous of his talent at painting and with music, and that came over! I remember John as always being very serious. I'm trying to remember the jokey side of John and I don't think I ever saw that, really. He was very driven and, outwardly at least, very confident, but I think looking back that was purely a front – I didn't think that at the time. I just thought, 'God, he's good at painting. God, he's good at playing the guitar.' He did used to like a drink, even then. He was just a really nice chap. I've nothing but great memories of him and of the time we all lived together. It was just a really nice time and a time when we thought anything was possible. It is a snapshot of time.

The great thing is, if you did what John did, then it's there. He's still there on the records – in that sense he's alive and he'll never go away. That's one of the ripples of the stone that was John McGeoch chucked in the pond. He's got the chance through the music. Listening to a Magazine album with my son and saying, 'Just listen to this bit,' with John's playing. Those ripples are still there. That's a good thing, in my eyes.

Paul Morley (author and music journalist)

I'LL TELL YOU something, you go through your life and you come across people and then you go through the rest of your life and you may not see them again – perhaps once or twice in passing. You find that you miss them. I didn't know John very well at all, but I would have conversations with him, knew his music very well and would say hi if ever I saw him, and we seemed to get on well. I know that I missed him even in the eighties and nineties, when I hadn't seen him in a while – 'I wonder how John's getting on?' To be honest, I missed those years he had when he was at the centre of things, you know? In a way they can only be what they were because they were short and brief, and maybe that's part of the magic, that they can only happen in intense periods of time. In the sense that people have gone missing and, as I get older, I will think of John. I love playing that music and hearing what I still hear of him. He was a special man, you really got that sense. I think of the times, I think of the people and I'm thrilled I was in that Manchester area in the late seventies when John was around, and then I knew the Siouxsie setting and John was part of my field of vision, which is exactly why I wanted him to feature on a record I was helping to make. He was always somebody I thought had made the world more interesting because of what he had decided to do with his life. I'm hesitating by saying that he was one of my favourite guitar players – but then, I know that every time I would compile a top ten list of my favourite guitarists John would be in there to this day.

Stuart Braithwaite (Mogwai)

JOHN MCGEOCH WAS *the* best post-punk guitarist. He played like no one else, totally distinct and with unyielding imagination. I hear his influence everywhere to this day. A total legend.

Emily McGeoch

HE ALWAYS HAD a studio and was doing things. He was never absent when he was at home; touring was naturally a different thing, but I was always included as a child when he was home. I used to spend a lot of time in the studio with him and the people he was working with – probably not really knowing what was happening other than it sounded like a lot of noise! I was always included. We did a lot of normal family things; it was never about fame. Wherever Dad was touring or working we would just go and make it a family holiday. There are pictures of me as a baby in America where he was working and my mum and me would go over, have a little break and a family holiday sort of thing. He didn't put his gold discs up in the house, and not because he wasn't proud of them – it was just that to him it was his job.

THE LIGHT POURS OUT OF ME

Ray Stevenson

AFTERWORD

JOHN MCGEOCH WAS a pioneer. Think of any genre, any period, and you will stumble across a handful of musicians who pushed the envelope and changed the way we perceive sound. For John, it was his approach to the guitar. When you go back to the advent of punk you are struck by what that meant not just musically, but socially and as an aesthetic, and then when you return to the musicianship you tend not to linger long. Punk had kicked the doors in and laid the groundwork for what came next.

John was at the front of the queue, a player who had taken notice of the energy, the ferocity, that punk stimulated, but brought to it something truly unique and so ahead of its time. He wasn't a rigid player – his style was loose, but it was loose by choice. McGeoch brought sophistication and a visual dynamic to his playing that set him apart. He was among a handful of guitarists who took what they knew, what they had heard, and developed it into something timeless – think Keith Levene, Andy Gill, Vini Reilly, Geordie Walker and, later, Johnny Marr.

When I think of McGeoch, I hear the unselfishness of his playing. The way he complemented and enhanced what the song asked of him. I think of songs like 'Shot by Both Sides', 'The Light Pours Out of Me', 'Permafrost', 'Philadelphia', 'Because You're Frightened', 'Happy House', 'Christine', 'Israel', 'Spellbound', 'Night Shift', 'Higher Than the World', 'Cruel', 'Brave New World'... I hear John's arpeggios, I hear his use of his beloved MXR 117 Flanger and his ability to harness feedback.

I wish I could have seen him live, up close, and allowed the canvas of my own mind to be filled with the colours and the textures of a master at work. John's playing was free, innovative, joyous, ominous, epic, sparse – and always cool. He was able to work with artists and groups as diverse as Magazine, Siouxsie and the Banshees, PiL, Visage, Ken Lockie, Billy

Idol and The Sugarcubes, to name a few. It says a lot, not just about him as a player, but as a man; it also shows you that John wasn't afraid of stepping outside of his comfort zone either creatively (if such a zone existed) or by extending himself to work on projects that, albeit lucrative, must have been exhausting.

John loved music – he loved to take part, to create, and he encouraged those around him. What of the records he produced without charging a fee, just to do his mates a favour? *The Wise Men,* anyone?

John has gone on to influence some of the most respected players in the game, some of whom have contributed to this book. They know what we all know: McGeoch was a one-off and a man brimming with creative energy and imagination.

John's story needed to be told, by those who knew him and by those who know just how special his talent was. For me, this is about passion and about honouring a legacy that should never be forgotten. It never will be forgotten – *Real Life*, *Secondhand Daylight* ('Permafrost'), *The Correct Use of Soap*, *Kaleidoscope*, *Juju* and *A Kiss in the Dreamhouse* will make sure of that.

I wanted to read a book about John and there wasn't one. That was my starting point. A random search on a train journey, travelling to collect my eldest daughter. For reasons I'm still trying to figure out, I felt I had to do it. I told my daughter of my plan and she was full of encouragement. The first move was to attempt to contact John's daughter, via social media. A couple of weeks later there was a response. From the very start, Emily was behind the project and her blessing and support have meant more than she will ever know. Her dad's wonderful legacy is also rightfully hers. I've never forgotten that. For a care worker with Asperger's syndrome, this was a bit of an 'Oh, shit' moment. Just how do you speak to some of the finest musicians and biggest names of the past forty odd years? That's two years longer than I've even been alive! You see, that is the other big drawback for me. Not only did I never see John play, I've never seen Magazine, Siouxsie and the Banshees (although we did meet briefly when I was 6, apparently) or PiL. Being a teenager in the late nineties and early noughties always felt like the shitty end of the stick as far as bands went.

Being an autistic child, music allowed me to name myself to myself. It gave me a frame of reference which has endured and, in no small way,

AFTERWORD

The Eastwood McGeoch 1000, a tribute to John and his Yamaha SG 1000.

enabled me to partake in and even occasionally enjoy social events! If music was involved, I had something to say. My own lack of ability to extend that to playing an instrument is a frustration that persists. John's music has been ever present in my life since I first discovered Magazine as a spotty teenager in the late 1990s. I was captivated by 'Shot by Both Sides', my first introduction to the band and the man behind the classic riff. Even if the song was a Buzzcocks hand-me-down, it is John's interpretation and performance that make it what it is. It is remembered as a killer record because of that guitar work. In many ways Magazine were an anomaly, almost unfairly talented but commercially misunderstood, and all too often overlooked. The same is true of John. Here was a true artist, the guitarist's guitarist. Far more famous players cite him as a major influence, yet he has seldom had the praise and recognition his prodigious talent and scope for inventiveness deserve.

The process of researching and writing this book came just in time for me. Working on the frontline of care during the most challenging and exhausting of years, unprecedented in our lifetime, was eased by getting to know and pull together the life of John McGeoch. For that alone I owe John a massive debt. I shudder to think how I would have navigated the turbulent waters of the past seventeen months had it not been for this, dare I say it, wonderful distraction. It has enhanced not just my own life, by giving me something to work towards and feel positive about, but by extension the lives of those dearest to me. Family and colleagues have been given near-daily updates (whether they wanted them or not) on the progress of the manuscript. Never once has this been a chore. I've never felt like switching the laptop off and jacking it in. It has been a pleasure from start to finish.

Somehow, be it through luck, determination or occasional harassment, I got the chance to speak with my idols. Eleven months after having the initial idea the interviews and manuscript were complete. There was no book and now there is, and I hope it entertains, informs and puts into perspective the brilliance, the triumphs, tragedies and legacy of a unique talent.

What I soon realised when writing the book is just how difficult and futile attempting to describe music is. Music, as art, is to be experienced. It is beyond description; the more you attempt to frame it the less sense it makes, and in doing so you either take away a bit of the magic or end up tying yourself in knots. Putting on paper what makes a sound so fascinating, so fresh and so challenging is beyond me. It would be as hard for me as trying to be as imaginative and as fluent a guitarist as John was. As a fan, the best you can do in breaking down the music you love is say how it makes you feel. How it moves you, how you can lose yourself in a world of someone else's creation. John's playing excites me, inspires me, blows my mind. Besides, I would much rather listen to brilliant musicians expound on the finer points of McGeoch's playing.

This is the book I wanted to read. I can never fully express my gratitude to all those who have been so generous in giving me their time so that this could be realised.

Bless you all.

Rory Sullivan-Burke
Yorkshire, 2021

THANKS

THIS BOOK WOULD not have been possible without the amazing contributions of all those who gave me their time and consideration. Huge thanks are due to all involved, but it would be remiss if I didn't single out some individuals who have not only greatly enhanced the writing of the book but have touched my heart.

Emily and her mother, Denise. I am honoured that, through John, I have been able to get to know these two beautiful souls who, without being presumptuous, I now consider friends. John's family must have, at times, found the whole process a challenging one but they have been incredibly generous.

Barry Adamson, an absolute legend in my eyes – a proper nice chap as well, and my God, doesn't just about everybody I speak to harp on about it!

Malcolm Garrett, a man I thoroughly enjoyed talking with. It was like an education in itself. Such a decent bloke, and humble as you like.

Siouxsie, who has been so giving to the project and more than prepared to give me extra insight over the phone whenever I have asked. A class act. She has consistently gone above and beyond, and all in the cause of celebrating John. In many ways I have come to view her not just as one of the greatest icons in popular culture, but as a mentor and someone who recognised that I was more than a little green when I first started the book. Put simply, she took me under her wing.

Michael Jobson, who I warmed to immediately due to him being a Celtic supporter. That and his readiness to casually drop the C-bomb into conversation very early on – possibly after hello. Although I do admit to suffering from a bit of beard envy – the man possesses a fine bit of face shrubbery!

Allan Dias, who I think gave me the best part of four hours. One of which was spent discussing the intricacies of Hendrix's solo on 'Machine Gun'... I think we have the makings of a PhD thesis there, Allan!

Phil Hamilton, otherwise known as Trigger, a refreshing change from all the northern and Scottish accents! A true geezer in every sense of the word and a man whose love for John was obvious from the very start.

Dave Formula, who I got the chance to speak with three times over the course of three weekends – 'Sundays with Dave' I called them. He has been a constant throughout this journey and always on hand to help where he could. So supportive and encouraging.

Keith Levene, an incredibly giving and interesting man and a contemporary of John's who I know McGeoch had the utmost respect for.

Johnny Marr, who will never know the overwhelming sense of excitement I felt when it was confirmed via email that he would phone me up for a chat. This was very early on in the process, and it was at that point that I knew this was really taking off and becoming something important. Brilliant.

Nigel Proktor, who has worked tirelessly to garner the necessary interest from publishing companies and has been a real blessing to both me and the book you now hold in your hands.

Omnibus Press, for seeing the merit in and need for this book.

Annie McGeoch – thank you always; Bill McGeoch; Tess Sullivan – for always being there and believing in me; Gemma Goddard – for your support and humour and creating the mantra 'Why not?'; Fianna Sullivan – for being the first person to support my ambition to do the book; Jessica Sullivan – for the smiles, cuddles and encouragement; Pam Goddard – for your help with my improving, albeit iffy, grammar; Eileen Bouziane – even though you are no longer here, I know this would have meant a lot to you; James Burke – proud to call you my father; Joseph King – the best mate a guy could have; Kala Ramsden – the second-best mate a guy could have; Donna, Ros, Sam, Mel, Jeanette, Gertrudi, Suzanne and all the guys – your support has been amazing; Shaz James; Tara 'Cone' Sullivan; Paul Morley – a contribution to be proud of.

Richard Jobson, John Doyle, Howard Devoto, Clive Farrington, Janet Shefras, Nicky Tesco, Doug Hart – thank you for being as supportive as you have been and putting up with my relentless emails!; Lu Edmonds,

Joe Barry, Budgie, Nick Launay – it has been a privilege to get to know you as a result of this; Glenn Gregory, Peter Mensch, Ed O'Brien, Jonny Greenwood, Peter Hook, John Leckie, Kate Cotter, Tom Sheehan, Jeff Singh, Billy Idol – I really appreciated the effort you made to be a part of this; Laurence Freedman, Murray 'Muzz' Mitchell, John Frusciante – fascinating conversation; Stephen Hague, Sammi Wild – you've been great from day one; Mille Petrozza, Lars Kronlund, Idde Schultz, Ralph Baker, Norman Fisher-Jones (Noko), Ken Lockie, Kelly Norris, Steve Matthews, Olivia Plunket, Rusty Egan, Emily Hockaday, Stephen Fry, Paul Lambden, Adi Newton, Sakis Tolis, Mark Arm, Bekah Zietz Flynn, Liddy Papageorgiou, Steve Albini, Andrew Harper, Billy 'Chainsaw' Houlston, Simon Draper, Andrew Graham-Stewart, Jon Webster, Pat Rowley, Roger Cleghorn, David Atherton, Kenny and Carl, Sinéad O'Connor, Jo Bench, David Barraclough – thank you for all the input; Imogen Gordon Clark – you have been wonderful ever since you became involved with the project; P. J. Harvey, Gillian at TheThe.com, Matt Johnson, Don Letts, Katie Nelson, David Byrne, Iggy Pop, Henry McGroggan, James Masters, Steven Severin, Don Ash, Ciaran Harte, Dave Barker, Nikki Law, Russell Webb, Charlie Renton, Tim Brooke, Ray Stevenson, Roddy Frame, Stuart Braithwaite. John Lydon was approached.

My biggest thanks of all are reserved for the man who made all of this possible: John Alexander McGeoch. I could never possibly sum up or repay what you have brought into my life, not just through your wonderful music but also courtesy of the amazing people you knew and loved and who I have had the opportunity to share time with. Thank you, John.

Rory x

The receipt for John's first Yamaha SG1000, November 1977.
Howard Devoto archive